Loyal Fana

Nancy Reagan

A SURGEON'S ODYSSEY

A Surgeon's Odyssey

DR. LOYAL DAVIS

DOUBLEDAY & COMPANY, INC., GARDEN CITY, NEW YORK
1973

ISBN: 0-385-02230-1
Library of Congress Catalog Card Number 73-79659

TO:
EDITH, NANCY, DICK, PATTI, AND RONNIE

ONE

THROUGH the years, people have asked me what influenced me to become a doctor. I'm not sure. A railroad engineer's son, no doctors in the family, not even high school graduates; what was the motivation? Was it my father's often repeated admonition that I should earn my living with my head and not my back? Were the chromosomes inherited from forgotten and unknown ancestors the reason? Was it the young Harvard medical student who worked alongside me in the passenger traffic office of the Burlington Railroad with his personal dignity and self-assurance that were so evident in his carriage, walk, and behavior?

It may have been all of these plus a subconscious appreciation and awe of old Dr. Horrell's professional talents and abilities, his stiffly starched shirt with detachable cuffs, his heavy gold watch chain draped across his vest, his neatly trimmed red Vandyke beard, his elegant manners, and the respect his patients paid him. Certainly, it was not a planned education and career, because in Galesburg, Illinois, it was assumed that the only male child of a railroad engineer on the Burlington would get a job with the railroad and stay on that job for the rest of his life. Nor was it the lesson I learned from my father when I worked for old Mr. Falk.

When I retired as professor and chairman of the department of surgery at Northwestern University Medical School in 1963, I began to think back and try to analyze what it was and who it was that influenced me to want to become a doctor. Certainly, my father's teaching and example influenced my future ethics and philosophies. He had to go to work when he was seven years old. He taught me by direct, practical applications of behavior and thinking.

We lived on Cottage Avenue in Galesburg in one of the houses built by the railroad during the strike in 1888. The short street had quickly been called Scab Alley. I became fascinated with railroad-

7

ing when I was six years old. Not frail, but slender, with a shock of blond hair topped by a white cap that advertised Pillsbury's flour, I often stood by the corner of the factory building that bordered the railroad tracks, and waited patiently. I listened for the two short warning toots of the engine's whistle, which my father would give as his freight train approached the Mulberry Street crossing. There she would come, moving smoothly and gracefully, beginning the climb out of town up the east grade without spinning her wheels and without the obvious lost effort that many engineers couldn't avoid with a long train of freight cars. This was the stock train that would get to Chicago early in the morning, stopping only for coal and water. The number, 1902, was on the engine's breastplate, one of a series of engines my father had broken in for the Burlington Railroad after they had been deadheaded from the Baldwin Locomotive Works in Philadelphia to Galesburg. Her bell would be ringing, and I could imagine the ease with which Pete Johnson, my father's fireman, was pulling and releasing the bell rope. I never looked up from the driving rods as she came along, swaying majestically, until the cab was opposite me. He would look down at me and flip his hand in salute.

I looked forward to the arrival of the new group of engines from Philadelphia. The master mechanic of the division asked Dad to adjust their valves and connecting rods before assigning them to be used in the road service. There had been more than a suggestion that I might be taken along for a ride; there was almost a promise. He would run the lone engine as far as thirty miles east and thirty miles south where there were sidings and double tracks. I could ride on either the fireman's or his side of the cab; I could watch the gauges and signal blocks; I could keep a copy of the flimsy paper order that governed the trips up and down the line.

The day finally came. My mother made a lunch for me and put it in Dad's dinner pail. We would share the coffee in the container in the lid. The metal gave a characteristic odor and taste to the food.

Bright and shiny and new, there she was. Faint smoke was coming from her stack, and just as we reached her, she popped off. Pete Johnson was already up. Dad let me climb up the steps first but didn't offer me a hand; he did give me a piece of clean waste to wipe my hands.

As we moved slowly out of the yards and onto the main-line tracks, I was fascinated with the accuracy of Pete's shovel as he spread the coal in the firebox; no wasted movements of his arms or legs as he swayed with the ponderous rhythm of the engine.

I watched my father out of the corner of my eye; he seemed to be looking ahead, to the side, across the cab, and backward at the same time. He released the grip on the vertical reverse and go-ahead lever with one big, powerful hand and in one smooth movement. The horizontal throttle was moved gently forward and backward, almost imperceptibly, and the engine responded immediately.

Up and down the line we went as Dad got the feel of the engine's movements. Regularly, we would pull on a sidetrack, while my Dad made adjustments with a big wrench. Noontime came, and we went in on a siding, took our lunch pails, and sat on the shady side of the engine on the grassy bank of the roadbed. The talk concerned railroading, and I listened attentively.

My father got up and walked around the front of the engine. Pete mounted the steps on the fireman's side. Instead of climbing up the same way or walking around the front or behind the tank to get to the engineer's side of the cab, I crawled beneath the tank wheels on my hands and knees. As I reached the other side, I raised my head and saw my father looking down from the cab window. Before I could straighten up, he was on the ground beside me. He picked me up by my overall straps and deposited me with a thud on the engine's gangway. No word was spoken. His face was ashen, and I instinctively knew it was a mixture of fear and angry disappointment. I had committed a stupid act. To act thoughtlessly and impulsively was not to use the brains God had given. To make an error in decision was human, he often said, but not a word was said on our way home.

Three weeks passed before I was invited again after I had answered "yes" to his question, "Do you think you know how to act on an engine?"

My mother was eight years younger than Dad. She was born and raised in Yates City, Illinois. Mother was emotional, quick-tempered, and wholly reliant on Dad. She and I were alone the nights Dad was away on his run, and although my aunt Bertha, Mother's sister, and her husband lived next door in a similar house, Mother was frightened at the thought of hobos and burglars, although nothing had ever happened. I am not sure whether this fear was transmitted to me and was the cause of my recurrent dream of riding a swiftly moving bicycle on the inside of a bowl and gradually and inexorably reaching the top edge just before I would awaken screaming in fright. I suppose a Freudian psychoanalyst would have interpreted this dream and my sleepwalking as a mother-fixation complex and connected it with my escape from the womb.

I entered grade school and came to realize that my father had decided that I should try to be perfect in my schoolwork. He would ask what I was studying as I sat at the kitchen table preparing my lessons. My father knew nothing about my studies and couldn't aid me, but he sat next to me as though his presence would help. My mother always signed my report cards but kept them until Dad came home.

I went to Sunday school at the Grace Episcopal Church. I sang in the choir, wearing the black cassock and white surplice. I carried the cross, heading the choir's procession, and was often pressed into service in pumping the organ. I was proud, scared, and quavery of voice when I sang a Te Deum.

A prayer book was to be awarded to the boy and girl who had been perfect in attendance at Sunday school for an entire year. I was the only boy to have such a record and I knew that. The prayer book was given to the son of the owner of the largest department store in town. I was angered and crushed in spirit. When I got home, I announced I would never go back to the church again. Mother cried and was angry about the unfairness of the action. Dad listened calmly.

"Did you miss one Sunday?"

"No, my teacher knows that but she didn't award the prayer book."

"I've always thought you could be good and follow the golden rule without having to go to church. You do what you think is right but don't keep talking about it to every Tom, Dick, and Harry."

I never joined a church. I have tried to practice the golden rule. I have never been able to subscribe to the divinity of Jesus Christ nor to his virgin birth. I don't believe in his resurrection, or a heaven or hell as places. If we are remembered and discussed with pleasure and happiness after death, this is our heavenly reward and mortality for having led a good life. I have never thought these beliefs necessary to the recognition of the great influence Christ's teachings have had and which I have tried to follow. I have wondered many times if my religious beliefs would have been different had the problem been discussed more thoroughly with others and if Dad had not given me the responsibility of making my own decision and living with it the rest of my life. I have always been affected by flagrant acts of injustice. Perhaps this is an inherited characteristic from my Welsh ancestors.

We moved from Cottage Avenue to a neighborhood two miles from the railroad yards. I was given a bicycle so I could ride back and forth to high school. I earned money that summer mowing lawns for the neighbors, and Dad made it fun to work with him painting the house, putting down cement for a curbing for the walk, and filling in and cultivating the yard to make a better lawn. We tore down and put back together an old two-cylinder automobile that always seemed to blow a tire when Mother joined us for a ride. It was a happy summer.

Mr. Falk was one of our new neighbors. His back yard was separated from ours by a fence. I was busying myself on our side of the fence when Mr. Falk called out to me.

"How'd you like to help me knock off some bugs from my potato plants, Loyal?"

Eager to earn some school money, I was over the fence and into his yard as fast as I could go. I worked all that afternoon under a hot August sun, picking off the bugs from Mr. Falk's potato plants and putting them into a tin pan. I was a dedicated worker, devoted to my task, trying to guess the amount of my reward for my labors. The sun was fierce in its intensity, and I perspired a lot, but at long last, the rows of potato plants were clean of bugs. I hadn't missed a single one. My job was finished, and I called to Mr. Falk.

"It's finished, Mr. Falk. I got every bug on every plant." Mr. Falk came out of his house and slowly surveyed the rows of potato plants. He carefully lifted the leaves and inspected them top and bottom.

"You've done a good job, Loyal. Come up on the porch with me."

I followed him up the stairs to his back porch.

"Yes, sir," he said, "you've done a good job. A very good job. You're a good boy, Loyal. Here."

Mr. Falk handed me two big white icicle radishes, opened the screen door, and walked into his house. My disappointment and anger brought tears to my eyes, and by the time I climbed the fence, rushed across the yard, and entered our kitchen, I was sobbing with frustration. I wanted to attack Mr. Falk bodily. As I told the story to my mother between sobs, her anger mounted, and our voices rose. The commotion awakened my father who was upstairs sleeping before going out on his ten o'clock night run. He came down the stairs pulling his pants over his nightgown and entered the kitchen just as my mother was rushing toward the back door with a broom in her hands.

"Where you going with that broom, Laura?"

"To see old man Falk. What a thing to do to a boy. Letting a boy work in the hot sun all afternoon, bugging those old potato plants. And paying him off with two miserable icicle radishes. He's no good, that Falk; letting his wife keep him with her millinery store and him cheating an innocent child. I'm going to give him a piece of my mind."

Dad deliberately finished adjusting his pants over his nightgown. "Both of you sit down." His voice and manner indicated that no questions were to be asked until we were seated.

We sat down around the kitchen table. Not a word was said. My sobs subsided as I watched Dad get up and get some lemons. He squeezed them into a pitcher, added sugar and water, and chipped off some ice from the cake in the top of the wooden icebox on the back porch. Then he poured our glasses full of cold lemonade, sweetened just right. There were several minutes of quiet as we enjoyed the drink.

"Now, tell me what happened," he said.

Mother began, but he stopped her.

"I asked him, Laura. Loyal, did you do a good job for Mr. Falk?"

"Of course he did, Al," Mother said. "What a thing to ask."

"I stayed until the job was finished," I said. "I picked off every bug."

"Did you ask Mr. Falk what the job would be worth before you started?"

"No."

"Well, Mr. Falk thought it was worth two icicle radishes. Next time, Loyal, you better find out what you're going to be paid for your work. Now, I don't want to hear another word from either of you about this whole thing." The matter was closed; he smiled and said, "Come on, let's take a spin in the country and see if we can cool off a bit. Then we'll be ready for supper."

Twenty years passed, and my father had retired from the railroad because of attacks of angina pectoris. I was a practicing neurological surgeon in Chicago. On a weekend visit to Galesburg, Dad and I were sitting on the front-porch swing. He smiled reminiscently. "You remember old Mr. Falk?"

"I sure as hell do." The forgotten hurt came back vividly.

"Well, he died last week." Father paused. "Falk hasn't been right for twenty years."

I knew instinctively that he didn't mean that Mr. Falk had been mentally ill. He meant that he had not been correct about something.

"I'm sorry he died," I said. "What do you mean he hasn't been right?"

"Well, Falk considered himself an expert on measuring rainfall. He'd keep talking about what he had measured in the pan he had fastened to his fence to collect rain water. Always said the weather bureau didn't know what they were talking about. When I'd come in off my early run in the morning, or go out late at night for a night run, I'd take a little water out of his pan or put a little in." He chuckled. "Falk wasn't right for twenty years, and he didn't know it."

My father smiled and gently nudged the swing we were on. That was his repayment to Mr. Falk for the miserable treatment of his twelve-year-old son.

Maybe subconsciously my experience with Mr. Falk governed me in my professional practice to sit down and discuss my surgical fee with the patient, or his family, and never send a statement out of the blue. More often than not, I initiated these discussions. Many patients didn't ask what the surgical fee and hospital expenses would be. I tried to make my fee commensurate with the patient's ability to pay and the services I gave. I never had more than one quality

13

overcoat to sell, regardless of what the patient could afford to pay for it. I believe that most differences between doctors and patients over fees can be avoided by a frank discussion between them before a cold, impersonal statement arrives in the mail.

I vividly remember my first experience with a doctor and my father's reaction to my injury. I was visiting Aunt Carrie's house in the Seventh Ward to play with my cousins. She was my father's sister, and I sensed that Dad sometimes made allowances for her. She had a Ouija board and said she could make the dead talk to her. My mother said Carrie and her husband, Curt, were spiritualists.

Aunt Carrie's three boys were older than I. The youngest, only a year older, was as black-haired as I was blond; we were called the Katzenjammer Kids by the family. On rainy days we would sit in a circle on the floor of the large living room in the old rambling house and read the funnies she had collected in large cheese boxes, a bowl of fresh popcorn in the center of the circle.

The house was located in the Bloody Seventh, as they called it, because it was in that ward that many fights took place during the strike of '88. Carl Sandburg's home was immediately behind it two blocks south. Somehow, the children tried to live up to the ward's name, though they had no idea how it originated.

I liked to visit my cousins, but my father was apprehensive because I was the youngest in the group. It embarrassed me to hear him tell Aunt Carrie, "Look after him."

There was ingenuity in the games played around the Bloody Seventh. Next to Aunt Carrie's house was an enormous, beautiful maple tree whose lowest branches were high from the ground. A rope was thrown over the lowest big branch, and to it was fastened a broomstick crossbar from which dangled a large hook, the sharp kind used by butchers to hang up a side of beef. This hung loose, out of reach of all except the tallest children. A wooden platform had been built high off the ground and big enough to hold a small four-wheeled wagon. From it, a slide of boards went to the ground and a runway. The game's rules were that one child pulled himself up and sat with the broomstick bar between his legs, the hook dangling below. He then began to swing harder and harder, and as he reached the height

14

of the platform, he would drop the hook into the handle on the end of the wagon tongue. His weight and the force of the forward swing would pull the wagon down the slide. At the proper moment as the swing reached its most forward point in the arc, the rider would pull out the hook and the wagon would go careening down the bare dirt runway. It was so complicated a scheme that it was a challenge to both the swing rider and the driver of the wagon.

When it came my turn on the swing, I had to jump up from the ground, grab for the bar, and then haul myself up by getting the bar under one arm, grabbing the rope, and repeating the maneuver until I had the bar between my legs. The hook grazed my face on the way up, but I got the swing going as hard as I could by pumping with my body and then neatly dropped the hook into the tongue handle. It was a good pull-off.

I stayed up on the swing for a dozen or more trips. It made me feel good to hear their praises. Finally, it came my turn to drive the wagon. I got the bar out from between my legs and let myself down so that I was holding it with my hands. Then I let go to drop to the ground. The sharp hook grazed my head and caught in the back of my right hand. There I hung suspended with the blood running down my arm and into my face. The rest were panicked and began to tell me just what to do. At last, my cousin George pushed me up by my legs so I could take the hook out of my hand.

Aunt Carrie heard the screams and came running across the yard. I had begun to sob from fright alone, because there wasn't any pain, although the blood was spurting from my hand in jets. Aunt Carrie tore a piece from her apron and bound it tightly around my forearm. With her arm around my shoulder, we started to walk the mile to my home. We went up Chambers Street, and as we came to the opening in the fence through which we would enter our back yard, Dad, carrying his lunch pail, was stooping to go through on his way to the roundhouse.

Mother was taking freshly baked bread from the oven as we came into the kitchen. Dad took me to the sink and poured a pitcher of water over my hand. Relaxing his pressure on my forearm, the blood spurted again.

Mother came from the telephone, sobbing. "Doctor Horrell will

15

be here as soon as he can. He said to keep something tight around his arm and to put alcohol on it. All we have is turpentine."

While my father held my hand, the turpentine was poured into the wound. I could not keep back my screams. Aunt Carrie slowly got up from her chair as the doctor came in. "I'll be going now, Al." Dad didn't answer.

Dr. Horrell took off his cutaway coat and removed the starched cuffs from his shirt sleeves. "Well, boy, looks like you got a real cut in your hand. When I was a boy, I was fooling around with a knife in Jim Hawk's store. Remember him, Al? The butcher over in Colchester. I picked it up just to look at it. Darned thing slipped out of my hand and went right through my shoe and foot. There I was, stuck to the floor. I couldn't have gotten away even if I'd tried."

As he talked, he was taking things out of his black bag. He put a piece of cotton over the wound. He brought out a small can, took off its top, and sprinkled some yellow powder into the wound. It didn't hurt, but it had a peculiar odor.

"Now, son, that powder will help a lot. I'm going to put a stitch in, and I don't think it'll hurt. It will stop the bleeding and help it heal."

He took a straight needle out of the bag and wiped it off with a green liquid he poured from a bottle. Then he took a piece of what looked like string, only it was yellow, and threaded it into the eye of the needle.

"Now, Al, if you'll let up the pressure a bit. That's it. I can see just where the blood is coming from. I bet you can't follow this with your eyes; the hand is faster than the eye. There you are! Didn't hurt, did it?"

Dr. Horrell had grasped the needle between his fingers, and in one swift motion it had gone through the edges of the wound. He tied the catgut and cut the ends. Years later, I knew that the iodoform couldn't stop pain and that the doctor's speed and conversation had been the anesthetic.

Dr. Horrell bandaged my hand. "You don't have to stay in the house. Go on and play. Charge everybody a penny if they want to get a good look at your bandage. In a week, come down to the office and I'll take it off. Don't get it wet. No use telling you not to get it

16

dirty. It'll be all right. The hook wasn't rusty, was it? Good. Guess hanging out there in the sun day after day, it'd be clean enough."

The doctor snapped his cuffs back on. He was short and round, with red hair and a mustache, and hair on his chin that quivered when he spoke. He had twinkly blue eyes and chuckled a lot. There were old, worn magazines on the table in his office, and the cardboard clock on the door had the hands set at the time the doctor would return. On sunny days it was a cheerful room, but when it was dark and cloudy, the room harbored ghosts. Dr. Horrell dispensed his medicine in different-colored little envelopes. Mother and Father laughed when they said that he often asked them the color of the last envelope he gave them.

"How would you like to take a ride around the block in my new Buick? Go out and get your pals. I've time to give you a short ride," Dr. Horrell said.

I didn't have far to go. Kent and Freddy were already walking around the bluish-white wonder with its brightly polished brass lamps and levers. I opened the door to the back seat, and they fell in; I was invited to sit up front. The doctor took us around the block twice.

"See you in a week, son. Don't be so silly again. Your father and I don't think people should do stupid things. Keep your wits about you. Hear me, boys?" He started his car with a series of bangs from the muffler exhaust, not waiting for our answer.

Dr. Horrell's cuffs, watch chain, Vandyke beard, and personality had to serve for the lack of medical knowledge in those days. The physiology of the endocrine glands was unknown; general anesthetics were limited to chloroform and ether; sulfonamides and antibiotics were far in the future; typhoid epidemics and carriers were commonplace; no one had ever heard of vitamin deficiencies. There were few good medical schools with a progressive curriculum in Dr. Horrell's student days. He had driven a country doctor's rig and kept his office clean. He sat through the same lectures two years in a row, and had he gone back for the third year, he would have been graduated cum laude.

There was no difficulty in getting Dr. Horrell to make a house call. He didn't direct that I be taken to the emergency department of

17

a hospital. The wound became infected, had laudable pus, and healed with a thick, ugly scar, which I still have. Lockjaw was a fearful term. I didn't receive antitetanus toxin. Dr. Horrell said the hook wasn't rusty and it had been hanging in the sun. No one questioned his actions or his advice; his personality and manner exuded confidence.

One evening I was doing my high school homework at the dining room table when Dad said: "I was walking home when this fella came up behind me. Said he was a professor at Knox College and just moved into a house on Garfield Avenue. He's got three boys younger than you. See if you can't help them have a little fun. He teaches Latin or Greek, something like that. They're important, aren't they?"

"You have to have courses in Latin to enter college. What's his name?"

"Drew. He wanted to know all about engines and trains. Asked questions about railroading like a kid."

At the end of the third year I led my class and graduated as valedictorian. I worked hard over the speech that eulogized former Governor Johnson, of Minnesota, and struck a popular note with the Swedish citizens of Galesburg. I can't remember now one single attribute, or characteristic, or cause he presented that made me choose him as a knight in shining armor. As I stood in the middle of the stage at the Auditorium Theater, I saw my mother and father sitting proudly in the middle of the second row. I had no doubts about what the problems of the United States were and how to solve them.

"Why don't you go back to high school next year, complete the fourth year, and prepare yourself for college?" Professor Drew asked me. "I'm sure you can get a scholarship if you apply. Your parents wouldn't object, would they? After all, you are young. You should take Latin, more German, and mathematics, and you can handle them. I expect the following summer you'd have to do some work to have enough subjects for college entrance credit. Your principal could arrange for that extra work. I'll speak to your father."

"Can you make good in the studies you have to take? If you think

18

so, go ahead. There's plenty of time for you to have to go to work. We'll manage it some way. Professor Drew's a fine man. You're lucky to have him interested in you; don't forget that all your life you'll be lucky if you have someone older who wants to give you a chance. That's how it should be, but it don't happen too often. You'll have to show him you deserve the chance. When you get it, you'll have to make good."

My parents could understand the work I had to do when studying shorthand, typing, and bookkeeping, but the sounds that came forth when I recited Latin verbs puzzled them. "What good will it do him to know Latin?" I heard my mother ask. "How can he use it, except maybe working in a drugstore."

"I don't think he knows what he wants to be, but he will someday. Right now he wants to learn more about everything. Just as long as he doesn't work with his back."

Going to college by a railroad man's son was being a dude in the minds of railroaders. It was comparable to smoking cigarettes, playing ragtime music, wearing peg-top pants with deep cuffs and button yellow shoes with knobby toes, and shaving with a safety razor.

One evening, my mother and I were invited to her brother's house for dinner. My father was out on his trip. Uncle Frank Hensler, his wife, Mary, Mother, her sister Bertha French, and I sat around the dining room table after the dishes had been cleared away. Aunt Mary began to tell fortunes with cards. I had heard the talk about Mary having some strange powers, and here she was performing. When my uncle proposed that she tell my fortune, Mother objected mildly.

"Now, take a card, any card, with your right hand and put it in front of you to your right. Keep doing this till you have six cards at your left, six cards at your right. The cards at your left tell of the present. The cards on the right tell about the future. Remember, the cards never lie." She glanced at those I had picked, closed her eyes, threw back her head, and let her hands wander over the cards, touching them, moving some. After a few impressive moments, she began.

"This card, the queen of clubs, right next to the jack of hearts, that's you, it's pretty plain. Are you seeing a young brunette lady? And this card, the first on your right, shows you're very ambitious. Looks like you want to shoot pretty high, get away from all your

19

relatives. Those other four cards look like foreigners to me. There are strangers in your future. You don't want to do the kind of work we do. You seem bent on spending all your father's hard-earned money, learning foolish things. This one here," she pointed to a card on my right. "Now, if you're not careful, you'll come to no good. You must be . . ."

My mother motioned for me to follow her as she walked toward the hall. Without a word to anyone, we walked out the front door. Dad came in off his run later that night. As always, Mother went downstairs to let him in. The next morning I helped my father jack up our Overland touring car before I left for my Saturday job, answering telephone calls for the horse-drawn cabs that met each train and carried passengers to the hotels; called for people at their homes and took them wherever they wished to go in town, for fifty cents. I made two fifty a week, working all day Saturday and two hours each evening.

"Your mother says our relatives don't like the idea that you're going to college. They're jealous. They believe in card tricks and spirits. They're against anyone who wants to get out of their groove. Don't let them bother you. They aren't worth it. It doesn't matter what people say about you; it doesn't make any difference if you're doing what you believe to be right. It sounds simple, but it's hard to do."

Not long after, my father's sister Carrie came hurrying up the street; her curious pigeon-toed gait seemed about to trip her. My father said you could always tell when Carrie had a juicy piece of gossip by the way she walked. Usually, she brought hearsay, but this day she had been told by someone who saw the whole thing.

"Al met Frank Hensler outside the roundhouse and asked him if he was there when Mary told Loyal's fortune. Frank said he was. Al grabbed him by the collar, slapped him in the face, shook him, and told him never to speak of his boy again."

I have often wondered if my father knew how much easier it would have been had he told me just what to do. Sometimes, I am sure, children anxiously wait for specific instructions and directions. These provide security. Wise parents, on the contrary, offer general advice and trust their children to implement their own decisions. The unwise child believes his parents don't care what happens to him unless he is told just what to do. Often, concerned parents have difficulty giving general advice without appearing to intimate that a specific course of action is what they really desire. It is an art to give a child advice and simultaneously appear confused, dumb, and unopinionated. If this attitude can be simulated, the child may often feel sorry for the parent, in his ignorance, and so decide to teach him the correct thing to do.

My father and mother never tried to possess me. They didn't want to live my life for me, or live their own again in me. They took pride in my school accomplishments. My father was savagely determined that if he could prevent it, nothing bad should happen to me. But even more, he judiciously influenced me to make every effort to avoid harming myself or erecting my own obstacles. He was fond of repeating the story about the idiot who found the lost horse after all the smart men in the village had failed. The idiot's secret of success was: "I thought if I was a horse where I'd go and he had."

I spent the summer studying Latin and ancient history. My credits had been forwarded to the registrar at Knox College with an application for a tuition scholarship. I sweated out the waiting period, and finally the letter came saying I had been accepted as a student for the freshman class and enclosing a receipt for the year's tuition. My thanks to Professor Drew were inadequate.

"You are welcome. I did very little. You did it with your work. It is not given to everyone to be curious, have an imagination, and be industrious. Sometimes, you will find that people will laugh at you; they may even become derisive in their comments; they seem to understand frivolity in youth more than a seriousness of purpose. Try to develop a sense of humor, and it will help you through some of the difficult days."

I thought how different were the backgrounds in education, knowledge, and culture of Professor Drew and my father. Yet each understood and appreciated the attributes of the other; there was a mutual respectful envy between them. With these completely diverse beginnings, Professor Drew's and Dad's similar philosophies about life amazed me. They had been able to communicate with each other. I had been the recipient of their interest in my future.

21

I was pledged to the Beta Theta Pi fraternity. My father and mother approved, I suppose, because their entire social life centered around the Masonic and Eastern Star lodges. Mother advanced through the various offices of Violet Chapter, memorized her speeches, became Worthy Matron, and later held an appointive office in the Grand Lodge. Lodges were important in Galesburg. They afforded the social life for the working class.

I made my first close personal friend, Abram Powelson, a fellow pledgeman. Abe was a year older, a fine football player in high school, and had won a reputation as a dash man in track meets. As a star student, he took more advanced courses than the other freshmen. We spent alternate Friday nights at each other's home, and it was an event to take the last interurban streetcar five miles to Knoxville with Abe after we had been to the Gaiety vaudeville show and had a bowl of graham crackers with half-and-half at Rowan's restaurant.

A new supply of cordwood for the big fireplace in the fraternity house arrived, and the freshmen were to carry it into the cellar, stack it, and make it available. Abe and I worked the following Saturday afternoon carrying in wood and arranging it neatly. We finally agreed that we had done more than our share and the rest could be left to the other pledgemen.

Sunday there was a note on the bulletin board that penalized me twenty-four strokes with a barrel-stave paddle for not carrying in my share of the cordwood. My anger mounted at the injustice and unfairness of the charge. I tore up the notice, threw it in the fireplace, left the fraternity house, and started home. Abe caught up with me.

"We carried in our share. I didn't get anything from my senior. What's eating Swede Olson, I wonder," Abe said. "Be sure and show up for the chapter meeting tomorrow night but make up your mind whether or not you're going to take the Omega. Don't talk to anyone, no matter what you decide to do."

When I got home, my father asked, "Something wrong?" I realized the gravity of the action I had taken in tearing up the penalty notice and throwing it into the fire. I felt shaken, weak, and uncertain. As I poured out the story, the injustice became more prominent. I hadn't been asked what the facts were.

"You're sure you carried in your share of the wood?"

"Yes, I did! Abe says so, too."

"I don't care what Abe says about it. You say you did. Now make up your mind how you're going to handle it. You've made your play. This is one time when you'll have to decide to stand by what you think right, or maybe decide that to be right isn't so important."

There was a confrontation at the fraternity house the next night between the upper classmen and the entire freshmen pledge class, which my actions had brought about. It was resolved by the son of an Irish coal miner, a senior at college on a football scholarship. He took the pledgemen to the vaudeville show at the Gaiety Theater. The next day at the supper table, my father said, "I see you're wearing your pledge button again." I told him what had happened, he asked no questions, and that was the end of the episode.

The annual fraternity dance was held in the Elk's ballroom. The dress suits had been rented. I was uncomfortable wearing a rented stiff shirt, wing collar, white tie, and gloves, with tails on the coat. My mother had made a black bag in which to carry my dancing pumps; it was the fashion. I had been told which girl to invite and escort. After the dance was over, the freshmen had been ordered to dress in warm clothing and report to the fraternity house. As the first pledgeman, I was the first to start out with a long roll of wrapping paper on which my instructions were written with repeated warnings to beware of ghosts and goblins. I was given a small lantern and a box of kitchen matches. My route went to the college through dark and wintry Standish Park, out the only street in town called a boulevard, to the Catholic cemetery. The lantern kept going out, and snow began to fall. I was to climb the iron fence surrounding the cemetery, advance to the center, kneel at the foot of the crucifix, and pray aloud to the legendary Wooglin.

It was hard to believe that anyone could be checking to see if I did all the things written on the scroll, especially on such a blustery winter night. There must be something at the end of the scroll that would prove whether I had been where I was instructed to go. I was scared as I climbed over the high iron picket fence. I felt surrounded by ghostly figures, all warning me to beware, as the wind blew through the bare trees. I reached the crucifix, bowed my head, but

23

no words came, and the cold wind filled my mouth. I left the cemetery in one big, vaulting jump over the fence and fell into a large ditch full of snow. The scroll unrolled, the lantern went out. After many attempts, I relighted the lantern and shielding the flame from the wind, read the scroll to the end. The talisman to be brought back was half of a railroad tie buried in a culvert nearly a mile west of the cemetery. I suppose the railroad tie represented my background. I found my way back in the dark of which I was no longer afraid and deposited the talisman as quietly as possible on the fraternity house front porch.

Cold, wet, tired, and sleepy, I knew a satisfaction I had never experienced. Coming up the street, I saw a light in our kitchen window, and Mother opened the door when I knocked.

"Abe has been here a long time. Get your things off, and I'll make some ham and eggs and coffee. A good thing your father isn't here, he'd think you were crazy."

I never asked Abe directly if he had carried out his instructions completely. I was reasonably sure, and it was strengthened by my father's silence when I told him my experience, that Abe had shortened his trip considerably and had waited with my mother at home. I never learned what my father thought of the fraternity preinitiation stunts. I have a suspicion that he thought Abe was smarter, but I also remember his insistence on telling the truth and acting honestly.

The lure of railroading was strong. There was no scholarship available for my second year. My shorthand and typing were assets; I wanted to go to Chicago and work for the Burlington. My father arranged an interview for me with his friend, Mr. Torrey, general superintendent of motive power. He was a short gray-haired man with a ruddy face who had come up through the operating side of the railroad. Immediately, he put me at ease.

"First, I want to tell you how much we respect your father's knowledge of engines and his loyalty to the company. Always willing to do anything we ask and at any time. More than that he goes out of his way to keep other engines besides his own working perfectly. Just the other day, his train was laid up behind a wreck, and there was trouble getting the wrecker equipment working. There came Al walking up the track to lend a hand. He got the equipment working in no time. Too bad your father doesn't think he can take more responsi-

24

bilities because of his lack of schooling. We've been urging him to do so. You know that he isn't limited in any other way, don't you?"

I did know, but he couldn't stand being embarrassed by his lack of schooling, if he was an official. I had told him there were people who could make records and write letters for him when he told them what to do. But, he said, if he couldn't do it, how could he honestly tell them what he wanted done?

There were no vacancies in Mr. Torrey's office, but he took me down to the passenger traffic manager's office and introduced me to the assistant chief clerk, Maurice Tanner. Mr. Tanner wore pince-nez glasses, was thin-lipped, precise in his speech, and immaculately dressed. I took his dictation of a letter in shorthand, transcribed my notes, and handed it back. Tanner took it and grunted, "Probably full of errors." I knew there wasn't a mistake and that it had a good format. Tanner put it down without comment and pulled a long typewritten letter from a drawer. "Let's see how quickly you can copy this, and when you're through, tell me what it said."

It was a form letter that could be sent to prospective travelers extolling the pleasures of scenic tours in Yellowstone and Glacier parks, the Royal Gorge, and beautiful California. Round-trip prices were quoted for various combinations of vacation trips.

"When do you want to start work? We'd put you on the correspondence desk, writing these form letters, but then you'd take some dictation from me, too, about passenger rates, routing of theatrical companies, and other odd jobs. Start you in at sixty dollars a month."

I couldn't afford to chance another experience like I had bugging potato plants for Mr. Falk and so was relieved when I didn't need to ask how much money the job would pay.

Soon, the form letters were left to others, and I was taking dictation from Tanner and the chief clerk, Albert Cotsworth, about the movements of theatrical companies over the railroad system. Some were complete special trains, others were several baggage and Pullman cars that were attached to regular passenger trains. All had to be routed accurately to get from one city to another in time for loading, unloading, and switching from one train to another. This was interesting work, more like railroading. I imagined the cars behind a switch engine, the switchmen with their hand and lantern signals, the engineer easing the cars on to make a smooth coupling, without

25

knocking the passengers out of their berths; the mysteriousness of a darkened passenger train at night standing in a station. I suppose I dramatized each letter I wrote in my imagination and enthusiasm.

"What do you mean, changing the switching instructions on these Red Mill company cars out of your home town headed for Peoria? Those were written by the old man himself. It's a good thing I caught this. It can't be a careless error; it looks to me like you deliberately made the change. Did you?" Tanner's voice was raised above the noise of the typewriters.

"The cars couldn't be switched that way in Galesburg. There is a Y on the southeast side of the yards that should be used. The cars would all be facing wrong if it was done the way it was written."

"You haven't any business changing things without orders."

"You mean not even things that are so wrong as that is?"

Tanner read the letter through again and smiled. "You're seventeen, and if the old man fires you, it won't do you too much damage. I've never had the nerve to correct a mistake just this way, but Lord knows I've wanted to. It saves a lot of time, but no face."

Tanner grinned in anticipation as he rose to take the letters into the passenger traffic manager; a tall, gaunt Scotsman who looked down on most people over his half-glasses. It was a common topic of wonderment how irascible, Scotch-drinking P. S. Eustis got the name of Percy.

It didn't seem quite fair to be made the offering to the old man's wrath by being corrected for a mistake, just so Tanner could see what would happen. I didn't have long to wait. P.S. plunged through the door of his office, his face red, clutching the letter in his upraised hand.

"Where's the fella who wrote this letter on the Red Mill company? Come in here."

The silence of the stopped typewriters was oppressive as I slowly pulled myself to my feet and went toward him. Mr. Eustis turned his back and re-entered his office. I followed timidly, leaving the office door open. P.S. was sitting behind his desk, and I stood before him. I didn't know whether Tanner's smile offered encouragement or was one of triumph.

"You can shut that door if you're afraid of everybody hearing."

I stood motionless and didn't answer. By now, I was angry and confident in the correctness of my knowledge about the switching problem. I felt calm and unafraid of the storm of words I knew was coming.

"What do you mean changing the switching plans on those cars? I wrote those down and they're right. Tanner didn't change them but you . . ." P.S. became speechless. "I suppose you think you know more about railroading than I do. It looks that way. I've moved more cars around on this road than you'll ever see. It's sheer impudence. Well, why don't you say something? Come on, say what's on your mind."

"You can move the cars the way you did on those switching orders, but they'll all be headed backward into Peoria. I did it an easier way, and they're headed in the right direction."

"How do you know all that?"

"I was born and raised there; my father is a locomotive engineer, and I know the yards."

"The hell you say! Why didn't you tell me that before? Tanner, did you know that?" I hadn't realized that Tanner had followed me into his office.

"Well, I did hear something about where he came from, but I didn't pay much attention to it." Tanner was enjoying himself in witnessing something he had never been able to afford to do.

"Sit down, boy, and take this piece of paper and show me just how it works. Go on, Morrie, get the hell out of here."

Tanner seemed pleased, surprised, wistful, discouraged, and hopelessly confused as he shrugged his shoulders and held his palms up.

"Son, I never knew that before. You stood up all right, too. When you believe you're right, stand up that way all the time. Damned few do. You know I could have fired you. Don't quite know right now why I didn't. Go on back to work and let's see if you have any judgment."

P.S. began to call me into his office and dictate letters. I had to stay beyond hours many evenings to finish the work and leave the letters on his desk so they'd be ready for his signature first thing in the morning. One evening, as a reward for diligence, I suppose, Mr. Eustis took me to dinner at De Jongh's, a famous restaurant on Monroe Street across from the Palmer House. I could hardly eat the sumptuous meal for looking at the room and the diners.

Finally, a buzzer was installed on my desk, and I would go into his office, notebook and pencil in hand. I learned a great deal about interdepartmental jealousies and ambitions; who was working to succeed Mr. Eustis and that he had his eye on a vice-presidency. I was startled by the methods used and the social obligations fulfilled to further their ends.

"Keep your eyes and ears open," P.S. said in answer to my question about the past railroading experience of the president of the Burlington. "You'll be able to decide for yourself how he got there. Let's just say there are several other capable railroaders around."

My father came into Chicago three times a week with a passenger train and on the westbound run took out the crack mail train. He had attained enough seniority so that he could hold these runs that paid him a better salary and required fewer hours away from home. He took pride in keeping his train on time and often complained about the train crews who, he said, had no idea how hard it was to make up the time they lost by strutting around depot platforms in their brass-buttoned uniforms. He kept his run on the mail train on time because he had a great sense of judging roadbed, time, and speed.

I went down to Union Station once each week to meet him. The gatekeepers soon learned I was a Burlington engineer's son and that I worked in the general offices. When the coaches were cut off, I would ride back in the cab to the Western Avenue yard, go into the bunkhouse while Dad washed up, and then we would go to the nearby railroad men's favorite restaurant for supper. A few questions and answers about home and my work usually left a major part of the time for us to sit silently, or for me to ask about some of the railroad officials. Many did not come up through the steps of railroading. Some were lawyers, others had banking experience. This probably accounted for some of Mr. Eustis' bitter remarks because he had gained promotion through the operating side of railroading. Albert Cotsworth had been the chief clerk in the office for fifteen years. I wondered what his future was.

There was a young man, older than I, who worked in the office that summer in the section on passenger rates. He was erect, tall, well built, and walked with, it seemed to me, a goal in mind. He was reserved, dignified, and appeared independently confident in himself. He was employed only for the summer, and railroad work was not his future. I learned he was a Harvard Medical School student. I was impressed by his air of self-confidence. I never met him, and he left in the fall.

I had been in the passenger traffic office for seven months; it was the middle of January, and I had been out of college almost the entire first semester. Many times, I had thought of Abe and the rest of the Betas; the fun of studying and being with friends.

The buzzer rang loudly on my desk. I was typing the same form letters after I had finished P.S.'s work. They had become so automatic I could let my imagination and thoughts move about without making a typing error. The buzzer became more insistent with repeated, short bursts. P.S. was impatient. I sat still. Suddenly, I realized I had made a decision that I couldn't quite account for, nor could I trace it back to any one particular event or any series of previous decisions. P.S.'s voice interrupted loudly and harshly.

"Come on in here. What the hell goes on?"

I got up slowly but left my notebook and pencil lying on the desk. I could feel the eyes of the men in the room follow me. There was an immediate recall of the first time I had been there. On both occasions I felt calm, confident, and completely at ease.

"What's the matter with you, boy? Where's your notebook? What's got into you?" The questions came fast without waiting for answers.

"I've decided to quit this job, Mr. Eustis."

"I'll be damned. When did that come into your head? Sit down. Tell me about it. What've you decided to do?"

"I've decided I can't jump to the sound of a buzzer all my life. I want to return to college; I want to study to become a doctor."

P.S. took off his glasses, polished the half lens, laid them on his desk, tipped back his chair, and wearily closed his eyes. After a moment he leaned forward. "You mean more than just not wanting to answer a buzzer, don't you? You mean the things I have to do that compromise my principles and beliefs because I'm trying to get a better position."

I nodded my head in agreement; that was exactly what I meant, and he had said it for me.

"D'you think you can make a good doctor? Quite a switch from railroading. Wherever did you get the idea?"

29

"I don't know. Maybe it's a lot of things; old Doctor Horrell, maybe." P.S. interrupted me.

"And the girl whose father was a doctor? Remember you told me about her the night we had dinner at De Jongh's? She's studying nursing, is that right?" I didn't answer because I didn't know.

"When do you want to leave?"

"I'd like to go the end of this week. That will give Mr. Tanner a chance to find someone. I'd like to take a trip to Salt Lake City and start back to college the first of February."

"How'd you like to have me arrange a pass; Pullman car and half rate in the dining car?"

"That would be quite a present, Mr. Eustis. Thank you for everything you've done for me."

"No thanks. Just see to it you do as well in your medical studies. And don't forget to come and see me when I'm vice-president."

I went to meet my father that evening and rode back on the engine with him to the Western Avenue roundhouse. I waited until we were in the restaurant and had ordered dinner before I spoke.

"I quit my job today, Dad."

My father kept on eating, and I wondered if he had heard. Finally, without turning his head to look at me, he asked, "Did you quit or were you fired?"

"I quit. I spoke to Mr. Eustis and told him I was planning to return to college in February; that I was going to study to be a doctor."

This time the silence was longer. At last, Dad finished and laid down his knife and fork. He pushed his plate away and drew the coffee cup toward him.

"I suppose you've figured out how to do it, as far as money's concerned? Your mother and I can give you the money for living expenses, but we'll need help for the college and medical school fees. Your mother will worry about how we can manage. Let me take care of her. You'd better get back now. Be home Saturday night?"

I could only nod my head. My father's acceptance of the challenging decision evidenced so much confidence in me that it was frightening. Was I doing the right thing? Should I step out of the niche in which I probably belonged?

30

A S I walked down the street in Chicago after getting off the early morning train, the fragrance of roasting coffee, mixed with the humidity of the June day, filled the air. The adventure of beginning a new experience became associated with that particular city odor. There was an element of fear in this sensation, fear of meeting the individuals with whom I must talk about registering in the medical school and doubt that I was prepared to start the study of medicine.

I had already registered by mail at the University of Chicago for three summer school courses which would leave only one other to be taken in the summer between the first and second years of medicine. The question was whether or not this would be permissible. There was no question about my lack of subjects, in one and a half years of college, which were admission requirements. My tenseness mounted, and I thought of what my father always prescribed: a cup of coffee. As I treated myself to freshly baked sweet rolls in Weegeman's armchair restaurant, my confidence returned with a satisfied stomach.

I took the streetcar out to the South Side, and since I was much too early for my appointment, I walked about the neighborhood of Twenty-fourth and Twenty-fifth streets, Indiana, Prairie, and Michigan avenues, and State Street. In the fall I would need to find a place to live within walking distance of the school. Some of the houses had seen better days, for this was the area of Chicago where the industrialists, packers, and merchants had built their mansions many years before, each trying to surpass the other in cost and ornateness. Many were deserted; others were occupied as boarding houses; others were inhabited by Negroes. The former owners had moved to the North Side and northern suburbs of the city. It was easy to imagine gay parties in the spacious halls and ballroom on the top floor.

I had walked several blocks aimlessly and now found myself on

Prairie Avenue opposite Mercy Hospital. Here the great surgeon, John B. Murphy, performed his famous operations and taught the Northwestern medical students in an enormous amphitheater that held almost five hundred spectators. I knew the doctor's name and reputation because several railroad men had been sent to him for his expert surgical opinion. I would have the chance to sit on the benches, watch Murphy operate, and be taught by him if I was accepted as a medical student.

A surgeon must have to be the center of the operating room scene, I thought. No division of duties could ever take the final, terrible responsibility for the patient's life away from him. I dramatized myself dressed in white from head to foot, masked and with rubber-gloved hands clasped before me; the operating room's silence broken only by the regular breathing of the anesthetized patient; the nurses and assistants poised like the players in a symphony orchestra.

I went up the steps, through the heavy glass-and-wood swinging doors, into a hallway with stairs in the center. It was rather dark, and I stood uncertainly, peering about for a directional sign. Charles Waggoner Patterson, the registrar of Northwestern University Medical School, was easy to meet. He smoked a big pipe with a long, curving stem which brought the bowl down below his chin. The office seemed more like a study, and his pleasant, soft-spoken manner encouraged me to speak of my aspirations. I expressed thoughts I had not put into words before. Mr. Patterson added just the right word or question now and again, but I did most of the talking. He spoke of the make-up courses I would take in the coming summer and agreed that the deficiency in one course in physics that would remain could be attended to between the first and second years of medicine.

The class of 1918 would be the first to enter the medical school, Mr. Patterson said, from whom they required two years of college work for entrance. Previously, a high school education had been enough. Dr. Horrell had told me that his medical education consisted of taking care of a doctor's horse and buggy, riding with him to call on patients, and reading about medicine. After two years of this, he sat on the benches of his medical school's amphitheater and listened to lectures that were repeated the second and last year.

What a difference between then and now. Mr. Patterson analyzed

32

the grades in entrance subjects; there was no aptitude test. Had one more applied, there would have been sixty-one in the class. With today's standards I would not have been qualified for consideration. Mr. Patterson knew every student personally and could give his college record without reference to his files. He was a graduate of the school of pharmacy and taught a course. I learned later that he was a balance wheel in the medical school faculty. He was satisfied to be regarded as a relatively unimportant man by the practicing physicians and surgeons who were the unpaid voluntary teachers in the medical school. They didn't realize how subtly and effectively he managed them.

Mr. Patterson accepted me for admission to the medical school in the fall of 1914. The only stipulations were that I have passing grades in the University of Chicago summer school courses and take the course in physics at Lewis Institute in the summer between my freshman and sophomore years of medicine. My application was not referred to an admission committee; Mr. Patterson accepted me. No one ever knew how he made his decisions; one thing was sure—a personal interview with him was very important.

I got a room in a boarding house at 5228 Cornell Avenue on the South Side. Mrs. Cheeseman was the divorced wife of a Milquetoast man, a violinist and leader of the pit orchestra at the Auditorium Theater in Galesburg. She was ambitious for their two daughters, and Mr. Cheeseman was content. Her boarding house consisted of two adjacent three-story flat buildings, joined on the first floor to provide living quarters for her family, a combination parlor and lobby office, the dining room and kitchen. I was assigned a small room with a closet and a window overlooking the court. I could barely get between the desk, chair, and bed. I paid nine dollars a week for the room and dinner.

The summer passed quickly; I became more confident in my studies. I had classes in an elementary course in botany, qualitative chemistry, and physics. There was a high proportion of laboratory work and few classroom lectures. We were almost completely responsible for our own progress; certainly, we were not spoon-fed. There was a total lack of comradeship between students; each was interested only in his own welfare. I don't recall the name of one fellow student who was in classes with me that summer. The university was a cold, lonely place.

My father and mother had saved three hundred dollars for the first year's medical school tuition, and we had figured I could pay my board and lodging on thirty-five a month. This meant sacrifices because they were making monthly payments on their house. I could save money for food and laundry by going home on the weekends using my railroad pass. My mother worried about meeting the financial obligations; not because she didn't want me to go to medical school but because she always imagined the worst that could happen.

"Your mother wants you to be a doctor just as much as I do, because that's what you have your heart set on. I've taken care of things so that if anything happens to me, you'll get your schooling." I had learned when not to ask questions of my father. "Nothing is going to happen to keep me from making my regular trips. I'll get the number nine and six run, or five and two, the first of next month by seniority, and I can't be bumped off them either. You'll never owe your mother and me anything. This is not a loan. We know you will be a good doctor. We'll get our money's worth."

On the morning of September 29, 1914, without introductory ceremonies, I met with my fellow freshmen in the class in gross anatomy in a lecture room. We were sixty strong.

There was tall, skinny John Claridge who inevitably became "Shorty"; short, broad-shouldered and -hipped Warren Ives came from Pecatonica, Illinois, and so was known as "Peck"; the blond, brusque Kansan's name was Warren Bernstorff, but for all time he became "Count von Bernstorff"; Ernest Berry was "Razz." Fat, thin, brilliant, lazy, ambitious to please and be noticed, serious, nonchalant, arrogant, we were all of these, but we were all seriously dedicated to becoming doctors. There were two Jews and two Negroes. One of each was liked and accepted totally by the class; the other two were wholly disliked. It was not a question of racism; it was character and personality. Another student was much older, had been a schoolteacher and had children; Pop Foster was set apart by his own choice. All were clean-shaven; all wore collars, neckties, and jackets. The era of peg-top trousers and pompadour haircuts

34

had passed. Vests and pocket watches were in vogue, a wrist watch was a rarity.

There we were, nervous, talking to hide our apprehension and waiting to meet Stephen Walter Ranson, the professor of anatomy. The meeting was short, and it seemed that the professor was as uncertain as we were.

"Gentlemen, ah, the dissection laboratory is on the top floor. There should be four students to a cadaver and—ah—if you make—ah—any attempts to observe—ah—what you may have heard—ah—are the traditions of the dissecting room—ah—you will be punished severely. Take your places at the tables as you wish—ah—and good luck." The professor had doctor of medicine and doctor of philosophy degrees. He had served an internship at the Cook County Hospital and decided to devote himself to research and teaching. He was shy, introverted, but not one of us ever questioned his knowledge, ability, or dedication. We had our opinions about his teaching talents and facilities for communication. We were not merely recipients, we had to do our part in extracting information and methods of procedure from him. In our infinite wisdom there was consensus that he never would have been able to practice the art of medicine. We were also agreed that he had respect and admiration for those who were practicing doctors but were lacking in scientific knowledge and investigative abilities in comparison. I didn't know it at the time, but this mutual regard between clinical and preclinical teachers was to become eroded to almost complete disappearance by jealousy over financial incomes, faculty ranks, personal empire building, lack of ordinary communication, curriculum dominance, and intolerance.

There was buzzing and confusion as Dr. Ranson abruptly left the room. It was soon apparent that some had already been pledged to medical school fraternities, and they paired off for the laboratory. I felt alone.

A hand on my shoulder turned me around, and I looked up into a moonface; a scanty mustache and thick lips called attention to a missing front tooth.

"Come on, kid, let's pair up for a stiff. My name's Howie Goodsmith. Over at the Nu Sig house they told their freshmen to look you up. Some old guy, practices up in Minnesota, named Grogan, told the bunch to try to sign you up 'cause you're smart. I figured I'd better pair up with you myself; I'm not so smart. I like the Phi Rhos better, but everyone to his taste, I say." The slurred, lisping speech made the merry, fat face more appealing.

The dissection laboratory had high, small, round windows. Electric light bulbs covered by green tin shades hung over the center of each black, slate-topped table on which was a body wrapped in white muslin, stained varying shades of yellow by the Vaseline that had soaked through. There was not much room between the tables when the four stools were in use. Two battered, silver-plated table knives were on each body, and a bucket hung beneath the center of the table. There were two doors to the oblong-shaped room, and between them on one wall was a blackboard. There were indentations in the black floor, and in warmer weather it would be soft, yielding, and greasy.

We stood off and looked at the messy mummy; the other two students were even less anxious to make the first move toward unwrapping the yards of bandages. Roy Crossen was a farmer boy from Kansas; Sam Durr, a native Chicagoan, had poise and an air of sophistication.

"I want to know what old number two sixty-five looks like," said Sam, as he cut through the Vaseline-caked bandages about the face and head. We watched wisps of gray hair appear. "Before we go any farther, let's place a bet whether our stiff is a he or a she. It's fair for everybody. These bandages hide any of the natural attributes of the female. No young ones get in here, you can bet, so don't start looking for the breasts, men. Pretty withered and shrunken, I'd guess."

"Suppose it is a female? What happens when we have to learn about the male organs?" I asked.

"We go visiting other tables, kid." Howie answered the question. "We'll trade specimens, maybe pick up some advantages here and there."

As I scraped the thick Vaseline away from the darkened, leathery skin and dug it out from the deep crevices made by folds of the skin, I could not keep my mind away from the identity of our specimen. Who had he been in life? What sort of work had he done? Did he have relatives, and had they, or fate, allowed him to end on a dissecting table? The odor of Formalin, carbolic acid, and other fixing fluids got more and more pungent. I had a sensation of sudden hunger followed by a wave of nausea. The last thing I wanted to do was vomit. Slowly, I edged off the stool and glanced around the room. Peck Ives was biting off a piece of chewing tobacco; Howie was silent, and several were walking toward the hallway where the windows were open. I didn't want to be the first to leave our table.

"Howie, let's join the bull session. We have the whole period to get Mr. Peabody cleaned up to start work tomorrow."

"Where'd you see his name was Peabody?"

"I didn't. It's the only name I can think of that's aristocratic. Maybe he was somebody, you know. Maybe he lost his money and ended on the poor farm."

Howie guffawed. "Hey, men, our stiff was once rich. I'll bet he wore striped pants and carried a gold watch chain. He probably was taken to the cleaners by a greedy floozie and landed on skid row."

"That's nothing. We got a dame, a blonde she was, too. She was one of the dancing girls on the midway at the World's Fair. She's got a heart tattooed right here," and Shorty Claridge pointed below his navel. "Can't make out the initials. Boy, I bet she could do the hootchie-kootchie."

Somehow, this bravura kind of loose talk helped us regain our perspective; we were trying to treat lightly an unanticipated shock. For me, the odor was the most disturbing physical sensation. I had been frightened by the dead I had seen in their coffins in the parlors of their homes just before the funeral services. The ritual of the gathering of the relatives and friends bringing food, and the morbid gossip conclave added to the fear, and I had often wondered just what happened when death came. Here was plain, matter-of-fact evidence that made belief in a physical hereafter impossible, certainly not in the same form. What kind of a personality did Mr. Peabody have? Would anybody remember and think of him kindly or with hatred, or not at all? Maybe this imprint that a person made upon his surroundings, friends and enemies, brought the only heaven or hell that was reached. These and many more questioning thoughts were in my mind as I began to clean up our specimen.

37

"There, he's as clean as a lily and ready to be picked as clean as a chicken," said Howie. "Now let's see if we can wash off this damned grease and odor."

No matter how hard we scrubbed, the odor of carbolic acid remained on our dried hands. It permeated my clothes, and I realized that I would have to ignore it and its association with Mr. Peabody and what he might have been in life.

Anatomy was my favorite subject. I had difficulty in bringing the benzene ring formulas into reality in chemistry. The stained microscopic slides of the structure of the tissues and organs we dissected were hard to visualize, since they represented only one plane of a complexity of cells multiplied thousands of times. I was fascinated by the formation of the embryo from the joining of the ovum and the sperm. What was it that made the fetal heart suddenly begin to beat at the fifth month? What were the chromosomes? We couldn't see them. Now they can be visualized and photographed with the electron microscope. What factor made the fetus a male or a female? I could understand how a harelip developed, but why did the embryonic processes fail to close properly? Would the answers ever be found? The use of the electron microscope, the discovery of deoxyribonucleic acid (DNA), ribonucleic acid (RNA), the chemical interaction of the enzymes, and the identification of vitamins are but a few of the many discoveries that have clarified the function of the structures dissected in the anatomy laboratory.

The professor of chemistry, J. H. Long, had gained a national reputation for his work in effecting a proper sewage disposal for Chicago, and his initials soon brought him the name of Johnny Hydrogen. His lectures were planned, unexciting affairs, and he never came into the laboratory. It was presided over by "Bush" Johnson, a hulk of a man who rushed about the laboratory awkwardly, his bushy hair sticking out in all directions. Bush's demonstration experiments never worked, and there were standing bets that he would blow up the laboratory and everyone in it. There was another assistant, a woman as broad-hipped as Bush was broad-shouldered, slovenly in her dress and always with reagent-stained fingers and a dirty face. We never knew her last name; the first, Sadie, was enough to be coupled with the one we gave her—Broadbutt.

38

Most of our studies in chemistry were concerned with what little was known about the gastric juice and the metabolism of ingested sugar, fats, and proteins. There were wide gaps of knowledge which became apparent during the second semester in the introductory course in physiology. This was given by an imposing, swallow-tailed-coated, red-bearded professor who delighted in giving his lectures upon the male and female reproductive system, but was obviously bored with the mechanisms of the gastrointestinal tract. There was so much to memorize and accept that the obvious questions we asked each other precipitated hot arguments during the lunch hour.

Russell McCurdy, a former all-American football star from Michigan State, helped finance his medical education by acting as tutor for the two small sons of the Drakes, who owned the Blackstone Hotel. He was the largest contributor to the noontime food pool, bringing more sandwiches, pickles, and hard-boiled eggs from the hotel than he could eat. Howie's mother was generous, and the rest of us picked up a sandwich and a bottle of milk from the nearby Greasy Spoon restaurant on our way to school in the morning.

I was one of the eight or ten who enjoyed those luncheon bull sessions. There were so many statements that had to be memorized because they couldn't be thought out logically; if only all those anatomical structures could be related to some patient in the future, perhaps we could then remember the most important and know where to refresh our knowledge when we needed to use the finer details. All of us began to feel the strain of learning so many important things so that they could be given back parrotlike in written and oral examinations. What would we do if we couldn't remember some of these details of anatomy later on when a patient was in the office? These were some of the questions answered with bravado and bluffing, with awkward humor, with silence, but always with the realization that we were working at our profession. All of us knew that what we put into our studies in our own way would influence what our worth would be as a doctor. None of us looked to our teachers to make us doctors.

There were times when the pressures were relieved by raw incidents that at the time appeared to be humorous. There was a veterinary school nearby, and as spring approached, the "horse doctors" came to visit the anatomical laboratory. They entered shyly, with their hats held behind them, and looked around with wide-eyed stares. It was simple enough to engage them in conversation and show them what they had come to see, while someone from another table walked casually behind the visitors and gently put pieces of greasy human fat, or organs, into their hats. Each group of "vets" seemed to get delight in keeping their experiences secret and sending another group of their fellow students over to see the human cadavers.

The same kind of hazing went on among ourselves, aided by Pete Zwalinski, the diener who had charge of the storage room where the cadavers were kept in a building adjacent to the school. Each of us, in turn, would point out what was to be learned from visiting Pete's workshop. Finally, after showing great reluctance, Pete would invite the uninitiated down alone, never in pairs. There were the wrapped frozen bodies in an ice-cold storage room, suspended by tongs placed in their ears. They could be moved about on an overhead trolley track. The dark room was lighted feebly by a single bulb hanging down from the center of the ceiling. Pete would begin his lecture on embalming, collecting, and storing, and gradually lead the student among the bodies. Listening intently, he would be unaware that Pete had moved near the entrance door. With sudden darkness and a closing of the door, the experience of being among the dead began. Often, Pete, who had his own ideas about each of our personalities and characteristics, would arrange additional entertainment. He would have posed a body on the route of escape to the door, with arms extended, offering an embrace. It required little imagination to believe in such a thing as resurrection.

When this experience came to me, I was seized with panic; each move in any direction brought me up against a swinging body. The tongs on the track made a clanging noise, and the bodies bumping together sounded like solid drums being beaten in rhythm with the clang. I could explain all these things logically, I thought; still, I was frightened. I hoped Pete was sober enough to remember if he had locked me in or not. The closeness of the room, the odors of the preservatives, and the rigidity with which I was holding myself caused my breath to come faster. I began to get mad at myself for being so gullible as to believe the sly remarks that had convinced me that there was something to be learned, that it was a part of the course in anatomy. I realized that each of the fellows who had been trapped was a part of the preparation to initiate the next candidate. I'd have to take it with a smile and with the idea that perhaps this was a way of showing that they liked me, that I was one of a small, select group. If Pete forgot I was there, got busy with his other duties, took another pull from his bottle, would I be missed? I'd better try to find the switch for the light; it must be somewhere near the door. I began to move more surely as my pupils dilated in the darkness; I could make out the rows of hanging mummies. I moved carefully to keep the bodies from swinging crazily against each other. My foot kicked a bucket which made a terrible racket as it slid along the floor; I stepped on a broom, and its handle struck me in the face. I kept straight on ahead, and my hands touched the cold brick wall. I began to move to the left, staying close to the wall, and I reached the corner. Still going to the left, I came to the door after passing the second corner of the room. I fumbled for the knob, turned it, pulled, and the thick, heavy door began to open. The daylight made me blink. My first reaction was to run, not even close the door, but I carefully shut it and then forced myself to walk away slowly, nonchalantly. I climbed the four flights to the laboratory and casually went back to the dissection table, sat down, and picked up my book and forceps. I knew that glances came my way from all over the room and from Howie, Roy, and Sam. After an interval, I opened a discussion about the origin and course of the internal mammary artery. I was determined not to mention my experience in the refrigerating room; surely, this was a part of the experience. I had found my way out, and this would be the test for others. I felt rewarded in some way; I had been accepted into a club that really didn't exist.

In February of the second semester, I accepted an offer from Howie Goodsmith's family and went to live at their home. The Goodsmiths owned a big brick house on Beacon Street on the North Side of the city. They lived on the second and third floors and rented the first. Howie and I had a big room and bath on the top floor and could be independent of his family by using a rear entrance at the bottom of the back stairs.

41

"I know more about you than you realize," said Dr. Goodsmith. "Howie is fond of you and has told me more than he realizes about your study habits, smartness, and determination. Howie is a good boy. I know he is not a good student. He was distracted easily in college, but now he can't afford it. Our father was a doctor, my brother is a doctor. Howie is the only boy in the family." Dr. Goodsmith slammed his fist on his desk. "Howie has got to be a doctor." The gold watch chain across his vest shook, and I could see his pencil, fountain pen, and thermometer in one upper pocket and a small leather book in the other. "This is a business proposition. If I know you, you'll want to pay your way. I'm really asking you to make Howie study. Study with him, help him with all the notebooks he'll have to turn in. Help me see to it that he gets through medical school. You can pay something, but it must be less than what you pay now, so you will be earning something for helping Howie."

"I don't know what to say. It's wonderful here. It would be great to live here. But what about Howie? Does he really want to go to medical school, Doctor?"

Dr. Goodsmith removed his glasses and looked at me a long moment. "You are shrewd, aren't you? I don't really know. Maybe he doesn't. I suppose I have talked a lot about him continuing the tradition. Maybe he feels it's his duty. But I would never insist. That's bad. Those fellows are the worst doctors in the world. Howie's never expressed a desire to be anything else. He made a free choice when he entered medical school. But I will not stand for laziness and not putting forth his best efforts."

I took the Burlington number five or fifty-five home each second Saturday evening, carrying my laundry and books, and returned early Monday morning on number twelve or fifty-six in time for classes. I seldom failed to meet my father as he came into Union Station during the alternate week. I would ride back on his engine and eat dinner with him. Riding on the engine and listening to the talk of the railroad men, watching the people in the gleaming dining cars of the crack passenger train, and sensing the mounting expectations among the travelers, visitors, and trainmen as the time of departure drew near, had not lost their attraction for me. Might I have been directing those trains someday, had I stayed; did I have the background, character,

42

temperament, judgment, and education to succeed in medicine? I never expressed these thoughts to anyone, but the desire to ride once again on an engine pulling a train going somewhere, anywhere, grew stronger.

The second semester had brought with it a new course: the introduction to physiology. We stimulated the sciatic nerve in a frog's leg. We recorded the contraction of the calf muscle attached to a writing lever on a revolving drum covered with a smoked shiny paper. We had been taught how to pith a frog, so that the spinal cord reflexes would still be present. The next year we would have Dr. Roy Hoskins, a younger professor, who was doing research on extracts made from the pituitary and adrenal glands of beef. These were pioneer experiments in a new field of medicine. Hoskins was not too preoccupied with his research; he taught in the laboratory and gave lectures packed with facts and their application to patients. He was highly respected but never had our affection, as did Daddy Zeit, the professor of pathology.

It had been snowing hard all that Saturday in March 1915, and it was cold and blustery. The wind was blowing strong enough to keep the railroad tracks clear, but if the snow became thicker and heavier, the trains wouldn't be able to move. Dad was due out at nine o'clock that evening on the fast mail train that carried no passengers. I had planned to go home on the six o'clock train.

I had been working in the laboratory and had finished pasting up the frog muscle-nerve tracings in my physiology notebook. If I hurried, I could catch a streetcar to the depot and make number fifty-five. If I didn't hurry, I could get supper near the depot, wait until my father backed the mail train onto the loading tracks, and ask to ride home on the engine with him. If I wasn't able to catch number fifty-five, there wasn't another passenger train until midnight. I wouldn't get home until four or five o'clock in the morning. The mail train would go down home in two hours and a half. I'd be there just an hour and a half after fifty-five got in.

I knew all the gatemen at Union Station. They had an interest and pride in the fact that I was going to school to be a doctor. My father

43

had bragged a bit. I never had trouble getting through the gates with my laundry and books.

Dad was coming down the engine's gangway steps with a wrench and oil can in his hands.

"Hi! What're you doing down here this time of night?"

"I had to work in the lab this afternoon and couldn't make fifty-five. There's nothing else out until number three, near midnight." I thought I gave a convincing reason which stretched the truth but was unassailable. Parents intuitively know when their children are evasively not telling the whole truth.

"Did you have in mind riding down with us?"

"Could I do that?" My quick response was a giveaway.

"Sure, sure. Stay where you are. I'll be back in a minute."

Dad walked around the front of the engine and disappeared. When he came back, he looked at his watch.

"Hugh Crane's firing for me on this run now. Just got seniority enough. You know him. Go on, get up."

My two bags made this awkward, but there was no help offered. I was supposed to know how to get up on an engine.

Dad had spoken often of Hugh Crane's skill, alertness, and strength. He taught Crane and was proud of what a good engineer he would be when they "set him up." His firemen could chew tobacco, smoke cigars and corncob pipes, but cigarettes were forbidden. They were smoked by pimps and ragtime players. He had a personal interest and investment in his firemen; something like that which existed in the surgical profession but has gradually been lost by increasing demands from interns and residents, who have insisted upon instant, unearned equality.

"Get up here on my side," said Crane. "I can use the edge of the seat, whenever there's a chance. I have to keep this baby popping all the time. This ain't no milk train."

I got settled on Crane's seat, my two bags in front of me on the floor of the cab, alongside the boiler. Dad was leaning out the side window looking back along the train for the highball from the trainmen. He pushed the big vertical lever forward and ever so gently pulled the throttle toward him. The start was smooth. The wheels didn't slip and revolve rapidly on the slick rails as they would have if too much steam had been let into the cylinders suddenly. I felt a warm flow of satisfaction; this was more evidence of what a great engineer my father was.

Gradually, the speed increased as we left the passenger yards and hit the open rails. The cab began to sway from side to side, and there was an up-and-down movement of the cab that was not synchronized with the movements of the coal and water tender. Hugh Crane's legs were straddling the apron that covered the loose connection between the two units. With his right hand he was getting a full shovel of coal, bringing it forward, simultaneously opening the firebox door with his left hand, then grabbing the scoop with that hand and smoothly hitting the open door. The steam pressure gauge stayed right at 210.

I had to grab the armrest to steady myself. I looked forward through a narrow long window that had no glass in its upper half. The wind and snow were coming directly in on me, and as the snow passed the boiler head it melted on my overcoat. Although the canvas side curtains were on the gangway, they were loose and flapping, the wind swirled through the engine, and coal dust blew on me and into my face. I could distinguish the red and green block lights ahead, but at times they were in front of me before I knew it. I began to close my eyes as we came to a curve; the sensation that the engine was leaving the track and was plunging straight on grew stronger and stronger. I tried to relax and let my body move with the engine. I was thrown up against the boiler head, and my father looked over and signaled me to keep a hold on the armrest. As mail sacks were picked up from the automatic arms that brought them to the cars from their stands beside the track, there was no slowing down, not until we reached Mendota, the halfway point, where a stop was made just long enough to take on water.

Before we came to a full stop, Hugh Crane had dropped off the gang steps, climbed the ladder on the tank, and had the cover up; Dad had stopped the engine, set the lever, dropped off, and turned the water spout over the tank. As Hugh filled it, my father quickly worked around the engine, dropping oil on the pistons and other moving parts. Then he was up in the cab, ready to get the highball, as Crane swung the water spout back into its position and came back into the cab. I could hear my father cursing the conductor's failure to signal him. Finally, he reached up and gave two short, impatient blasts on the whistle.

"How's it going? We'll be hitting around seventy-five on this last stretch. Watch yourself. Don't land in the firebox," he shouted over the noise of the engine. Hugh got up on the seat beside me as the engine began to move. I hunched forward.

It was different from riding a lone engine and breaking it in, but here I was. The pace grew faster as the engine plunged against the wind and snow. I had to hang on tighter and tighter until my neck, back, arm, and leg muscles were tiring and ached. My eyes smarted, and I couldn't watch the block signals ahead; they were dancing and seemed to be over the wrong set of tracks. I knew the road and began to count off the depots with their light of a single lantern in the window. They looked lonely and ghostlike because the speed of the train tore them away before realization. I was brought out of this daze by the familiar greeting: two long and two short blasts of the whistle. We were near Center Point and home. My overcoat and trousers were wet through. The train slowed gradually, and we were passing across Mulberry Street and arriving at the depot. As we came to a stop, Dad looked at his watch and shouted, "Right on the button, Hugh."

I climbed down painfully from the seat, picked up my bags, and started across the gangway.

"Where you going, son?"

I mumbled, "Thought I'd wait in the depot for you."

Dad looked almost as fresh as when we left Chicago. "I have to cut her off, leave her on the pit, walk back to the roundhouse, change clothes, and walk home. Guess you'd better keep me company."

I crawled back on the seat. We threaded our way through the yards and pulled onto the pit where the engine's fire grates would be cleaned. I carried my bags, trying to keep stride with my father and Crane who were loaded down with oil cans, wrenches, and cases. I stumbled over the uneven ties. The snow was frozen and slippery. I never looked up from the ground, fearful that I might step into an open pit. The warm, lighted roundhouse was a welcome sight. I sat mutely as Dad made out his trip reports, took off his overalls, washed his face and hands, and, finally, was ready to start the mile-and-a-half walk home. I made no effort to clean up; I was worn out.

My father didn't talk as we made our way home, but he did carry my laundry bag. As we reached the porch door, he rapped with the three rhythmic knocks of recognition he and my mother had used for years. I was dimly aware that the light went on and that mother had unlocked the door and was standing there looking at me.

Her voice rose. "What have you done to him, Al?"

"Not a damned thing, Laura. He wanted a ride and got it. Let's have something hot to eat."

I dropped my overcoat and books, splashed some cold water over my face at the kitchen sink, and slumped down at the kitchen table.

Mother was silent as she prepared bacon and eggs with toast and coffee. As my father set the table, he asked the usual questions about her day and complimented her on the neat job she had done sweeping the sidewalks free of snow.

The food made me feel better and relaxed me so much I could barely keep from falling off the chair. Finally, as I waited for my father to finish, Mother said quietly, "Go to bed, son." I took off my clothes as I climbed the stairs and fell into bed.

My father was reading the Sunday paper when I came downstairs. The oven was emitting the tantalizing odor of pork and baked beans.

I was sure as I could be that when Dad had told me to wait by the side of the engine steps, and had gone around the pilot with his wrench and oil can, he had climbed up beside the boiler on the fireman's side. He must have knocked out the pane of glass in the door in front of the seat. I knew that he would have had it replaced had it been broken on the trip into Chicago.

"Have you decided for sure whether you want to work with your head or your back?"

"I've decided all right. Guess it was worth it."

"Sure, it was worth it if you'll never have any more doubts about railroading."

The second year of medical school required hours of work and study in physiology, pathology, bacteriology, chemistry, physical diagnosis, and neurological anatomy. We had to submit notebooks of our experiments and drawings of our microscopic studies every week. Occasionally, I made drawings of the slides we examined and described for both Howie and myself.

Sam Durr spent a weekend at the Goodsmiths' with us, and in preparation for Monday morning and neurological anatomy, we rehearsed Howie in the names and functions of the cranial nerves. We thought he was letter-perfect. If Steve Ranson asked him the names of the fifth cranial nerve, or if he asked which cranial nerve was the trigeminal, Howie could answer perfectly. We sat in the front row with Howie between us. We rehearsed Howie quickly and finally, and sat back hoping.

Dr. Ranson came into the room, stood in front of us, and asked: "Andt, Mr. Goodsmith, give me the name of the fifth pair of cranial nerves."

Howie gulped and stuttered, "Optic." Sam groaned aloud and said in a loud whisper, "That's the second, you dope."

"You're correct, Mr. Durr," said the professor. "It is difficult to teach without losing patience, isn't it?"

The entire class attended post-mortem examinations and sat in the lecture amphitheater while the kindly, old Swiss, the professor of pathology, made his bold and extravagant incisions, held up the organs, and sliced them to show the disease process. Clinicians would be there to explain the symptoms of the patient, how they had been treated, and what they expected the professor to find. It was a stimulating game to understand Dr. Zeit's accent. His manner of saying things, which we would never forget, made me feel I was getting closer and closer to the day I would be a doctor.

Dr. Zeit never tried to push things into our heads in an outlined fashion. He illustrated how hard the cirrhotic liver may become by telling a story of a maiden lady who was an ardent member of the Women's Christian Temperance Union. She had a fresh bottle of Peruna, a popular tonic, on her table each day. He said, "Gentlemen, zis lady's liver was made so hard by ze alcoholic content of Peruna, zat ven she died her liver had to be beaten to death wiz a club." This story was so illogical but so vivid in description we did not forget cirrhosis and one of its causes.

We drew the shapes of the bacilli of typhoid fever and tubercu-

48

losis, the diplococci of pneumonia, and the cocci of the pus-forming bacteria. We inoculated these bacteria on culture media, incubated them, killed them, and stained them so we could look at them on slides and determine which stains they took. There were times when I was sure that I had become infected, and I would awaken in the night to go over the steps I had used in handling the culture tubes to avoid their contamination and my infection. I learned to keep my fingers away from my mouth and to scrub my hands carefully. I also had to guard against acquiring a soap-and-water fetish.

The assistant in the course in physiology was a redheaded Kansan who was older but took other courses with us because he was working his way toward his M.D. degree. After he had given some of the physiology lectures, we all agreed that Bob Gunning was an excellent teacher. He was helpful and patient with us in our laboratory experiments. We had to put glass cannulas into the veins and arteries of dogs and record blood pressure changes. First, we had to etherize the dogs, and sometimes the confusion was chaotic.

Big Jim Skolka, the Bohemian diener, had shown us how to hold the dogs between our knees so the hind legs couldn't get loose; how to get the front legs in one hand and then quickly clap the paper and towel cone, soaked with ether, over the dog's snout. It seemed to be easy when he did it, but the words of advice from the other members of the five-student team only complicated the assigned student-anesthetist's attempts to control the wild struggles of the animal in the second stage. As the animals emptied their bladders and bowels, pandemonium occurred as the etherizer attempted to save his trousers from ruin and the dog from breaking loose.

I made up my mind that when the job was mine, I would have a smoother induction for the animal. I went to Big Jim and asked his help and advice. The awkward Bohemian spoke broken English but understood what I was asking. "All the years, nobody ask me to help him. I show you, thank you. Take it easy, nice and slow. He must get the ether and air at the first; little ether, much air. Then more ether, little air; more and more ether but slow. At the last, you got him nice and loose. Careful, no choke him."

I spent as much time as I could watching the experiments of Professor Hoskins and Gunning with the new extracts of the adrenal and pituitary glands of internal secretion. By observation, I was learning about methods and techniques of experimentation. I was impressed by the meticulous manner in which they prepared for the experiment. Any one of the preparations, if not perfect, could destroy the results. Even Big Jim could place a carotid artery cannula with those big spatulalike fingers. Later, my surprise at Jim's dexterity was dispelled when I saw him repairing a watch during the noon hour.

Professor Hoskins asked me into his office. "Gunning tells me you are the student who types out his experiment notes. How would you like to earn some money working for us in this department? You could do most of it on Saturday afternoons when you have no classes."

"I'd like it. If it would pay for my tuition, that would be all I would need."

"Maybe you're cheating yourself, but if you put in more time than that, I'll arrange to pay you thirty cents an hour extra."

It was difficult to find a job in Galesburg during the summer vacation. Finally, I got a night job in a lumberyard, cutting and assembling boards for grain silos. I bought a copy of Edward's textbook of medicine which we would be studying in the fall. Occasionally, I accompanied Dr. Ben Baird on his hospital rounds. He delivered babies, treated medical diseases, performed operations, and, as I learned later, rarely admitted his limitations as a surgeon.

One afternoon, Dr. Baird invited me to come to St. Mary's Hospital to watch a young bone-and-joint surgeon from Chicago, Dr. Paul B. Magnuson, operate upon one of his patients with a fractured femur.

I waited in the lobby with Sister Mary Rita. Dr. Magnuson was tall, vigorous, and had a loud and rasping voice.

"Are you the young fellow Doctor Baird has been telling me about? Here, get these instruments sterilized. Come back to the patient's room." He didn't pause for me to answer. In the room he summarized the patient's findings for me after he had introduced me as "Doctor." He talked to the patient in a quiet, confident tone as he sat by his bed.

"Doctor Baird has told me all about your injury, and I've seen the X-ray pictures of your leg, Mr. Hinman. You've had excellent care, and in the beginning there was a good chance for your thigh bone to knit together. But sometimes this doesn't happen, and we have to operate and fix the broken bone with plates. You're in good shape, and I agree with Doctor Baird that is what should be done. You and your wife know that's why I'm here, don't you?"

The patient smiled and nodded.

"Fine. Now, I'll tell your wife the same facts I've told you. No more and no less. See you upstairs, soon. One other thing. You'll be in the best of hands after the operation. Doctor Baird will be in on the operation with me and will look after you just as he has. He'll keep in touch with me, and if it's necessary, but I'm sure it won't be, I'll be down to see you again."

Magnuson repeated patiently and slowly to Mrs. Hinman all that he had just said to her husband. She listened without interrupting and then took his hands in hers. Dr. Magnuson looked embarrassed as he put his arm around her shoulders.

Dr. Baird handed me a pair of white pants and a white shirt. The pants were held up with a cord.

"Turn up the bottom of your pant legs, son. Your pants will fall down no matter what you do with that string. I can't stand to see a surgeon walking on the bottom of his pant legs. You've got to look like a surgeon. Go on into the operating room and stay up against the wall, out of trouble." Dr. Magnuson had taken charge. It was the first time I had been in an operating room.

Mary Sandburg, sister of the poet, Carl, was a registered nurse and gave anesthetics to Dr. Baird's surgical patients besides being his office nurse and laboratory technician.

"Ready for us to begin, Sandy?"

Sandy raised one of the patient's upper eyelids and was looking at the pupil. "He's all right; good pulse. I'll keep him quiet for you."

"And you, Sister? All the instruments I brought along on the table?"

"We're ready, Doctor."

Magnuson cut through the skin in one bold stroke. I had never seen living tissue cut into deliberately before. I saw the fatty tissue just beneath the skin, and then the doctors were busy with hemostats, clamping the bleeding vessels. The surgical Sister was fast with her hands, putting hemostats into the outstretched hand of each of them.

I wondered how Dr. Magnuson could tell one muscle from another. It certainly looked different than in the dissecting room.

My reverie was broken by Magnuson's harsh voice.

"Go down to the foot of the table. Don't touch the outer sheet. Reach under it and get the tails of the half-hitch sling."

My heart began to beat rapidly. I held myself rigidly for fear I would touch a sterile sheet or instrument. Gingerly, I reached under the sheet and groped for the tails of the sling.

"Come on, boy! Don't take all day. I want a pull so I can get these fractured ends in line. Relax, boy, relax. You're going to have to pull steady and easy for a long time. Don't press. Got the bandage? Good! Now, pull steady and gently. That's it. There they are. Now, hold steady, don't jerk, don't loosen your pull and then tighten it. Just keep it steady."

I never looked up from my hands holding the bandage tails; I realized I was holding my breath and that wouldn't do. I began to breathe easily and naturally and found that my forearms weren't so rigid. I could hold the two strips of muslin taut without gripping so hard that my knuckles were white. My mouth got dry, and I wondered if the whole operation might fail if I relaxed my pull. I could feel drops of sweat running down my face under the mask. Sweat trickled down my back and legs. I was only vaguely aware that Magnuson had a bit and brace in his hands and asked for screws.

"Good." It was Magnuson's voice. "Don't let go, boy, until we get the plaster cast on and it gets set. You just hold the leg steady. You don't have to pull quite so hard now."

I held the traction for two hours. When the operation was completed, Magnuson patted me on the back.

"You were a great help. This is one way to find out if you ever can be a surgeon. I hope you enjoyed your first experience. Come see me when you get back to school."

Eight years later, Paul Magnuson sent me my first patient in consultation and gave me a lecture about evaluating my talents when I asked him if a fee of ten dollars would be correct.

In the junior year in medical school we had classes in medicine, surgery, gynecology, obstetrics, pediatrics, attended the dispensaries, and were taught how to get histories from patients, examine them properly, and record our findings accurately. How to interpret the patient's symptoms and physical signs in the light of the family background, the patient's personality and characteristics offered a real and new challenge.

I discovered that the men in practice who volunteered to give their time in teaching without compensation had a different attitude from the professors who taught anatomy, physiology, bacteriology, and pathology. They were realistic and pragmatic. There were more differences between them in their teaching techniques.

There was John Wolfer, a young surgeon, slight in stature, immaculately dressed with an aesthetic face, precise in his knowledge, and efficient in his presentation of surgical diseases. We were also taught surgery by William Cubbins, the antithesis of Wolfer. Tall, big, he immediately told us he had won fame as a football player at Centre College in Kentucky. A loud voice proclaimed that we couldn't learn surgery until we saw blood flow. He spent the greater part of each hour telling us about his patients and how successful he was in practice. Wolfer lived at the Blackstone Hotel where he served as the hotel doctor to help him get started in practice.

Cubbins taught the course in operative surgery, in which operations were performed on dogs to treat simulated clinical surgical conditions. Since we could perform operations legally after obtaining a license and without internship, Cubbins emphasized the importance of the course. It had been handed down from class to class that the high point was when Cubbins shot the dogs in the abdomen and students had to resect the damaged intestine and perform an anastomosis. The anticipated day came. We stood around expectantly as Cubbins with a flourish aimed his gun. The shot missed the animal, went through the partition, and struck the laboratory diener in the leg. The class was dismissed promptly and the exercise never repeated.

Twenty years after graduation, I realized that Cubbins was not the great surgical teacher we thought him to be when we were students. Wolfer, in his undramatic, quiet way, taught us more about surgical principles, but at that time he ran a poor second to Cubbins. How inaccurate it would have been for the dean to have paid atten-

53

tion to a vote of the students upon the teaching abilities of Wolfer and Cubbins. Medical students today are no more capable of mature evaluation of teaching than we were.

At first, I tried to memorize the signs and symptoms of typhoid fever, pneumonia, tuberculosis, appendicitis, and uterine tumors. One morning, as my half of the class sat waiting for Dr. Wolfer to meet us at eight o'clock, a man entered the door briskly, walked across the room, and stopped in front of me. It was Allen Kanavel, a surgeon we had all heard about, who had written a classic upon the diagnosis and treatment of infections of the hand from the careful studies he had made upon his patients at the Cook County Hospital and from dissections he had carried out in the anatomical laboratory.

"Young man, will you describe for me the signs and symptoms of a patient who has osteomyelitis of the left tibia?"

We had prepared to recite about appendicitis that morning; we hadn't come to infections of the bones. I rose from my chair and began to stammer.

"I don't know anything about osteomyelitis, Doctor Kanavel. We haven't had it yet."

"Oh, you haven't had it yet? You have had anatomy, haven't you?"

"Yes, sir."

"And you have had physiology, bacteriology, pathology, and histology? Or am I mistaken?" I could only nod my head in response.

"Well, then, describe the gross and microscopic structure of the left tibia."

For an entire hour, Kanavel led me on to discuss the tibia, the organisms that could infect bone, the pathological changes that would result from infection. Finally, I had to summarize the signs and symptoms that would be present in the hypothetical patient, stating that the infecting bacteria could have come from an open wound or through the blood stream.

"Now, you see, young man, you did know. I compliment you upon your poise under the fire of my demanding and pointed questions. All of you must remember that surgery is the art of the application of the knowledge you gain from your study of the basic scientific subjects. It is not a separate science as are bacteriology, anatomy, or physiology. Learn to use your knowledge. Good day and thank you." With that, Kanavel left the room, and we could hear his rapid steps going down the corridor, breaking the silence behind him in staccato bursts.

Kanavel had planted the seed of a real idea. Now I could be free of the driving urge that made me feel that I would have to recall from memory the exact answer to every question that might ever be asked me in medicine. Here was the way to be able to figure out the proper answer, or the approach to a complex problem that the patient might present. The thing to do was to imagine problems and see if I couldn't bring my knowledge of the basic subjects into play.

I decided to leave the Goodsmiths' and room with Bob Gunning in one of the old mansions on Michigan Avenue at Twenty-ninth Street. It had been built at the time of the Columbian Exposition in 1893, by Henry Higginbotham. Princess Eulalie of Spain was a guest of the Higginbotham's during her visit to the exposition. The woodwork was beautifully grained oak; the hardwood floors and tiled bathrooms were examples of affluence and artistic workmanship. The house had been converted into a rooming house and a tea room.

Howie Goodsmith's father talked to me when I made my decision. He hoped that my friendship with Howie would not end; he wished me good luck. He emphasized that Howie had a sense of humor, a personality that attracted people, the ability to relax, all of which, he said, I didn't possess but should try to develop. He ended by saying, "Unfortunately for Howard, it will be easier for you to do than it will be for him to become a student."

Bob Gunning accepted my invitation to spend a weekend in Galesburg. It was a pleasant visit, and Bob made a favorable impression upon my parents and Dr. Baird, who suggested we think about joining him in a small group clinic practice after graduation.

Bob and I discussed Baird's offer and agreed it was something to consider when the time came, but Gunning had reservations.

"I doubt if I would ever want to go into practice. Likely, I'll stay in teaching or research."

"You mean not to see patients at all?" I asked.

"Right. Most of the practice of medicine now is by guess and by God. You have to wear a big gold watch chain, look pleasant and appear to know everything, read a thermometer with a flourish, and write a prescription so no one can make it out. I'd like to know more about the movements of the stomach and intestines by taking X-ray plates; really, what it is that makes people tick."

"All of us would like to know everything about the body. Someone has to look after people while these things are being discovered, and they are the ones that will have to put them to use. If you never see patients, how can you put things you are learning in the laboratory to work?"

"Who said they wanted everybody in a laboratory? Not many know how to do an experiment anyway, you ought to know that. Babies will keep coming with or without doctors. People will get well from colds, and either they get well or die from pneumonia, regardless of what doctors give them. Maybe sometime we'll know more about pneumonia, but right now, this fall, you'll learn that there is a crisis in the disease and the patient either gets well or promptly dies."

On the weekends I didn't go home, I joined Bob, Sam Durr, Shorty Claridge, Ralph Eisaman, and Peck Ives in making the rounds of the cabarets. There were the Drexel, the Vernon, the two owned by the Collins brothers, the Friar's Inn, Fritzels, and the Elite Cafe, a black and tan cabaret. Jazz bands were coming into their own in Chicago. It had come up the Mississippi, got a Chicago touch with just enough restraint to appear sophisticated. Then, there was Colosimo's on Wabash Avenue near Twenty-second Street where Big Jim enjoyed giving us a seat near the dance floor and a glass of beer. When Dale Winters sang, neither waiters nor customers stirred. When she finished her act, he would politely and firmly usher us out, invariably saying we were always welcome.

The youngest, I felt like the kid brother who was taken along because he couldn't be left at home, but I soon progressed from a horse's neck to a whiskey sour or a Bourbon and water and learned to beat out the rhythm of the New Orleans jazz. The popular song of the day was, "Oh, Johnny, Oh, Johnny, How You Can Love."

The war in Europe had settled down to a stalemate fought in muddy trenches; the *Lusitania* had been sunk off the Head of Kinsale, Ireland, by a submarine after the German ambassador, Count von Bernstorff, had warned United States citizens to cancel their passages on the ship. It appeared more and more likely that the United States would go to war, particularly after the Germans began unrestricted submarine warfare and diplomatic relations were broken. An executive order by President Wilson armed merchant ships after the Senate had defeated a bill to that effect. Finally, the selective military conscription bill was signed, and every male between the ages of twenty-one and thirty had to register for military service.

There was unbridled speculation as to what would happen to medical students; would their education be interrupted and would they serve in the line, or would they continue on to graduation and then serve in the medical corps? I had a chance to make the honorary scholarship society.

With a young linotype operator, Berry Davis, who lived with his wife, Marie, across the street from my parents, we started a collection agency that would handle long-past-due bills of the doctors in Galesburg. My job was to get the accounts, and Berry's was to write the dunning letters. We charged a 20 per cent fee. This business venture was short-lived and unsuccessful, but I gained valuable experience in my talks with the doctors and learned some of the reasons why patients didn't pay their bills.

Quite often, they said, patients felt they had been overcharged either because they believed their doctor hadn't needed to make as many calls as he had, or because he hadn't given thought to the amount of their income. I suggested to Dr. Longbrake that the doctors should discuss their fees with their patients and not just routinely mail a bill. I asked him why he didn't charge a lump fee instead of three dollars for each home call he made. The good doctor reminded me that he had been in practice for thirty-five years and when he wanted business advice he knew where to get it.

I glanced around his office waiting room that must have looked much the same for years: the old, ragged, and torn magazines, the worn-out floor covering, the broken springs in the cracked leather chairs. A dim light sifted through a grimy ceiling window. The muted voices coming from the doctor's examining room would suddenly cease, and he would jerk the door open fiercely and call out, "Next!" Then began a struggle between politeness, urgency, and importance of real or imagined complaints, as each patient in the room would rise, start toward the doctor, hesitate, then fall back as the doctor's voice boomed out, "You all know damned well who got here before you. Next!" The preceding patient in the examining room seemed to have disappeared, noiselessly, through another door, but still the air of mysteriousness was there.

Dr. Longbrake didn't bother too much about examining his patients. They stuck out their tongues, he heard their complaints briefly, then sent them on their way with their medicine. He was patient, gentle, rough, loved, and hated; I felt sure his head and heart had carried many of the problems of the patients in his large practice. This good doctor had delivered into the world many who now came to see him, bringing their own children. There was little more he could learn about them by taking out his pencil and writing down the personal and family history as I had been taught to do last year in school. Still, the fact remained. Almost all of them didn't pay the doctor when they were financially able to settle his fee promptly. And as I watched him, I wasn't sure how much this really concerned him.

All of us felt a bit more important as seniors and carried our stethoscopes in our coat or trouser hip pocket, carelessly allowing the ends to peek out. We would not have the opportunity to hear the famous teaching clinics in surgery given by John B. Murphy because of his death the previous year. We had our favorites who could present patients interestingly and hold our attention as they taught the clinical art of medicine. Kanavel's quiz had shown me that surgery and medicine were not new subjects at all; they were the art of the application of what I had learned in anatomy, physiology, and the other basic science subjects. Diagnosis became a game of detection; the criminal hid behind all kinds of false identifying signs. I began the task of using my knowledge logically and without extraneous decorations. I studied and restudied questions I imagined might be asked in the Cook County Hospital examination that I planned to take, even though I might accept an internship elsewhere. This examination, by tradition, had become a matter of real competition between all of us in the class and the students of Rush and the University of Illinois medical schools.

We were finishing our services in the outpatient clinics, and we added our own contributions to the scuttlebutt that was handed down year by year about the talents of each group of dispensary teachers. The children's dispensary rated high among us; the clinicians were young men, good teachers, but most important of all, Flossie Olmstead was there.

Florence Olmstead was a graduate nurse who had spent her life in the pediatrics clinic. She bossed the making of the feeding formulas, the sterilization of the bottles and rubber nipples, and the distribution of the finished product to a mother or older child, when they came to carry the bottles home in their small wire-basket containers. Flossie could make a diagnosis upon a sick baby quicker than a clinician could get out his stethoscope. Her voice was sharp and incisive, but mothers, children, and students loved her.

The supply of fresh milk from which the feeding formulas were prepared was kept in a large old-fashioned icebox, and Flossie always had an oversupply because a game went on between her and the students assigned for three weeks at a time to the dispensary to learn about sick babies. If they could steal a bottle of milk each day and sneak out and drink it, all was fair, but this wasn't as easy to do as it sounded. Flossie had an eagle eye. She saw everything everywhere, and her hearing was remarkable. The limit, imposed by Flossie, was two bottles a day.

My group of six were planners, and we worked out an elaborate scheme, using different tactics each day, to engage Flossie's attention. There was a bit of sleight of hand involved, too, and the bribing of student nurses in manners and methods not quite ethical. Flossie was becoming irritated by our complete success. We became bolder and raised the take to three bottles.

One day a woman brought her infant to the dispensary just after noon when all of the doctors had gone. I alone remained of the students because I had been kept a bit longer with my last patient. The child was gasping for breath; its face and fingers were blue. The mother was crying and sobbing. Flossie took one look at the baby, heard the stridor as it tried to get its breath, saw the nasal openings dilated with each attempt to breathe. She took the baby and sat down in a straight-backed chair.

59

"Doctor, pick up that bistoury knife. That's it, the one with the long handle. I'll hold the baby facing you so it won't move its arms or its head. Now, listen carefully. Don't get excited. You're a doctor now, or you never will be. Put your index finger over its tongue back to the pharynx. It will feel swollen, bulging. Keep that finger there. Now, pass the knife on top of your finger and incise the abscess. You have one chance to open it properly and get drainage. Bring the knife out along your finger quickly but steadily. Then get out of the way because I'm going to tip the baby's head forward so the pus and blood will drain out and not choke it to death. Understand?"

I nodded dumbly. My heart began to pound and sweat broke out on my forehead, but my index finger wasn't shaking. The operation was over in a few seconds, and the pus rolled out of the baby's mouth. Flossie gave the child back to its mother, quickly made out a card for entrance to the pediatric ward in Wesley Memorial Hospital, which adjoined the medical school, instructed the mother where to go, explaining she would need to leave her baby there but she could stop worrying because already he was breathing better. "And when he is discharged from the hospital, bring him to see us." I had stood, quite unable to move while all this went on, still holding the knife between my fingers.

"Well done, Doctor! Run along and get your lunch. By the way, let me know how all you boys enjoyed that extra bottle of milk you've been taking each day. The last three were mothers' milk. Didn't you recognize some difference? You're all so clever; I wondered."

The United States had finally entered the war against Germany; the war to end wars. My friends at Knox College had entered the candidate officers' groups in training. All medical students were exempted from the draft and prohibited from volunteering for any type of service. The slurring charges of "draft dodger" and "slacker" were used indiscriminately. The medical students had been organized into companies for drills, and three times a week we went to a neighborhood playground to march energetically but badly. We had no identification to set us apart as those being held over by the government so that the supply of doctors might be kept intact. Relaxation on Saturday evenings was restricted to places where we were known as medical students. We were embarrassed to be seen with a young lady, so we went in groups to cabarets, avoided arguments as to the right or wrong of the war, and read about the use of bismuth paste and Dakin's solution in the treatment of infected war wounds. Each of us took a physical examination, answered a few questions about medicine, and was commissioned as a first lieutenant in the enlisted medical reserve corps. We were to be held out until we had finished an internship; the army and navy weren't willing to trust us without the experience we would get from a year's work in a hospital, but without an internship we could get a license to practice on the civilian population by passing a state board examination.

Bob and I talked many times about where we should serve an internship. Surely, we thought we needed to get the experience of different teaching methods and ideas that would prevail in a hospital on the Atlantic seaboard. We decided to write the Cook County examination and take the St. Luke's oral, just for experience, then send our applications to the Kings County Hospital in Brooklyn. Neither of us had ever seen this hospital, no graduate of Northwestern had ever served there, and we had not talked with any of the professors about Kings County. We had read a small circular that set forth the advantages of the internship and carried a picture of the imposing buildings set back from the street and surrounded by lawns and trees. It offered an adventure that information and facts might discourage.

The same approach to internships has prevailed through the years; the grass is greener elsewhere; one has to learn from doctors in another section of the country, or a hospital should be chosen in the community or state where one intends to practice. These are the illogical reasons set forth by medical students. Little or no data are gathered regarding the teaching abilities of the attending staff or their continuing interest in the futures of their young, aspiring physicians or surgeons.

We were accepted by return mail, but we agreed we must meet the challenge of the county's written examination. The oral at St. Luke's had been a matter of a few questions by two of the attending staff and a review of the application. The final question to me, "If you are successful in the county examination, will you accept it in preference to this internship?" closed the interview. I did not believe that Bob's vacillating answer to the same question had been completely honest; my quick affirmative answer sealed my fate.

We were accepted by Kings County Hospital. I made seventh place in the Cook County examination; Bob placed in the second group. Our trip to Brooklyn started the day after the graduation exercises. It was filled with frustrating experiences in finding our way on the subway; arriving at dusk at the hospital, hungry, hot, and homesick. We stayed overnight, resigned our internships the next morning, and returned to Chicago. A kind fate had kept us from refusing our acceptances at Cook County. The wards to which we were assigned at Kings County, the late dinner we were given reluctantly, the county poor farm appearance the hospital had as it sat back from the road in a large expanse of land, influenced our decision. They were not logically thought out reasons. Remembering this experience, I have been less critical of the reasons my own students have given for and against choosing hospitals for internships.

THREE

TEN of our class were in the first group of thirty interns who entered the Cook County Hospital on July 1, 1918. We were assigned sleeping quarters in a sun parlor on the roof of the main building until rooms became available in the interns' quarters. We changed into our stiff, unlaundered white suits. Wire coat hangers were the only clothes closet, and a white enameled table beside each bed was our desk. A telephone was placed on a long wooden table which sat in the middle of the room on a small rug. The remainder of the floor was tile.

"Did you guys notice where Eisie chose his bed? Just as far away from that telephone as he can get," said Count von Bernstorff. "No soap, my boy! What about making a roster so that everyone takes a day in rotation at answering the telephone when he's here, and particularly at night?" Bernie looked around and without waiting for discussion made it an accomplished fact.

I began to inspect the walls and door casings. "What gives, Gyppo?" said Sam.

"Well, maybe there's a bullet mark here somewhere. This is where Tony Jindra's girl shot and killed him."

"My God, that's right," George Hahn yelled as he jumped from his chair and joined the search. "Whoever got Tony's bed may not have a good night if his ghost starts prowling."

"Boy, you have to hand it to Tony. How the devil did he get through medical school and have such a stable of good-looking girls? Where'd he get the mazuma?"

"Listen to who's talking. Mazel the manipulator. That's a real tribute coming from you, Morrie," said Sam. "The warden better lock up everything that's loose in your ward. You guys all know that this slicker will have his office furnished before he leaves here, don't you?"

Morrie Mazel laughed at Sam and broke the momentary strained silence. He had been a chronic irritant to the whole class throughout our four years. Pushing, aggressive, confident, and smart, he pre-empted a front-row seat in every clinic. Being picked up and bodily passed back over the heads of his fellow students to a rear row didn't stop Morrie. The next time he'd take a front-row seat, grinning and inviting battle. The other Jewish boy in the class was jolly, fat Meyer Chapman; well liked, quiet, friendly, and one of us. Morrie had been thrust upon us as a temporary roommate.

"Just watch your step, at least while you're in here with us, Jew boy," said Sam. "No dames in here and nothing but silence from you. Any questions?" Flack, a broad-shouldered country boy from Iowa, and Morrie had fought out in front of Michael Reese Hospital where we had classes in pediatrics, after Morrie had persisted in baiting Flack about his dumb answer to a question asked by Daddy Abt. No one had gone to help Morrie get up from the frozen, icy pavement when Flack had hit him. Morrie grinned and walked out of the room.

"Wonder who'll get the first call to his ward? What'll it be? Maybe we should all go down in consultation."

"Just use your heads," advised Bernie. "Some of these characters are going to come in here breathing their last. Just use common sense. What's important now is, when do we eat?"

"Yeah, where's the grub?" said Sam.

"The dining room's on the second floor, but I don't mind telling you I don't look forward to walking in there with this fresh monkey suit on in front of the middlers and seniors." Eisie, as usual, was frank. "Mazel is probably there right now, sitting at the warden's table and telling him what's wrong with this joint. What about it? Let's go down in a group and sit at a table together till we get used to it. Most of them have finished eating by now." I had been dreading that first entrance into the dining room as much as the anticipation of the first call to a patient.

There was silence as we entered in a platoon led by Eisie and headed for a large round unoccupied table. Our immaculate, white, starched uniforms crackled as we walked. Soon, the murmur of con-

64

versation began again, and we relaxed, realizing there would be no hazing incident.

None of us had been approached by our senior intern, and we had been told that it was an unwritten rule that we should not be fresh and seek him out. It was understood that the senior had to agree to accept his junior, but Bernie had said the idea was ridiculous. He had won first place in the examination, had first choice of his service and intended to keep it, senior or no senior. In spite of Bernie's assurance, it was a bit nerve-racking to have to wait until a senior, out of school and in the hospital a year, who must be full of experience, condescended to help us go to work.

The food was good. I had purchased three suits of whites, shirts, and underwear which should last the eighteen months I would be on service. Board, room, and laundry furnished by the hospital would reduce the amount of money my parents sent me. We received no remuneration from the hospital; we were there to continue our education and training to become good doctors. Our biological urges were the same as they are today, and if we considered marriage, we also had to plan how to finance the adventure; we did not hold the attending staff, or the administration of the hospital, responsible for our personal ambitions. No one but ourselves was responsible for continuing our education. We did not consider that our care of patients should be paid for. We were not in professional practice; we were still anxious to be taught and to learn.

Back to the eighth-floor sun parlor we trooped, each of us silent and impressed in our way with the seriousness of the responsibilities that the donning of the white, starched suits had thrust upon us. Sam Durr began to titillate our imaginations with speculations about what had led to the fatal shooting of Tony Jindra. Evidently, Sam concluded, whatever she had in the beginning wasn't enough to hold Tony. We marveled at Tony's audacity in bringing the girl into the intern's living quarters at the hospital.

The telephone interrupted our speculations. Eisie drew our admiration when he answered, "Doctor Eiseman speaking. Yes, he's here. Just a second." He turned to me. "Boy, you win the prize. First one up. Hurry up, get off your can and speak up now with a loud voice."

"You're wanted right away in Ward Thirty-four, Doctor Davis." The telephone operator's voice was soft and had a warm, personal tone. "Your senior, Doctor Lavolette, isn't in the hospital, so it's all yours, Doctor Davis." I wondered how she knew my senior intern's name. I hadn't even met him. "It's always a good idea to answer your calls promptly, Doctor Davis. It impresses the nurses."

"You look a little scared, old topper," said Eisie. "Why don't all of us go down and see Gyp's patient with him. Between us, we ought to come up with a pretty good consultation."

In spite of my protests that I didn't need their advice or help, they followed me in a body to Ward 34. It was a long walk from the elevator down a high-ceilinged, white-tiled, wide corridor. The sound of our heels marching in step echoed off the walls. The night nursing supervisor, immaculate in her white uniform and pert cap, which reminded me of the frilled paper collars I had seen florists put around a bouquet of flowers, met us as we entered the open doorway.

"Which one of you is Doctor Davis?" If she was surprised that so many doctors had answered her call, there was not the slightest suggestion in her voice or manner. I stepped toward her. "I'm Miss Glauber, Doctor Davis, nurse in charge of this ward at night." She was a bit taller than me, had nice dark brown hair, a round face, and red cheeks. She was comfortably rounded in the right places, which lent her an air of authority, capability, command, and maturity. I judged her at about twenty-five years of age. She reached for my hand and shook it.

"Glad to have you on the ward, Doctor. Your patient is in the dressing room. There isn't room for all your consultants. Why don't you go back to your quarters?" She smiled as she shooed them out and opened the dressing room door. "Doctor Davis will tell you all about it when he's through. We'll get along all right. Good night!"

I felt totally alone as the boys reluctantly, but without protest, left the ward. As I looked down at the thin, frail man with scanty, wispy, dirty white hair lying on the examining table, I had a moment of panic. The patient was grayish pale, and his color was accentuated by the white hospital gown tied loosely at his neck. There was a sheet over him, and this was covered by two bluish-gray blankets carrying the words "Cook County Hospital" stenciled in the corner.

66

I stood and looked at him. Where and how should I begin? Miss Glauber must have undressed the patient. His dirty blue shirt, overalls, and heavy shoes were on a chair at the side of the room.

The man's eyes were closed, his lips were blue, and he would breathe regularly and rapidly for less than a minute and then stop. I was frightened by the sudden realization that I was seeing Cheyne-Stokes respiration for the first time. That was a bad sign. I put my hand on his neck and felt his carotid artery pulse. It was rapid and weak; I could not feel his radial pulse at the wrist. His skin felt cold and clammy.

I heard Miss Glauber's voice which seemed to come from far away. "I've sent for Father Cook, Doctor, to give him the last rites." I looked at her dumbly and slowly understood that she had concluded the patient was going to die. I felt a moment of resentment. How could she, a nurse, not a doctor, come to such an opinion so quickly and with such finality? She had discounted completely what I might be able to do for the patient.

"If you don't mind a suggestion, Doctor?" It was a question, but I knew I would get the suggestion whether or not I minded. "Examine the man carefully and record minutely everything you see and find right down to every mole he has, and how large and where it is." A knock came on the dressing room door. "Remember now, everything—pupils, pulse, respirations, skin marks, scalp, face, chest, abdomen—everything in detail."

She turned and opened the door. Quietly, in her soft voice, she said, "Come in, Father Cook. This is Doctor Davis, our new junior on the ward, and this is his first patient. Excuse me."

Father Cook was a small, slender man whose head and face seemed too large for the rest of his body. He came to the head of the examining table, looked into the face of the patient, and said, "Too bad, Doctor." I went on with my examination, jotting down notes as I went along. I felt nauseated, and my movements were stiff and tense. Inwardly, I felt an urgency to do something more than examine the man. Anybody could see he was unconscious, but I couldn't find a wound on his scalp, not even a bump. The man wouldn't be able to swallow anything I might think to give him by mouth. He did seem to breathe easier when his jaw was held forward, but the rhythm of his respirations remained the same; slowly, they would become faster until they were gasps, then slowly they would decrease and finally disappear. I timed the interval, which was getting longer, during which not a movement of the chest or even of the sides of the nose occurred.

My attention to the patient was broken by Father Cook who had gone to the sink and was filling a small vial from the water tap. I heard mumbled words as the priest held the vial before him. Father Cook came to the head of the table, sprinkled water from the vial over the man's head, and after saying a prayer, which I couldn't quite hear, made the sign of the cross. The priest had given the patient the last rites of the Catholic Church. First, Miss Glauber and now the Catholic priest. Both had in a matter-of-fact way made a final decision that my patient was going to die in spite of anything I could do. I looked up into Father Cook's eyes; I was embarrassed. I turned back to my examination and heard more soft mumbling in the background. Finally, the dressing room door opened and closed, and I was alone with my patient.

I was alone with a dying man for the first time. Why couldn't I think of something to do to save his life? I felt the carotid pulse become fainter and fainter during the period when there were no respirations. Then, as a convulsive intake of breath would occur and respirations would begin again, the pulse would become stronger, but I knew that each time the heart was not responding as strongly as it had in the beginning. His left pupil appeared slightly larger than his right. All of his extremities were flaccid, and I couldn't detect more muscle tone on one side or the other which might tell me that he was paralyzed on one side and had a stroke.

What would I see or feel when the patient's heart stopped beating? I would be the only one to say that the man was dead. I didn't even know his name or where he lived. No relative had come to ask about him. I, a perfect stranger to an old, unwashed, unkempt man lying on a table in a bare hospital dressing room, was the only person who would be with him when he died.

The pulse stopped beating after the respirations had at last failed to resume. I placed my stethoscope over the chest wall and listened long and intently for the heartbeat. I was in a room alone with a human being who had just died. This was different from being at the anatomy dissecting table. The electric light bulb threw eerie shadows of the furniture on the white-tiled walls. Again, I felt a moment of panic and wanted to get out quickly. I started for the door and stopped. What would I say to Miss Glauber? I hadn't finished recording my examination; I'd have to note the time of death; I'd have to record that I didn't know the cause of death. I sat down at the small table and found she had provided a pad of history sheets on which to write.

I concentrated upon recording every detail of my examination just as Miss Glauber had suggested; ordered, in fact. It helped to have a task assigned to carry out. I wrote carefully, reverting to the type of penmanship I had been taught and had practiced laboriously in high school. I found myself thinking of the still, warm body with the gray, ashen skin, the open, staring eyes, lying in front of me on the examining table. Just a few hours before, this man had been talking with people, going about his job. I doubted that the Catholic priest could explain any more than I could, but the examining room had become a different place in just a few seconds.

I wondered if I should have performed a spinal puncture to see if the cerebrospinal fluid was bloody because of a brain hemorrhage. I had never put a needle between the spines of the vertebrae to take fluid out of the dural sac. The man had died before I had even thought of doing it. I should record exactly how the patient had come to the ward; all I knew was the few words written on a card by the police who had put him on a stretcher and loaded him into a paddy wagon.

I finished the record after midnight, and Miss Glauber asked me to help her wrap the man in a sheet which she brought up around his face and pinned securely. She placed a tag on the body and called the morgue attendant.

"You'd better go on to bed, Doctor. All in all, you've had a big day, haven't you?"

I took off my clothes in the dark room, laid them on a chair, and stumbled into bed. I was tired, but my mind was a kaleidoscope of faces, movements, words, and thoughts. I tossed and turned. It seemed only a short time until the telephone rang, and reflexly I jumped out of bed and had the receiver off.

A rough, gruff voice greeted me. "Davis?"

"Hello." I wasn't quite sure that I was awake and had heard correctly.

"Stop the nonsense and wake up. Listen, now. Get on down here to the morgue and be quick about it. This is Le Count. Hurry up!"

I had heard of Dr. Le Count but had never seen him. He taught pathology at Rush Medical College and was the pathologist for the county coroner's office. The gossip had it that he was mean, sarcastic, and just downright ornery. But it was admitted that he was a fine pathologist and had made some outstanding scientific contributions. He was an impatient teacher who demanded a lot from his students and got it.

As I went down the dimly lighted corridor to the elevator, I wondered if I had done something wrong. Did old Le Count think I was responsible for the patient's death? Somehow would I be taken to court? My apprehension increased, and my mouth was dry.

"You're up early, Doctor." The small, wizened figure sitting on the elevator stool looked up at me with kindly, blue eyes. I stepped in, and as he closed the iron-latticed door, the gnomelike man took his pipe out of his mouth. Slowly, the elevator descended.

"I'm Charlie, Doctor. Been here thirty years. I've seen a lot of you come and go. You're Lavolette's junior, right?"

"Yes." My voice was a hoarse croak. "What time is it?"

Charlie pulled out a thick, large watch and held it close to his eyes. "Five-thirty, Doctor Davis."

"How'd you know my name?"

Charlie chuckled. "Oh, I know all of you. It's a little secret I keep to myself."

The elevator reached the ground floor and bounced slightly. I stood confused and bewildered.

"Hurry along now, he'll be waitin' for you. Go down the hall to the right as far as you can, turn, and then take the first hall to the left. Keep right on straight. The door'll be open. Walk right in and there'll be the perfessor. Just remember, you're a doctor, too. Good luck."

I began to trot down the hall, and then, as I realized that Charlie knew I had been called to the morgue, who I was, and had given me directions and advice, I slowed down, straightened my shoulders,

70

and walked through the door with a false air of assurance and confidence.

I was in a brightly lighted room which momentarily blinded me. A body was on the autopsy table placed in the center of the cement floor in which there was a large drain opening. I recognized my patient over whom I had agonized in the dressing room of Ward 34. Standing at the opposite side of the table was a tall man with a cigar in his mouth. The sleeves of his undershirt were rolled above the elbows, a derby hat was perched rakishly on his head, and a black, heavy rubber apron hung from a slender cord around his neck. He had a big autopsy knife in one bare hand and a kidney in the other. The long hideous autopsy incision had been made in the body from the suprasternal notch to the pubis. The liver, sliced in many layers, lay on the table with the opened stomach and intestines.

This was the famous Dr. Le Count. I felt nauseated and my fears increased. I saw the refrigerator doors that lined one wall of the room. There was a sink in the corner but no other furniture. A fecal odor pervaded the air. I knew that I was being scrutinized from head to foot, and a feeling of anger came over me. I brought my eyes back to look at the professor squarely.

"Davis?" The cigar didn't move as Le Count's hoarse, guttural voice asked the question. All I could see was a slight parting of the lips on one side of his mouth and the tobacco-stained teeth.

"Yes, sir."

There was a grunt. "Best record I've had down here for a long time. You must have learned something. That head nurse on Thirty-four should have been a doctor. Pay attention to her and you'll learn more than you can from your attendings. Now, look here."

Le Count reviewed the pathologic changes that he had found, pointing out the widespread arteriosclerosis, the firm atrophied liver, and the enlarged left side of the heart.

"Now, I'll show you how to take out the brain. That's where we'll find the cause of his sudden death. Just remember I wouldn't do it this way if I wanted to preserve the brain for future studies. This is a coroner's case, and according to the damned fool law, I've got to section the brain right now. It'll spoil all the anatomical relations. Should suspend it accurately."

He made an incision across the top of the head and pulled down the scalp in the front and back with a few deft movements of his strong hands.

"Here, hold the head still." I placed my hands flat on the vertex of the skull and steadied it while Le Count sawed through the bone on the sides, across the front and back. Then, with a broad chisel, he pried off the skullcap. Cutting through the dura mater boldly and across the venous sinuses, the blood ran down onto the floor and spattered on his apron. Soon, the cranial nerves were cut at their foramina, and the brain was resting in his left hand.

He turned it over and looked at the base. "First thing to look for is an aneurysm of the circle of Willis. Didn't think there would be one. Not enough blood beneath the dura. Vessel probably ruptured within the brain."

Le Count made sections through the brain like he was slicing ham. This was the organ whose development made man different from apes. I felt a wave of faintness and disgust. My thoughts were interrupted by an explosive cry of discovery from the big man.

"There it is! Look how that blood has ploughed right through the brain tissue into the ventricle. It all came from that little vessel, too, but under terrific pressure. Tell me its name."

Momentarily, I felt a complete loss of everything I might have been expected to know. Then with a rush the answer came. "The lenticulo-striate."

"Lenticulostriate what?"

"Lenticulostriate artery, sir."

"That's better. Make sentences and use language accurately. You'll do all right. Go on back to bed or breakfast now. If you keep making good records on all of your patients, you can't help but succeed. You're not supposed to be here by law, you know, so remember that. There wasn't anything you could have done in that dressing room to have saved your first patient's life; if you'll get any comfort out of it."

Le Count began to put back the viscera within the abdominal cavity; he spit out the dead stub of the cigar onto the floor.

"Thank you, Doctor, I . . ."

"Go on, get out."

There was a knock on the door, and Father Cook entered hesitantly. "Sorry, if I disturb you, Doctor Davis, but . . ."

"Come in, Father. I'm here to put a new uniform on after last night's session. The other men are on their wards."

The priest sat down, drew his pipe from his pocket, and lighted it. "I did something in the dressing room that shocked you last night, Doctor. What was it?"

For a moment, I was unable to understand what the priest was saying. Then quite vividly I recalled my surprise that tap water could become holy water with such ease. I became embarrassed because of my evident lack of knowledge about religious customs.

"It was nothing, Father. I'm afraid I know little about your church customs."

"What is your religion, my son?"

"I have no formal religion, Father Cook."

Father Cook regarded me quizzically. "I don't think it is necessary for some people, and particularly the rightly motivated men in your profession. May I ask, did you have a displeasing experience with your church?"

"You're psychic, Father." Somehow I found myself telling the priest about the failure to receive the prayer book when I had been perfect in attendance. It now sounded childish, but it had happened, it seemed, a long time ago. Father Cook nodded his head sympathetically.

"A blow to a young lad and a stupid error it was, indeed. Now, what was it I did last night?"

"I don't understand how you can get holy water from a city water tap."

Father Cook chuckled. "And I suppose you thought it should come direct from our Holy Father in Rome."

"Well, yes, I guess I did."

The priest became serious. "You see, Doctor, as chaplain of the hospital, I have the right to bless water and administer the rites. If I had been the man's parish priest and had no vial of holy water, blessed at the altar of my church, I could not have done what I did. Thank you for your time, Doctor Davis. I must be going about my work. I, also, spent a great part of the night out of my bed. Perhaps

I can come again. Often, patients' relatives bring me home-baked cakes, cookies, and homemade wine. I'll bring some along next time. Of course, I'll call beforehand. We can talk about religion at greater length some other time; I would enjoy discussing the questions in your mind with you."

On the first of October I transferred to a medical ward where the pace was slower and the tensions less. There were a number of patients being admitted who had coughs, aches, pains, fever, and were sicker than the physical findings would suggest. Some of them came to the hospital cyanotic and died in spite of the drugs given them. Autopsy showed scattered areas of pneumonia in their lungs, but not the typical involvement of one or more lobes as we had been taught occurred most commonly.

It became known that such patients were increasing in numbers in Europe, and that army hospitals were filled with soldiers with the same symptoms. The death rate was climbing alarmingly. The disease was called the flu, and it was recognized as an epidemic. There wasn't much to do for the patients other than to give them salicylates, which didn't seem to influence the course of the illness.

More senior interns had been called into military service. Bob Gunning left Mercy Hospital where he served in the interim and took his place as an intern in November. Dr. Wesley Woolston, who was substituting for Dr. Karl Meyer, as medical warden, arranged for him to work with me on Medical Ward 60.

Some of the surgical wards were closed and converted into medical wards to take care of the influx of influenza patients. Only patients with acute emergency conditions were admitted to the surgical wards. Often, patients would die a few hours after admission. We were working night and day and were sobered by the news that four former county hospital interns had died in military camps.

Bob and I tried to use screens between patients' beds to separate them into cubicles, but this was not feasible for so many patients, some of whose beds were in the dressing room, in the middle of the ward, and in the halls. We were able to get surgical gauze to make face masks for ourselves, the ward nurses, and the patients. We tried to keep the sicker patients in one part of the ward partially isolated from the others, but often the patient's condition would change in a few minutes, and our best-laid plans would be upset.

It was a helpless and hopeless feeling to be unable to do something definitive for our patients. Bob said they should have oxygen, but how? Should we open the windows of the ward widely? We decided to put two patients outside on a screened-in porch and cover them with blankets and put hot-water bottles around them. This was the way tuberculosis was being treated in Switzerland in the mountains, but there the air was dry and there was sun. I felt encouraged that some of the patients put on the porch got well, but Bob asked how I knew they wouldn't have recovered no matter what was done.

Armistice Day was celebrated prematurely and later officially. The examining room of the hospital was filled with the celebrants. Lacerations were sutured and the patients sent home or taken to the city jail. The dressing rooms and halls were filled with raucous laughter, loud voices, scuffling, and arguments. For twenty-four hours all the interns were involved in a confusion of alcohol, scalp wounds, blood, harsh dry coughs, gasping breaths, death, and squalling babies being delivered from mothers dying from influenza.

There were long futile arguments in the dining room and after we had gone back to our quarters, tired and exhausted, about the effectiveness of the masking program. The best argument was that if masking in the operating room was practiced to prevent contamination from the nose and throat of the surgeon and the rest of the operating room team, why wasn't it sound to apply on the ward to help control the spread of infection? The number of patients began to diminish as the winter wore on; the epidemic had apparently run its course.

I thought for some time that I, alone, was often awakened from sleep by the thought that perhaps I had acquired each new disease with which I came in contact. I had run the gamut of meningitis, pneumonia, Bright's disease, and recently typhoid fever. The only patient in the hospital with the suspected diagnosis of typhoid fever was on our ward. The patient was a curiosity, and there was a parade of interns to look at the temperature chart, follow the blood counts and the Widal tests. I succeeded in getting Dr. Frederick Tice, a distinguished internist in the city, to come over and examine the patient. He confirmed our diagnosis and entertained a group of us at the dinner table with stories of how the wards were crowded with typhoid patients during his intern days, twenty years before. His accounts of carriers of the disease, like typhoid Mary of New York City, were fascinating tales of the detective work that was required to discover them.

Cassie Kost, our medical nursing supervisor, called me to Ward 60 late one wintry afternoon. I found an old lady on the examining room table, in coma and with brick-red cheeks and hands. Bob reached the ward almost simultaneously and as he saw the patient, uttered a cry of astonishment and glee.

"She's got carbon monoxide poisoning. Come on, let's get her out to one of the beds on the porch where she can get some oxygen."

We picked her up, fully clothed as she was, and put her in a bed on the screened-in porch. She had on layers of underskirts, underwear, and two outside dresses. Her reticule was fastened to the waistline of the inner dress and hung open. As we undressed her, so we could examine her chest and abdomen, I saw Bob quickly put a small leather purse in his pocket.

The scrawny body was dirty, and the soles of the feet were caked with callus and dirt. The atrophied, wrinkled breasts were only folds of skin, and there were striated lines of previous pregnancies on the thin abdominal wall through which we could plainly see the pulsations of the aorta. The heart was beating regularly, slowly, and rhythmically. The respirations were long, sighing, and infrequent, but as the fresh air reached her lungs, the cherry-red color of the face began to fade and her breathing became more regular and the pulse increased in rate.

"The old girl must've turned on her gas stove and stuck her head in the oven," said Bob.

"The janitor smelled the escaping gas, broke down the door, and called the police. I wonder if she has any relatives. The police report doesn't say. Let's get some more blankets on her, put some hot-water bottles in the bed, and leave her here for a couple of hours." I was thinking out loud and began to wonder about her lonely and miserly existence.

"You do that and I'll go up to the room. Come on up as soon as you can." Bob hurried out of the ward with his customary rapid, short-spaced, listing gait. Miss Kost sorted the woman's clothing and put tags on each item.

The door to our room was locked, and I turned the heavy Yale lock knob back and forth roughly, thinking the door might have become stuck. The unrelated thought flashed through my mind of the stories that the locks on each door, including the bathrooms and clothes closets, had cost the county twelve dollars apiece. As we sat around in the evenings, all of us had been amazed at the evidence and stories of grafting between contractors and county commissioners.

Bob opened the door carefully and furtively. "Come here, let me show you something. You won't believe it."

The bathroom door was closed, which was unusual because there was always an open passage through the bathroom into Eisie and Sam's room next door. On the table in the center of our room, Bob had emptied the contents of the old lady's purse. A rosary of purple glass beads was caught on the clasps and was partly inside the purse; obviously, he had turned it upside down and emptied it hurriedly. There was a pile of dirty, crumpled paper money which he had straightened and counted. I was scared and my mouth was dry.

"There's over a hundred dollars there, and no one but you and I know about it. We'll divide it fifty-fifty."

I shook my head from side to side. I couldn't find the words to express my thoughts.

"Don't give me a lot of conversation about what's wrong about it. I need the money—I've always needed money—and the old girl isn't going to miss it. We'll earn it taking care of her. She'll never remember she had it, if she does get well."

I couldn't look at Bob, whose voice became louder and angry. "Don't forget I paid more than half the room rent at Mrs. De Grazia's. You haven't any reason to criticize me. You either split or shut up about it. One or the other."

Suddenly, I realized that the thought of stealing the money was not uppermost in my mind; it was the fear of being caught and punished. It was as if my thoughts had been spoken aloud when Bob said, "You're scared; that's the only reason you act so damned pious.

77

You'd take the money in a second if you were sure you'd never be found out, wouldn't you?"

I couldn't deny Bob's tirade. I was confused and stunned by his attack. This was a side of him I had never encountered.

Bob walked about the room. "Christ, should the policemen get it instead of us? You know damned well if it's turned in with her clothes, the purse'll be empty when she gets it back. You're going to have to wake up some time to what's going on around you."

"Yeah, you're right. I'm scared to take it, so scared it couldn't be worth it. I'm going on back to the ward. You do whatever you want with the money; I'll never mention it again to you or anyone else. I've never seen it, you can be sure of that."

As I walked down the long, empty, wide corridor to the wards, I made up my mind that I wouldn't try to decide whether I didn't take half the money because I was scared or because I believed it to be wrong. There seemed to be logic in much of what Bob said, and I needed money, too. I was more and more ashamed to take money from my mother and father to buy shirts, socks, and underwear. My father always stopped me from talking about how much money they had spent on my education. "One of these days, you'll be having patients and you'll be a respected doctor; that will more than repay your mother and me."

The picture of meeting my grandfather Hensler on the street when my cousin and I had snitched a piece of candy from the general store in Yates City, having to return it, and admit we had stolen it, came before me vividly. I was just scared.

As I turned into the ward, Miss Kost had a slip of paper and the old lady's clothes in her hands. "She must have been wearing all of her possessions. Strange that she didn't have money hidden about her somewhere; they usually do."

I stayed on the ward the rest of the evening, examining patients, watching the old lady's color come back to normal, and following her return to consciousness. I didn't go to the dining room; I decided to stay on the ward late and then go back to the room. In the morning I saw Bob's empty bed; his white uniform was hanging on a hook.

For two days I ran the ward alone and told Miss Kost that Bob had been called home by the illness of his mother. Early in the morning of the third day, Bob came into the room just as I was answering a telephone call from the ward.

I put the receiver up slowly. "Maggie Monahan was just found dead in bed." Bob turned and said inquiringly, "Yeah?"

"She's the old woman who came in with gas poisoning. She's been out of bed and doing fine. I was going to let her go home today. She was all right at six o'clock when the night nurse took her temperature. Must have had a pulmonary embolism."

Bob stood still for a moment. "Maybe a massive coronary occlusion. Take your time, I'll go right on down." Bob took his keys from his pocket, opened his dresser drawer, changed into his whites, and stuffed an object into his coat pocket.

I dressed and went to the ward. I met Miss Kost in the doorway as she was coming on duty.

"Maggie Monahan died suddenly just a few minutes ago. Miss Thompson found her dead in bed."

"What a shame. You worked hard to save her, I know. She'll be a coroner's case. I'll get her things together right away and send them down to the county agent's office."

Bob was coming out of the storeroom where patients' clothing was kept.

"Good morning, Doctor Gunning, glad to see you back. I hope your mother is feeling better."

"Yeah, thanks. I've put a note on the chart; she's a coroner's case. I was trying to find her clothing for Miss Thompson. I'll call the morgue."

Cassie Kost came into the dressing room with two bags of clothing. "Check these items off on the list, Miss Thompson, as I go through them." Piece by piece, all of Maggie Monahan's possessions were checked. "Here's her purse." She held it up and looked at it in surprise.

"There isn't a purse listed," said Miss Thompson.

Cassie Kost smiled and said quietly, "There was a lot of confusion when she came in and I guess I just didn't mark it down. It got all mixed up with her skirts." She opened the purse, took out the money, and counted it. "Write down purse and contents: a rosary and a hundred and thirty-seven dollars in paper money." She stuffed the bills into the purse. "That'll go to the public administrator's office along with her other belongings unless someone steals it before it's a matter of record. Our ward list will show it, Miss Thompson."

My middler service began in the examining room on the ground floor of the hospital, adjacent to the county agent's office. It was an enormous room, partitioned only by curtains that surrounded examining tables. A head mirror, an electric bulb in an extension bracket, a flashlight, and tongue depressors supplemented the equipment that each intern could carry in his pocket. There were only two blood pressure outfits for the entire area. In slack periods we would estimate systolic pressures by feeling and compressing the pulse and then check our guesses with the blood pressure apparatus. I became expert at detecting the high systolic, low diastolic pulse that we had learned as the Corrigan, or water-hammer, pulse.

The examining room was a busy place, and many patients were so ill that they were hurried to the proper ward with only a cursory examination. It simply became an exercise in determining whether or not some of the patients should go to a surgical or a medical ward.

There were many who had to go through the county agent's office and provide information about their financial and family status before they could be accepted as indigents. It was traditional that during the winter months the examining room would be crowded with derelicts from the nearby skid-row streets who would seek admission to a bed in a warm ward. Once admitted, they were hard to discharge until the spring months came.

I came to my next patient who was sitting on a chair in the screened-off cubicle. He held the county agent's slip of paper in his hand.

"Here's the slip, Doc. Send me up to the ward. I'm sick."

I looked at the loose, lax skin of his face, the small venules on the nose and cheeks, the blood-shot conjunctivas of the eyes, and the filthy clothes. The thin overcoat was held together at the throat with a large horse-blanket safety pin.

"Better take off your clothes and get up on the table so I can examine you. It won't take long and then I'll know where you should go."

"Look, Doc, I've been here before. Just send me up to Fifty-four, I'm sick. Got an ulcer that's acting up."

"Take off your clothes and let me examine you. We've got a lot of sick patients coming in this morning, maybe sicker than you are, so be a good fellow and get your clothes off."

Reluctantly and with mutterings, the patient began to take off his outer garments and finally got down to his shirt. I waited patiently ignoring the scattered words of insult and threat. There was no use trying to get a detailed history from the man; the question was whether or not he showed any physical signs of an acute illness. If not, I could give him a note to the Rush Medical School dispensary three blocks away where he could be registered, examined thoroughly as an outpatient, and be treated.

Finally, the patient got up on the table in his one-piece underwear which was dirty and ragged. Carefully, I examined him without finding any reason to admit him to the overcrowded hospital as an acutely ill patient. I told him to put on his clothes and wrote a note stating that I thought he should be studied carefully with X-ray and laboratory examinations and that provisionally I would regard him as a chronic alcoholic with beginning cirrhosis of the liver.

"The hospital is crowded, and we have beds only for acutely ill patients. Now, I've written a note for you to take to the Rush dispensary down the street. They'll start an examination, and then if they think you need hospitalization, you can get on the list here and be admitted for further study when the beds open up. I think they'll be able to help you without it being necessary for you to come into the hospital."

"Yuh think you're smart, don't yuh, Doc? Well, you're nothing but a punk. I've got connections, see! Yuh'd better send me up if yuh want to keep your job."

"I've examined you, mister, and I think you'd better move along now and let some sick people get some attention. Just go on over to the dispensary. You'll get good care there and more time can be spent on you."

I turned to leave. "You're a dirty son of a bitch. I'll show yuh."

Reflexly, I hit him with my open hand across the face, and he stumbled against the table. I got behind him and took his collar and coattail in my hands and pushed him toward the door that opened onto the street. There was silence in the examining room, and I quickly recovered from my anger. I was embarrassed and mortified. It was the last thing I should have done. The county agent, standing in his doorway, broke the silence. "I should have thrown him out before he got to you, Doctor. He's a no-good bum looking for a bed for the winter. Forget about him."

My red-faced anger had been replaced by pallor and a physical weakness. I had done the wrong thing and let a patient take advantage of my tiredness and lack of patience. Dully, I went to the next patient.

I heard the shouting voice of the man before I heard the door open and looked up to see the hospital warden, Michael Zimmer, advancing toward me.

"That's him, Warden, that's the dirty little bastard that won't give me a bed in the hospital. I'm deathly sick I tell yuh. He don't believe me. You'll regret it, Warden, if I die on the street. Jim Rappucci won't stand for it, he'll get your job, Warden."

"The hell he will. Now, shut up! Look here, Doctor, you have no right to strike a patient no matter what the provocation. I'm ashamed of you. Why didn't you admit him?"

"There are only a few beds left, Warden. We've got beds in the halls; you know that. I've given him a note to the Rush Medical School dispensary, and he can get a good examination there. No, I shouldn't have slapped him, but he called me a son of a bitch and I won't take that from anybody."

Mike Zimmer glared at me. "I can throw you out of the hospital, you know that, don't you, Doctor?"

"Look, Warden, I'm sorrier than you'll ever know for losing my temper with this character, but I'll save you the trouble of making any more threats. I'm leaving the hospital as soon as I can get upstairs and pack my clothes."

"Now, wait a minute, Doctor. Don't get sore. Take it easy."

"Let him go, Mike, he's a no-good bastard anyway. He hit me, remember?"

"Listen, you! Don't tell me what to do. Shut up, or I'll throw you out myself."

82

"Yuh try it, Warden, and I'll have yer job before yuh can get back upstairs."

"Take your slip and go on over to the dispensary. After they examine you, if they think you should be admitted, come on back and I'll put you in."

The man's voice rose again to a scream. "You lousy fink, you're a bigger son of a bitch than the doc."

Zimmer turned quickly, and with one hand on his coat collar and the other grasping the seat of his pants, he lifted the man off the floor and rushed him out the door into the street.

"Now, you bum, go on and see the committeeman and tell him Mike Zimmer threw you out of the County Hospital."

I watched the performance with a mixture of satisfaction, chagrin, and discouragement. I opened the door to leave the examining room.

"Wait a minute, Doctor, I'll go along with you."

The older man walked along with me in silence. "Come on into my office and have a cup of coffee with me." The memory of my father recommending a cup of coffee for my mother when she was distraught crossed my mind and somehow helped me maintain my poise. We sat silently and sipped coffee.

"We both acted hastily, Doctor. I shouldn't have come down to the examining room with the stiff. You shouldn't have slapped him. You're tired and working hard. I'm trying to get along with politicians who want a rake-off on every contract the hospital has, but what's worse are the two-bit ward heelers that tell guys like this one to come over and spend the winter here. Forget what I said, what do you say? I know about your record here; you're a good doctor. We need you and you need us. Don't worry about the punk. Just mark it down to experience. Nobody really got hurt. The only thing I ask is, don't talk about it."

Dr. Baird repeatedly renewed his suggestion that Bob and I join him in practice. We could start a group clinic. He and I would practice surgery, and Bob, because of his background in physiology, would be the diagnostician and internist. It was understood that we would deliver babies and make house calls as well as carry on a general office practice. Bob should learn all he could about roentgenology; we could purchase X-ray equipment and have the most up-to-date office in Galesburg. Bob and I would receive one-fourth each of the net income, and later the division would be one-third each.

The proposal was attractive, but I was concerned about returning to my birthplace to practice medicine. I wondered if I would be thought of as a doctor. Would I be asked to deliver babies if I was unmarried? I knew if I didn't make house calls, treat colds, and rheumatism, and deliver babies as well as or better than the old midwife who had spanked the first breath into many infants, I just wouldn't be asked to take out their appendixes.

I'm convinced now that the thought of practicing in Galesburg as a single man fortified my emotional reaction when I first met Pearl McElroy. She was beautifully impressive in her black velvet dress with her black hair and brown eyes, the first time we met as the result of a date arranged by telephone by a mutual friend. Our courtship was short, and there was no chance to learn about each other's idiosyncrasies. Pearl seemed enthusiastic about living in Galesburg; we were married in the Fourth Presbyterian Church chapel without our parents' attendance. It was an illogical, unnecessary, inexcusable evasion of decent manners. There was no objection from her or my parents after the fact; what was even more poignant was that there was no criticism of our neglect of their feelings.

To compound a beginning, which, to say the least, was inauspicious, I rented an apartment and without consulting Pearl furnished and decorated it with my mother's help. Although she never said so, I'm sure this was an important factor in her dislike of Galesburg and housekeeping. I thought at the time how nice it would be for her to come into her home and rationalized the feeling by the fact that she preferred to delay coming to Galesburg after I joined Dr. Baird in practice after the first of July, when I finished a year's internship.

It became more and more difficult for us to discuss our problems of adjustment. I was unable to accept her dislike and ineptitude for housekeeping. She had left a small town for the attractions in Chicago; she was not prepared to settle down to life in Galesburg. I had borrowed money to furnish the apartment and buy a Velie coupe automobile. The indebtedness worried me, as it always has, and my driving urge to be successful as a doctor in my home town was too much for my immaturity to combine successfully with our marriage. Pearl regularly and frequently left to visit her sister in Chicago; I didn't object strenuously enough, and this gave the impression of favoring the mistress—Medicine.

I was proud of our private examining and consulting rooms. Dr. Baird had rented more space, which provided an X-ray room and a clinical laboratory. Rapidly, I became busy. Dr. Baird praised me to patients who called and asked him to come to their homes on house calls. I was a young man with all the latest knowledge and they would be lucky to have me come and see them, he said. Sooner than I had expected, I answered calls that came to me directly. I soon forgot the embarrassment I first suffered when I had patients in families I had known all my life. Occasionally, they used my first name when they addressed me but quickly corrected themselves, and I was quite aware of their respect for my education and profession.

I assisted Dr. Baird in all of his surgical operations. He was facile with his hands and had a grace of movement that was efficient and timesaving. He was calm and at times almost nonchalant in his attitude and approach to the patient's problem. It took me some time to figure out how he managed the chew of tobacco he bit off his plug just before he put on his mask and began to scrub his hands. He certainly had no opportunity to spit out the tobacco juice, and I couldn't conceive of how he could swallow it throughout the operation. I watched carefully to see if there was any tobacco-juice stain at the corner of his mask. I never discovered any and, finally, had to conclude that Dr. Baird must have an awfully strong stomach or that his salivary glands didn't function.

Ben Baird was a bold surgeon. He had learned surgical procedures by doing and by watching others with more experience operate. He was particularly proud of the fact that he regularly attended John B. Murphy's clinic at Mercy Hospital in Chicago. He was enthusiastic about Murphy's surgical technique and his ability to make surgical problems clear and simple. He repeatedly emphasized his belief that a doctor must have self-confidence and show this to his patients.

If they didn't believe in him, he wouldn't be successful as their doctor, and if he didn't believe in himself, how could he expect them to think he always knew what was the matter with them and just what should be done?

The first clash between us came over an obstetrical patient. I had delivered several babies in the homes of Dr. Baird's patients. Baird had made it quite clear that he would not accept any more obstetrical patients but he could recommend me as a capable and experienced baby doctor. I was about to protest when I heard him tell a patient and her husband about my great abilities as an obstetrician. I was silenced by a look from Baird. I had driven far out into the country and stayed all night waiting for the baby to deliver on several occasions in the short time I had been in practice. I had gathered more assurance when I remembered the teaching that 90 per cent of the time, exercising patience and waiting watchfully, as Dr. De Lee, our teacher, expressed it, would result in a successful delivery.

Dr. Baird's niece was waiting the arrival of her first baby. She was in her thirties, and she realized that this was an added difficulty, as I did. Dr. Baird had turned her over to me because he was going on a combined visit to A. J. Ochsner's and Arthur Dean Bevan's clinics in Chicago and on a vacation at the time she was due to deliver. I was particularly concerned because I was sure that the baby was in an unusual position. Dr. Baird told me to stop worrying, the position would change and she would deliver without trouble; she had a large pelvis, like all the Baird women, and there'd be nothing to it.

The labor was long, and progress was arrested. I could feel the face presentation, and I had little experience in the use of forceps. I would have to use high forceps. As the hours wore on, the patient was becoming exhausted and the uterine contractions were weaker. I knew I should have help in consultation to save the baby and the mother. Dr. Edwin Nash was an experienced obstetrician of Dr. Baird's age; I had known Dr. Nash all my life. When I called him and told him the situation, I asked if he would come in consultation.

"Who is the patient?"

"Dr. Baird's niece and she's in her late thirties. She's a primipara. I think she should have a high-forceps delivery and your help."

"I'll come right over and help you, but remember, Ben Baird won't like it."

It was a difficult forceps delivery, and all of Dr. Nash's skill and my assistance were necessary to get a live baby and repair the surgical incisions and tears that had become necessary in the delivery. I had explained to her husband, and later to the patient, that I had called Dr. Nash in consultation without asking their permission. They would receive a bill for his services. The proud mother and father were so delighted with their baby that they showered me with their thanks for my judgment and honesty.

I recited all of the details to Dr. Baird when he returned. "Why didn't you go ahead, put on the forceps, and get that baby yourself? It'll be all over town that you had to call in that damned fool Nash."

"Doctor Nash has had more experience than I. This was a difficult face presentation that couldn't be rotated. The patient was your niece, but I would have done the same thing for any other patient. Your niece has a fine, live baby and is all right herself; it seems to me that's what counts. I'm not crazy about being an obstetrician, but I can take care of most deliveries because they're normal and easy. I don't understand why you think I shouldn't have called Doctor Nash in consultation."

"My God, don't you know he's our competitor? He's a damned poor surgeon. He's probably laughing up his sleeve at me right now. 'Baird and his bright young boys,' he'll say. You'll hear about it, don't worry. You'll have to live that down and you'd better change your tune about getting consultation from your competitors."

I walked away fearful that I would say words that should be left unsaid. I was disappointed and discouraged by Baird's attitude and criticisms. I was completely convinced that I had done the right thing. I knew I would have a hard time to forget the incident and keep from showing my disappointment in my expectations of Dr. Baird's ethics and practices.

All of my work was not surgical operations, house calls, and obstetrics. Often, I felt an embarrassment sitting in my private office doing nothing while patients filled the reception room waiting to see Dr. Baird. One day, I felt the contagiousness of Mary Sandburg's interest in my future, which was reflected in her smile and eyes as she stood in the doorway and announced that there was a new patient to see me. Her parents had come from Sweden and her father worked for the Burlington Railroad. One brother was a city fireman; Carl, about whom she talked with a mixture of pride and worry, had gone to Lombard, the smaller college on the east side of town, and then had taken his guitar and was "bumming around the country," as Sandy put it. He liked to sing folk songs and philosophize; he was the smart one in the family, said Sandy, but not a bit practical. She was worried about how he'd get along in the world and make a living writing poetry.

The woman who came into my office was tall, dark-haired, and had an angular face. Her eyes were dark brown and shining. She looked at me, and her gaze darted about the office. She was dressed in an old-fashioned black dress and wore a long coat with a collar that could be brought over her head like a hood. She held a large black purse with a long handle so that it fell below her knees.

"Please sit down. Is it Miss or Mrs. Ostrander?"

"Miss Lydia Ostrander!" Her response was clipped and harsh.

"How can I help you, Miss Ostrander?" I had learned not to ask patients what was wrong. The average patient couldn't resist answering that this was what he had come to find out.

"It's not about me. I'm surprised you're so young, but no one else has been able to help us, so maybe you know about the new things in medicine."

I didn't answer; it would be better to wait until she wished to state the problem.

"It's my sister who is very ill, Doctor. I had to use all my persuasion to get her to come to see you. I'm not sure she won't leave before I can tell you about her troubles. She didn't want to come at all. We're alone; our parents are dead. We take in sewing and have had to work hard, but we have a good clientele." She leaned forward and peered into my face. "Oh, we can afford to pay your fee, Doctor, don't let that worry you."

I told her I wasn't worrying about the fee and suggested it would be better if her sister came in and told me about her complaints.

"That's just the trouble, Doctor. She says she hasn't a thing wrong with her, but I know better. She hears voices talking to her and gets angry when I question her. She thinks they are Mother's and Father's voices." Miss Ostrander stopped and gazed out the window reflectively. "Mostly my dear father's voice. She becomes angry and tears up the dress-goods material our customers have brought us, so it costs us money to replace it, to say nothing of the embarrassment. For days, she won't speak at all. She doesn't eat properly, either. She sometimes hides our money in the strangest places around the house and then forgets where she has put it." Her voice lowered and became more confidential. "You know she was married and her husband died after a year. We all lived together; that is, Mother, sister and Oliver, and me. Father died some years ago. I've never been married."

Abruptly, she rose, opened the door, and spoke sharply to a small, oval-faced woman sitting quietly with her hands folded in her lap. "Come here, Amelia. The doctor wants you."

Amelia was small, petite, and was dressed neatly and stylishly. Her hair was light brown and streaked with gray. She smiled as she held out her hand. "I'm Amelia Cox, Doctor." She pressed my hand firmly, as if she were trying to convey a message.

I asked Lydia if she would wait in the reception room, saying it was rather crowded and assuring her that Amelia and I would get along and she would tell me about her complaints.

"I don't think she will and I'm here to make her."

Amelia Cox grasped her sister's arm and turned her toward the door. "I will tell Doctor everything, my dear, don't worry. I want to get well just as much as you wish me to."

Reluctantly, with the pallor of her face even more severely contrasted with the somber black of her clothes, Lydia Ostrander stepped into the reception room. I sat down at my desk and turned toward Mrs. Cox. She sat with her hands grasping the pocketbook in her lap. Her manner, smile, and appearance contradicted the fact that they were sisters.

"It won't be necessary to keep a record on me, Doctor. Lydia has insisted that we come to see you. But, really, there's nothing wrong with me. I'm just as well as you are. All the trouble is in Lydia's mind. I'm sure she told you that I hear voices, particularly Father's voice; that I become angry, unmanageable, and destructive. My sister Lydia

89

and I were the only children. She is the older and was the favorite of my father. She never married; my father discouraged beaus from calling on her. We take in sewing to provide a living for ourselves after my husband's and our mother's deaths. Lydia was quite unhappy when I married. Now she is in her menopause, Doctor. Sometimes I am frightened by her ravings; I'm not sure that she won't take her own life or mine. Have you any suggestions as to how we can solve this immediate situation? I'm sure you find it a confusing one."

Amelia Cox had put it mildly. I was greatly confused, and I would need some time to straighten out the contradictory statements. I was not a psychiatrist, but perhaps some common sense would be helpful. "I will examine you now as the first step in a complete examination, including X-ray and laboratory work. It will be necessary for you to return tomorrow and the next day. Perhaps later your sister will agree to the same kind of an examination."

I knocked on the door of my examining room.

"Come in, Doctor, I'm quite ready."

Mrs. Cox was sitting on the side of the examining table, one leg crossed over the other and with the sheet loosely draped over her shoulders. I hesitated momentarily when I saw that she was completely nude beneath the sheet. I should have asked Sandy to prepare her for examination; if I called her, it would be too apparent. I recovered my poise as I turned to get my reflex hammer and stethoscope. Amelia's body had none of the angularities so apparent in her sister. She wasn't coy in mannerisms to protect her body; neither was she vulgarly exhibiting herself.

I could find no evidence of an organic disease upon my physical examination. "Open the door when you are dressed, Mrs. Cox, and I'll ask your sister to come in when I talk with you about my plans for completing your examination."

I went back to Sandy's laboratory and sat down on a stool.

"Which one's the patient?"

Sandy's question crystallized my thoughts. I really didn't know, and I had been afraid to acknowledge it.

I explained to Lydia Ostrander that I wished to have certain laboratory and X-ray studies made on Amelia, to which she had agreed. I had examined her but had found no objective findings.

"It would be an excellent idea to allow me to examine you, Miss Lydia, when I have completed your sister's examination. Even though your sister's examination may prove to be quite negative, it is to her advantage to have a base line examination on record for the future."

Lydia Ostrander eyed me suspiciously. "We'll see. Right now, Amelia is the one with all the trouble, and I don't want anything to happen to her." Tears came to her eyes and ran down her cheeks.

Quickly, Mrs. Cox put her arm around her. "Now, now, sister dear, don't cry. I'll be quite all right. We'll go now, Doctor, and I'll be here tomorrow at the time marked on this slip. Come, Lydia."

That night I got a telephone call from Amelia Cox asking me to come to their home immediately. Lydia was screaming, unmanageable, and was throwing herself about the room. I called an ambulance and had her taken to Cottage Hospital in restraints. As I walked into her room, she was in a convulsive seizure. Her face was purple, her jaws clenched, her eyes rolled upward, her arms and legs rigidly extended. Her sister and the ambulance attendants were holding her down on the bed. The seizure progressed into the clonic phase. It was not localized to any one extremity or to one side of the body. I protected her tongue as her jaws opened and closed clonically. It seemed an interminable interval before the sphincters relaxed and her breathing became more regular. Her blood pressure was high. I had to get the convulsions stopped. Immediately another seizure began. The pulse was now more rapid and thready. I forced the tongue depressor between her teeth and brought her jaw forward to help her breathing. Her fingernails turned blue and her respirations stopped. Her pupils dilated and her face and lips became a deep purple color. There was suddenly a long expiration of air, and Lydia Ostrander's heart stopped beating.

I took Amelia Cox by the hand and led her from the room. I explained that, undoubtedly, the attacks in which Lydia had appeared to be dangerously angry, destructive, and had frothed at the mouth, "like a crazed animal," had been convulsions. It was important, I said, that as her closest living relative she give permission for an autopsy to be performed. It could be determined whether or not she had a brain tumor which would explain all of her symptoms.

Amelia listened politely and offered no objections to my persua-

91

sive arguments, but when I finished, she shook her head and said, "No, Doctor, I understand all of the good reasons you have given, but Papa and Mama wouldn't like it."

I continued to plead logically and sincerely that the knowledge gained would help unfortunate patients in the future; that I could not sign the death certificate with accurate information. Amelia Cox retained her pleasant demeanor, did not lose her patience, but continued to refuse. Finally, I admitted defeat. I was angry and concerned over any shortcomings I may have shown in handling the problem that Lydia Ostrander had presented. True, I had been given such little time in which to work, but without an autopsy to show the facts, how could medical knowledge be advanced? How could I know whether or not I had been remiss or ignorant? I learned later that there were more practical and cynical ways of obtaining an autopsy permit which appealed to the avariciousness in relatives.

Bob Gunning joined us in practice in January 1920. He entered into the Baird, Davis & Gunning clinic with enthusiasm, and there was no question that, between the three of us, we were giving our patients good care. I found it difficult to adjust myself to the fact that Bob made rounds of all the patients in the hospital even though they were surgical patients and he had not assisted in the operation on them. Sometimes he countermanded orders that I had left previously. Dr. Baird had stopped making rounds of the patients in the evenings soon after I joined him.

The winter months gave way to raw, windy days, and the deep, packed snow, which had brought out almost forgotten bobsleds and sleighs pulled by horses, was replaced by ankle-deep slush and hub-deep muddy roads. I learned where the rich black soil of Knox County, which produced corn that was taller than "knee high by the Fourth of July," was streaked with gumbo, a dirt that stuck like mucilage and mired my car so that twice I had to be pulled out by a team of horses.

Bob had made friends rapidly. He accepted my mother and father's invitation to make his home with them. Sometimes my mother complained that she couldn't find Bob when calls came in for him. He seemed to disappear, and the best she could do was to leave messages at the hospitals.

I suspected that Bob was unhappy about the routine office consultations and X-ray examinations he was doing. Surgery was more glamourous and dramatic. He spoke more and more about how his training in physiology fitted him to be a surgeon. There was no doubt that he was impressing Ben Baird with his discussions about patients. I wondered if I wasn't a bit envious; I had a feeling that I was the outsider in the partnership between Baird and Bob which was based on a worldliness that they thought I lacked. Often, they didn't trouble to let me know when they couldn't be reached.

All of my doubts were magnified one Sunday when I had a call from Maquon, a small village of three hundred people twenty miles away. I was proud that the call had come from a farmer, named Swigart, who said that his seventy-year-old mother was so sick that she couldn't be moved. Would I come to see her and Doc Hensley said to tell me that I should bring my tools along to operate upon her. No, the doctor wasn't there. He had left to answer another call. It took me an hour before I got Dr. Hensley on the telephone.

"Yes, that's right. Vern Swigart's mother has had a big inguinal hernia for years. Never would get it fixed. Now it's strangulated and I can't reduce it. Always could before. She's been vomiting and looks like hell. They didn't call me till this morning. Swigart knows your mother; comes from down around here, don't she?"

"Wouldn't it be better to bring her up here to the hospital, Doctor Hensley?"

"Sure it would, but she wouldn't stand the trip. Her only chance is for someone to operate real quick and get that bowel back—that is, providing it isn't gangrenous already. Can't you bring your instruments down and someone with you? I'll give her the ether."

"I'll be down as soon as possible." I hoped that the hesitation I felt didn't show in my voice.

I couldn't locate Bob or Ben Baird. Mary Sandburg listened to my story. "I'll skip right over to the hospital, Doctor. Glad to help. It's exciting, isn't it?"

It was a small house on a farm just on the edge of the village. The coat of white paint had probably been put on when the house was built; it was cracked and dirty, and in places the bare wood showed. The yard was surrounded by a fence of pieces of irregularly shaped wood laid in a zigzag pattern. The front porch slanted crazily.

"Drive around to the back door, Doctor. The front door is never used. Besides, your patient will be in the parlor."

Without a word, I obeyed Mary's instructions. Without knocking, Sandy opened the kitchen door, and we put our bags of supplies and instruments on the floor. She surveyed the kitchen stove, sink, and table critically.

Sandy was right. There was a bed in the parlor, but there were so many people standing around the room silently that I stopped precipitately. There was no movement and no sound. It seemed that I had entered the camp of an enemy. There could be no reason why they should not like me; I had never seen any of them before. Perhaps they distrusted doctors. Maybe they were all just frightened and so shy they didn't know what to do and each was waiting for the other to begin.

"Vern Swigart called me and I've talked with Doctor Hensley. Will two of you ladies stay in the room with me while I examine Grandma? I wish the rest of you would go outside. Please don't stop in the kitchen; Miss Sandburg will be busy there. I'll talk to all of you after I've finished my examination. I'm sure Doctor Hensley won't mind if I go ahead; he'll be here soon and we can consult."

There was no discussion about who should remain. There were looks from one to another, and I was left with two women who waited expectantly. They were neatly dressed, clean, and obviously sisters. There was no expression in their faces, but I felt their kindness and motherliness. They were people who didn't talk much; day after day they went about their chores. They had become withdrawn and had lost the art of spoken expression.

"We are her two oldest daughters, Doctor."

The bed was low, and I had to bend over uncomfortably. I felt a chair touch the back of my legs and sat down without turning. The patient was an emaciated woman in her seventies with thin white hair. The loose skin of her neck hung in folds, and her face was wrinkled with lines of hard work, worry, and privation. Her eyelids were partially closed, and her eyes moved slowly and searchingly.

Her lips were dry, and her tongue was coated and swollen. There was the distinctive odor of breath that follows repeated vomiting and lack of water. Her respirations were regular, slightly increased, and her skin was hot and dry. Her arms and legs were like pipestems, with the skin hanging loosely from the bones. I picked up a fold of skin and released it. All the elasticity of her tissues had disappeared; there was no tone left.

"The trouble's is her stummick, Doctor."

I heard the impatience in the voice of the woman standing over me. A stray thought flashed through my mind. Why couldn't people learn the difference between the abdomen and the stomach and then stop saying "stummick"? I went on with my examination of the heart and lungs. Finally, I pulled down the layers of sheets, blankets, and comforters toward the foot of the bed, keeping her legs covered and leaving her abdomen free. I picked up a crocheted fascinator off an upholstered rocking chair and covered her chest. Gently and slowly, I raised the coarse, soiled, white flannel nightgown. The coarse striae in the skin of the abdomen testified to the large number of children she had borne. I could see the violent movements of the intestine in the upper part of the abdomen and the protrusion in the right lower quadrant. Gently, I placed the flat of my hand on the abdomen and moved my fingers gently. I searched over the abdominal wall carefully. It was not rigid, but as I palpated more firmly below, an expression of pain showed in the patient's face. There was a protrusion through a hernial ring, and the bowel was strangulating in the hernial sac. It would have to be relieved or the obstruction would be complete and the bowel would become gangrenous. Perhaps it was necrotic already. I was sure my patient wouldn't need a great deal of ether; she was semiconscious. The obstruction should be relieved; I should pray that the bowel was viable and could be replaced in the abdominal cavity. She needed fluids more than anything. Sandy and I could get saline solution started by putting needles under her skin, and in lieu of a standard I could fasten it to a high-backed chair and get the correct height for the solution to flow.

It would be better if I injected a local anesthetic, gave her a small dose of morphine, and not administer ether. Local anesthetics were just coming into use, and Dr. Baird and I had used Novocain in simple hernia operations. Would the morphine depress her respirations too much? She'd need only a few whiffs of ether; perhaps I shouldn't use morphine.

Dr. Hensley was a small, rotund man with a physician's beard on his upper lip and chin. As he entered the kitchen door, his small button eyes took in the preparations for an operation.

"You've decided I was right about an operation, have you, Doctor?"

Before I could answer, Hensley grabbed my hand and shook it. "Nice to meet you. Baird has done a lot of operations for me. We've worked together pretty close. What do you think about the old lady?"

"I think you're absolutely right, Doctor. She has a strangulated hernia and it should be relieved. Her condition is pretty poor, though."

"She's been vomiting. Course, she's been complaining of pain for days before they called me. Just like her, though. I've delivered most of her kids. But she's a tough one. Where are all of them? Let's tell them and get at it."

"I asked them to wait outside."

It was an unusual place for a medical consultation. The odor of the milk cows was mixed with hay, and several chickens stepped daintily between our feet and pecked at the dirt floor. Dr. Hensley came into the group without a nod of recognition to any of them. They were standing and sitting on milk stools, boxes, and wooden horses.

"Doctor says she has to be operated on for that hernia. Should have called me earlier, but I've already told you that. She's old, worn-out, and hasn't had any food or drink. It's a risk, but she'll die if we don't do something right away. I think she's tough enough to make it. He'll use a local anesthetic, and I'll stand by to give a few whiffs of ether if she needs it. Any questions?"

I was overwhelmed by the older doctor's presentation. He was sure he wouldn't have any questions. They appeared to be accustomed to being bossed by Dr. Hensley, but it was because of their confidence in him built up by past experiences when he saw them through all of their problems of sickness and health. Hensley knew more about each of them than they, themselves, knew. Their silence

96

was broken only by one voice that came from a slender, primly dressed, and tight-lipped woman.

"I don't understand about her rupture. Why should Ma have such a thing at this time of life?" She addressed herself to me, I thought, but Dr. Hensley answered.

"Don't suppose you do, Em, but we haven't got time to stop and take you through a course in anatomy right now. C'mon, Doctor."

The operation went along smoothly and quickly, thanks to Sandy's anticipation of my every step. She was actually performing the operation through my hands. The three of us were alone with our patient in the small kitchen, which had only the wood-burning cook stove and the cistern water pump in the sink to mar the appearance of an efficient, small operating room. I whealed the skin with the local anesthetic, and the loose subcutaneous tissue ballooned out as I injected it into the deeper tissue. I made the incision and with Sandy's help freed the small knuckle of bowel from the constriction of the hernial sac. I breathed a sigh of relief when I saw that only a small piece of intestine had been forced down into the sac. It was bluish-gray in color. Sandy quickly put a hot gauze pack in my hand, and automatically I placed it gently around the exposed bowel and waited. I repeated this three times, and each time was encouraged by the slow but gradual return of color to the wall of the intestine as the circulation in its vessels returned. Dr. Hensley peered over his glasses which he had pushed down on his nose.

"That looks viable to me." I glanced at Sandy and detected the faint smile behind her mask. I had not had the courage to insist that Dr. Hensley put on a mask and gown. I was sure that the old doctor was approving of me as a surgeon. The operation was finished quickly as I replaced the extruded intestine into the abdominal cavity, closed the hernial ring, and sutured the thin fascia, subcutaneous tissues, and skin.

Dr. Hensley waited until the patient was in bed and Sandy was arranging the furniture so it would be a more effective room for nursing, while the two daughters looked on passively.

"C'mon, you two, we'll talk to all of you about it at the same time; then there won't be any garbled and half-baked stories going the rounds afterward. You'll all hear the same story."

He stood in the center of the group. "The doctor did a fine operation, slick as a whistle and quick, too. The rupture's repaired, the gut will live and is back where it belongs. She didn't need any ether. I think she'll make it if you all don't congregate around her bed so she don't have any air to breathe. Two of you women at a time can take turns seeing that she gets food and water. Don't let her stay on her back all the time; turn her and prop her up. I don't want to see any bed sores, understand? Her bones are sticking out right through her skin, so watch that. Any questions?"

I could see the relief on their faces. There was a smile here and there among them as they began to realize the good news that their doctor had brought to them.

"I'll thank Doctor and his nurse for you; it's not easy to bring all their equipment and operate on a kitchen table. He'll send you an honest bill. See that you pay it right away." He turned, shook my hand, clapped me on the back, and said, "Good job, Doctor. I'll remember it. Tell Baird I won't need him any more. Gotta go now, one of the girls I delivered is having her first baby and I don't want to miss it."

Dr. Baird did not show interest in the account of my experiences with Grandma Swigart's operation, Dr. Hensley, and her family. Dr. Hensley had called me the next morning to tell me that she was taking liquid foods and "perking up." Both Bob and Dr. Baird listened politely but expressed no regret about their absence and failure to give me support. In fact, there was no word of commendation or questions that showed curiosity. I felt as if I were telling an interesting patient's story to professional competitors, who were bored. My resentment rose when I overheard Baird talking with Dr. Hensley about Grandma Swigart the next day. How could he discuss a patient he had never seen; the only facts he had were what I had told him; why didn't he call me to the telephone? It was an insult that angered me beyond any understanding of Baird's actions.

Ben Baird came out of his office as I passed his door. "Just talked to Ben Hensley about the old lady."

I stopped, looked him in the eyes, and turned away without a word. I was shaking with anger; my voice was tremulous and loud as I asked our secretary to get Dr. Hensley on the telephone so I could talk with him and check on Mrs. Swigart's condition. I returned to my own office, closed the door, and was chagrined that my anger had tricked me into acting impulsively and immaturely. Why hadn't Hensley insisted on talking with me about the patient? I left the office before the call went through, got into my automobile, and drove out into the country. There was no reason why I shouldn't keep on driving and make a postoperative call on my patient. My worries over her would be less if I could judge her condition for myself. It wasn't right, I reasoned, to have operated upon her and then never see her again. I ruefully admitted, as I drove on toward Maquon, that it would help establish my predominance in the situation.

Our practice was increasing, and so it was a shock when Dr. Baird announced our income for May. "Our collections and our work fell off in May and I think I know why. I don't want you fellows to have anything to do with that damned Clyde Finley from here out. He's a snake in the grass."

I had known Dr. Finley since I was a boy. Everybody called him the new redheaded doctor.

"You men should get smart. Have you noticed that we haven't had as many patients sent to us for operations from Rapuzzi over at Abingdon in the last two months? Hell's fire, Rapuzzi has been a good feeder."

It was true that there had not been as many patients from Abingdon as previously. "Has Doctor Rapuzzi been away or sick?"

Baird shook his head in disgust. "I'll tell you what's happened. Rapuzzi has sent just as many patients to town for operation as ever. They've gone to Finley, that's what's happened. Do you know why? Finley, the double-crosser, gives that Italian a fifty-fifty split on the surgical fee, and we've only given him forty per cent. But Rapuzzi doesn't come and tell me that. He just took the deal without giving me a chance to meet his price."

I had noticed that each month, checks were sent to certain doctors in the smaller communities and listed the patient's surgical fee and the amount sent to the referring doctor. Dr. Baird had explained that this was the way surgical practice was carried on. I had to admit that Finley was a good surgeon, dextrous and with good judgment.

99

Another doctor in town was the anesthetist, and he worked with the Sister who ran the operating room at St. Mary's as his assistant. The patients got good surgical care and Rapuzzi got 10 per cent more, but what if Finley wasn't a good surgeon, then what would happen to the patient?

Professional ethics, or how to charge patients, were not taught to us in medical school. This practice of returning a part of the fee charged the patient to the referring doctor, without the patient's knowledge, was nothing more nor less than selling the patient to the highest bidder. I knew that lawyers received a percentage of a fee charged when they referred a client to another lawyer, but this involved human life, not money and properties.

"Why worry about it?" was Bob's reaction. "These country doctors figure it's the only way they can get what's coming to them from the patient. They get sore when they see the surgeon get a single fee that is more than they can charge. So they want us to collect it for them."

"Don't they think their services are worth charging for when they make the diagnosis and advise an operation?"

"They don't think of charging a patient that way. They are strictly house call and office call chargers."

"But still they want a part of the surgical fee."

"Certainly. Why do you suppose they come here with the patient just as often as they can, or at least appear on the day of the operation and go through the motions of scrubbing their hands and putting on a sterile gown? It's so they can say that they assisted at the operation and this saves any conscience they have about taking their forty or fifty per cent of the fee."

I had never heard of the American College of Surgeons, which had been organized in 1913 by Franklin H. Martin, a gynecologist in Chicago. Opposition to fee-splitting was one of the principles upon which the college was founded. I was to have my second experience with the problem of fee-splitting thirty-two years later.

Gradually, conflict developed between Bob Gunning, Ben Baird, and me regarding surgical practices. A confrontation occurred about Baird's decision to operate upon a patient with tuberculosis. John B. Murphy had popularized the Forlanini method of collapsing a lung

100

by the introduction of gas. This had been followed by the surgical method of collapsing the lung and chest wall by removal of several ribs. The operation was termed a thoracoplasty. Ben Baird had never performed the operation; I had advised that the patient be referred to Dr. Carl Hedblom in Chicago, a young surgeon educated at the Mayo Clinic, who was specializing in thoracic surgery. Baird and I had a heated argument. He insisted that he could perform the operation as well as Hedblom. Bob agreed with him, saying we couldn't refer all of our surgical patients to specialists.

After weeks of indecision, weighing the financial advantages, beginning a postgraduate education in surgery if I could find such an opportunity, security as against an indefinite future, knowing that Pearl would welcome a move from Galesburg, anticipating the criticism that was bound to follow, I wrote to Dr. Sumner Koch and asked if he thought I might have an opportunity to study and work with Dr. Allen B. Kanavel. The answer was encouraging, and I made an appointment with Dr. Kanavel at Wesley Memorial Hospital in Chicago.

Two years before, I had sat on the narrow concrete amphitheater benches. Now I felt in a different professional status as I went up to the operating room floor. Dr. Kanavel's greeting was warm as he invited me into the surgeon's dressing room and gave me a cap, gown, and mask.

"We have another operation to perform, and you can watch if you wish. It's an infected tendon sheath of the hand, and, as usual, the incisions for drainage were made in the wrong places. The poor fellow will be lucky if we can get a useful hand for him."

Kanavel's study of hand infections as a young attending man at the Cook County Hospital and his dissections and injections of the fascial spaces and tendon sheaths in the hands of cadavers had become a classic piece of clinical investigation. His studies were being continued, and he had published a book that was recognized everywhere as the authority on how to treat injuries of the hand to prevent infection, how to drain pus without injuring the tendons and sheaths, and how to bring back the functions of stiff joints and muscles by properly directed exercises.

I remembered vividly how he had quizzed me the morning he

101

held our junior class in surgery. As a senior student, I was called down into the pit of the amphitheater to examine a patient he was demonstrating who had a palpable, discrete mass in his groin. He was discussing undescended testicles. I felt the swelling easily and agreed it was an undescended testes. Dr. Kanavel removed the sheet from the patient's legs, disclosing a badly infected ingrown toenail—what I had felt was a swollen lymph gland. His comment was simple, direct, and impressive. "You must never forget to examine the patient and never take anything for granted." I wondered if these two experiences didn't prejudice my case and if I wasn't presumptuous.

When the nurses had removed their instruments and the patient was out of the operating room, Dr. Kanavel motioned for me to come onto the floor and pointed to an operating room stool for me to sit on. As I sat down, it was much too high and put me in an awkward position with my feet hardly touching the floor. I turned the seat down to a proper height so I could sit and face Dr. Kanavel squarely. There was a faint smile on his face as he sat in a comfortable metal chair, twirling his mask and cap in his gloved hands.

"You said in your letter you want to be taught to be a surgeon. Why?"

"The short experience I've had since graduation makes me sure in my mind that I want to be a surgeon. I want to have an opportunity to be taught more about surgery rather than try to learn by performing operations on patients and making mistakes."

"The residency system of education and training surgeons has been going for more than twenty years at a few hospitals in the East. We don't have that system in Chicago, but I want to take individual young men and educate them in accordance with those principles," said Dr. Kanavel. "It's a long, hard path. The first year you should work over in a laboratory of the medical school. Anatomy, pathology, and if you have any flair for it, chemistry in particular. Surgery has grown up through anatomy, pathology, and now it's in its physiological stage, but in another twenty years or less, the top surgeons will have to know a great deal more than we do about the chemistry of the body. You worked in the physiology laboratory while you were in medical school. How old are you?"

"I'll be twenty-four next January."

"I'll be able to give you a hundred dollars a month and wish I could make it more. Sumner Koch speaks highly of you, and I've gone over your grades in medical school. Do you want to think it over?"

"No, sir. I have thought about it before writing. I'd like to study and work under you. When may I start?"

"How about the first of September? Too early? School will start soon after that, and you should get to work in the laboratory before it opens. I can arrange for you to work under Doctor Ranson in the gross anatomy laboratory. Helping teach freshmen medical students will be a fine experience. We'll get you started on a problem, and I want you to learn about investigative and experimental methods. Let me know when you are settled and are ready to go to work. Nice to see you and I'm flattered that you want to work with me." He shook my hand firmly, turned, and was out the door and down the hall before I could thank him.

It was not as difficult as I thought it might be to tell Bob and Dr. Baird I had made up my mind to leave the partnership and go to Chicago and work with Dr. Kanavel. Pearl accepted my decision without expressing approval or disapproval, though I was sure she was happy to leave Galesburg. Without delay she made arrangements to rent a room and bath in the three-flat apartment building where she had lived with her sister. Then she announced she had applied for and had been accepted for a job as a filing clerk in the offices of a soap manufacturer. I knew my income wouldn't support us; I resented having to accept financial support particularly when I couldn't be sure Pearl understood why I wished more education and training to become a surgeon. I was a doctor, wasn't I? Why did I want to be a professor?

103

DR. KANAVEL'S advice was brief and to the point. His homely face was forgotten because his cheery voice seemed to carry so much interest in my future. It generated a feeling of enthusiasm that I was about to start the most important step in my life. There was also an unspoken confidence in my ability to become a surgeon.

His hands were covered with powder that had remained when he removed his rubber gloves. It had been smeared around the collar of his coat and on the fly of his trousers. His brown coat didn't match his dark green trousers. He followed my gaze and looked up grinning broadly.

"Pretty observant, aren't you? When I get home, Olive'll give me hell for putting on the wrong coat. It was a bit dark in the bedroom, and I didn't want to put on a light and awaken her. But maybe I'm getting just a bit absent-minded. Never paid much attention to clothes on the farm in Kansas. Come on, let's go over and see Ranson and get you started."

He took my arm, and we walked down the corridor to the passageway that led to the medical school. I had to walk fast to keep up and pay attention to the rapidly spoken instructions.

"I've spoken to Ranson and he remembers you. Seems you made an A in neuroanatomy. I think you should help in his laboratory with gross anatomy. Show the freshmen students what you learned about dissection, help them by questions that lead them on to find out the answers for themselves. Don't recite lectures to them. Make them do some mental work on their own. Ranson says he'll welcome your help. I don't need to tell you to show Ranson he can count on you. I want you to choose an experimental problem to work on. It should be related to anatomy, and it isn't important right at the moment that it has any application to patients. I want you to learn the experimental method. Maybe Dr. Ranson will have a suggestion for you. Start thinking right away about which particular field of surgery you want to know the most about. It won't be long before you young fellows will have surgery divided up into special fields of interest. You have to be a surgeon first, of course, but there's going to be so much to know about each part of the body that my kind of surgeon will be a thing of the past. No one will be able to know everything about the chemistry of the body fluids, the workings of the glands of internal secretion, and just think of the opportunities in the surgery of the nervous system."

We stopped at the foot of the broad wooden stairs that continued up to the gross anatomy dissection laboratory. Momentarily, the long walk up those worn steps on warm, humid, spring afternoons when I was a freshman flashed across my mind. I had done well in Dr. Ranson's course in the anatomy of the nervous system, and I remembered my thrill when I stimulated the sciatic nerve of a frog and watched the instantaneous contraction of the gastrocnemius muscle recorded on the smoked drum in the physiology laboratory.

"A group of about a dozen of us who are general surgeons have a real interest in the development of surgery of the brain, spinal cord, and nerves." With a deprecatory smile and a wave of his hand, he said, "Of course, Cushing is the one who knows more about the anatomy and physiology of the nervous system than the rest of us, but an awful lot was learned during the war in France. We want to get young men interested in the field. They've got to be good sound surgeons, first, no short cuts."

Dr. Ranson sat behind a flat table on which were spread drawings and typewritten pages. His old-fashioned roll-top desk was behind him so he could turn his swivel chair from one work area to the other. His highly polished, unrimmed glasses partially hid his unblinking, bright blue eyes. The collar of his white laboratory gown came up high under his chin and bulged over his shirt collar and necktie. Dr. Ranson had a soft, pale skin, and when he lectured, bright red areas appeared over his prominent cheekbones. I remembered our discussions on how often "Old Ranson" shaved; we were never able to detect much of a beard. We didn't know much about glands of internal secretion, but there were plenty of surmises that he couldn't be a "stud," as Eisie put it. But then again he had fathered two girls and a boy.

I heard the familiar voice and speech. "Good morning, Dr. Kanavel, andt here is Davis again."

"Perhaps Davis could fill in by helping with the freshmen in gross anatomy," Dr. Kanavel said. "Arrangements have been made for his salary. He wants to be a surgeon, and I've planned a progressive program of study and training for him. The first year will be given over to the study of anatomy, and I hope you will get him started on an investigative problem. We'll ask him to see an occasional patient to keep his touch."

"Well, this is the first time I've ever had an addition to my teaching staff without having to scrounge around for some money."

"Thank you, Doctor Ranson, I'll be back this afternoon and settle in with my books. I hope you'll be good enough to start me to work on a problem."

Ranson was moving the papers on his desk absently and, without looking up, nodded his head. Dr. Kanavel and I left his office, partly backing out, sliding around chairs and bumping as we went through the door. As we walked down the long hall, Dr. Kanavel looked back over his shoulder almost surreptitiously.

"I think he likes you and is pleased that you want to come with him in preparation to be a surgeon. Don't expect him to ever say so. It's a great opportunity to work in his laboratory."

I stopped at the bottom of the stairs. "I would like to start in learning more about the anatomy and physiology of the nervous system, Dr. Kanavel. I believe I want to be a neurological surgeon."

"You couldn't work in a better laboratory, if that's what you want, than Ranson's. You should examine and follow every patient I have on my service with a neurological disease. I don't want you to operate on them with me, yet. Keep good preoperative and postoperative records on each one. Look up a young fellow named Lewis Pollock, the best neurologist around here, and spend some time with him. Learn how he examines patients and comes to a conclusion about a diagnosis. There's no guesswork about him. More often than not, what seems to be a quick decision isn't at all. What's more

106

important, they are usually the right ones. Miss Spencer, my secretary, will mail a check for a hundred dollars to you each month."

Dr. Kanavel turned and hurriedly walked away toward the hospital, his coattails flying. Momentarily, I was overwhelmed by a deep sense of loneliness. I hoped it would disappear if I got busy and started to grow into that desk and chair in Dr. Ranson's laboratory.

I was reluctant to call Dr. Pollock at his office and ask for an appointment to discuss how I could learn neurology with him. I hoped that I might find him when he made rounds at the hospital, but I always missed him. I knew that he was a close friend of William Holmes's who taught clinical pathology and who ran the laboratory at Wesley Hospital to augment his income from a practice he had recently started.

I peeked in the hospital laboratory for the second time that day. Holmes saw me. "Are you still trying to find Pollock? He's hard to pin down, but I'm interested in how persistent you are. He just left here and said he was going to the library at the school. You'd better get there before he's gone again. He isn't worth it." Holmes's voice was mocking and sarcastic.

I hurried across the passageway to the crowded, inadequate library stacked with shelves of books between which there was just room enough for one person to walk. I looked into the semidarkness of the aisles and found Dr. Pollock perched on a stepladder, holding a book on his knees. He was turning the pages rapidly, and the big cigar tilted upward in his mouth was emitting a cloud of smoke that almost obscured his head. I approached slowly and stood near the ladder without speaking. Pollock closed the book sharply, put it back, took another, rapidly skimmed its pages, and returned it. This procedure was repeated several times until finally he grunted, put one finger between the pages to mark the place, removed the cigar from his mouth, and regarded its long unbroken ash speculatively. He hopped down from his perch and stood looking at me.

"Sorry you've had a hard time finding me. You're Davis, aren't you? My wife's from your home town, did you know?"

"Yes, sir, she's the daughter of Doctor Percy, and you practiced with him for a short time, didn't you?"

Pollock grinned and waved his cigar like a Roman candle, which I thought might explode in a display of fireworks at any moment. "I did that until I decided that the old man's ideas of heat treatment for cancer, by using a soldering iron, burned too many holes in normal tissue. He's a zealot, all right, but my start wasn't too good anyway. He objects to Jews, particularly if they're smarter than he is." All of this came out rapidly and cockily as if he dared me to disagree but expected an answer.

"I don't know Doctor Percy or his family except by name; I came from the other side of the tracks."

Pollock looked at me quizzically. "Why have you been dogging my trail?"

"Doctor Kanavel advised me to spend time with you in clinical neurology. Of course, provided you would take me on. I want to become a neurological surgeon."

"Kanavel's smart enough to know that it's time that the surgeon is something more than a mechanic who stands at the table and has the neurologist tell him where to make the incision and then what to do. There are many diseases of the nervous system that lend themselves to good surgical treatment. Surgeons should be trained in neurology enough to know what we are talking about when we make a diagnosis. There'll be a lot of disappointments and discouraging happenings. It's no field for a timid soul, or one without dedication. If you mean what you say, be at the County, Ward Four, tomorrow afternoon at two o'clock."

I had not had service as an intern on Ward 4. It was in the County Psychopathic Hospital which was separate from the general hospital but on the grounds. Barred windows distinguished it from the rest of the building, and its dirty, brown bricks gave it the appearance of a prison from which there was no return. Its dirty, disorganized lobby, crowded always with psychotic patients, half-dressed, unkempt, depressed or manic, brought in by the police and accompanied by distraught relatives, half of whom believed their relative was as sane as anybody and the other half frightened of bodily harm to themselves, was a confused mixture of babbling voices, purposeless movements, and immobility.

On the top floor were fifty beds for patients with diseases of the nervous system, many of them chronically ill, but experiencing intervals of improvement that gave them false hopes, always shattered by relapses that brought them back for readmission. There were many with what their relatives and neighbors called strokes; some could not speak more than to utter a guttural "yes" or "no" with which they responded to every question with an appropriate facial expression. They swung their paralyzed, stiff leg forward in a wide semicircle and carried their useless arm and hand tightly flexed against their body. There were those with congenital defects of the nervous system, paralyzed at birth from injuries to which every human being is susceptible when the process of delivering him into the world begins.

As I stood in the doorway promptly on time, I felt the depression that my fellow interns had spoken about when they griped about having to spend a part of their service on Ward 4. This was regarded as a penalty for not having written a higher place in the intern examination. I did not see a supervising nurse to whom I could introduce myself, but suddenly a small, thin, wizen-faced woman dressed in an ill-fitting wrapper, wearing felt house slippers, stood before me and peered up into my face.

"Are you a doctor?" I nodded, wondering what would come next. "I'm Gracie Wilson and my bed is that one there." She pointed to the first bed on the right nearest the nurses' office. I knew that this favored position made her the accepted boss of the rest of the ward's patients. She had won the place by her long tenure of occupancy in the hospital, probably because she suffered from an unusual and interesting disease and because there were no relatives to care for her on the outside.

"I've got Wilson's disease." She threw back her head and laughed deeply and loudly, as if she genuinely enjoyed the humor of a family name similar to that of the distinguished British neurologist who had described the symptoms of a disease that bore his name. "Who're you here to see, Doctor?"

"I'm to meet Doctor Pollock here at two o'clock. Where are the interns and the nurse in charge?"

"You don't expect Doctor Pollock to be here at two o'clock, do you? He's never on time. We'll get the signal when he comes in the front door, and then we'll have the interns skip over here real quick."

I had never examined a patient with Wilson's disease, and I wasn't sure what Gracie would say when I asked if she would tell me her story and let me examine her.

"I figured you wouldn't have come up here unless you were really interested. Right?" Suddenly, she turned to the rest of the patients and shouted, half crying and half laughing, "See, don't you ever try to fool Gracie. I knew this one would be interested in us; now see that you do what he wants when he gets around to examining you."

I was not aware of the passing of the afternoon hours until a cart was brought into the ward carrying the evening meals. It was getting dark quickly, and Pollock hadn't come. Six o'clock seemed a reasonable time to wait, and I left. I worried because Dr. Pollock had told me specifically to be there, and though I knew that perhaps he had been detained by a patient, or had to go on a consultation, I wondered if he took my determination to learn all I could about neurology seriously. Should I call him and tell him I was there? If I did, it could be taken as an implied criticism that he had broken the appointment. I decided to go back to the County on his next regular visiting day, examine patients, and keep on doing that until he came. For three weeks I visited Ward 4 without seeing Dr. Pollock. Finally, the fourth week he arrived shortly after I reached the ward. He was accompanied by the two interns whom I had seen on rare occasions come to the nurses' station and soon leave. Neither of them had ever seemed curious as to why I was on the ward examining their patients.

"Well, Doctor, I understand you have kept yourself busy whether or not I've been here. Splendid. Now, let's see what you've learned. Should we start here with our friend Gracie? She seems to think very highly of you."

I was embarrassed by the effusive remarks and was apprehensive of the implied challenge. My attention didn't wander for long.

"Now, I'm going to show you how to make a correct neurological examination. This is an art, and the first thing you must learn is to use a reflex hammer, properly. Let's see your hammer." Pollock's face showed his disgust and dismissal of the triangular piece of hard red rubber fastened onto a metal handle. He tossed it aside. "Perfectly atrocious. No weight in the head, no balance. You can't possibly get the feel of the reflex response without using wrist action and letting the weight of the resilient rubber head stimulate the tendon. Take this hammer and keep it. I have an extra one. Nurse, throw that thing in the garbage can. Don't let me see it on the ward."

We went from bed to bed. He demonstrated the niceties of bringing out ataxia, weakness of muscles, and atonia. The logical way to think about a diagnosis was emphasized over and over; it was not a guessing game. When certain signs were present, a lesion existed at a definite level within the central or peripheral nervous systems. Such a lesion, once anatomically located, could then be pinpointed as due to definite causes and pathological conditions. It was a brilliant performance of a demonstration of physical findings and local interpretation of their significance.

It was six-thirty and dark outside as Dr. Pollock stopped and lighted the stub of his cigar. Throughout the afternoon he had lighted and smoked three, carefully balancing them on the edge of a bedside table, gesticulating with the cigar in his hand, puffing furiously at times so that it seemed it was emitting sparks, holding it between his clenched teeth as he gazed across the ward occupied with his own thoughts about the disease that the particular patient had. Without a word, almost as if the afternoon had drained him of all conversation, we descended in the elevator and walked toward the street. Suddenly, he stopped, turned and bowed slightly to the interns, and with a gracious smile said, "Thank you gentlemen for your time and attention. I trust you have learned something, or have been stimulated to read this evening. I would be desolated were you to conclude that you had wasted an afternoon. Now, my young friend, I invite you to dinner."

Pollock took me to the Oak Forest hospital for chronically ill patients, one Sunday, walking the wards and playing the game of making a diagnosis purely from observation. I was fascinated by a dwarfed woman, her face wrinkled and with black, buttonlike eyes which darted around the room constantly. She was confined to a wheel chair with a tall back, which accentuated her smallness. Her short legs with their clubbed feet stuck out straight from the seat. She did remarkable things with the chair, as she used her hands to turn its wheels.

111

Pollock immediately paid his respects to her. He introduced us, and she appraised me deliberately. Her voice was high-pitched, and she seemed to cackle with glee. "I suppose he's planning to be a nutcracker like you, Doctor Louie."

"Mattie and I are old friends. She's a favorite patient of mine, isn't that so, Mattie?"

The little misshapen creature grabbed Dr. Pollock's hand and held it against her cheek. "He has always been kind to Mattie, and you'll be all right if you'll pattern after him."

"The highest compliment I could be paid, my dear. Now, how's your family getting along?"

As we dropped behind Mattie's fast-moving chair, Pollock explained. "Every ward like this has its boss. This doesn't come by appointment from the nurses or the hospital superintendent; it just happens because they are the leaders, and that quality shows itself quickly. You see, Mattie has the responsibility of their good, deep in her heart, and they all know this."

We saw patient after patient chronically ill with heart disease; paralyzed by thrombosis of the blood vessels of the brain; adults paralyzed since birth and mentally retarded; and epileptics who bragged that they suffered from the sacred disease. Pollock emphasized that there were probably many patients among them with brain tumors that had never been diagnosed. If we could only take the newer methods of visualizing the ventricles of the brain to them, or bring them to our hospital for these studies, perhaps we could help many of them by a surgical operation. We stopped at each bed, and my depression became more and more marked. I was glad when Pollock said, "That's enough for today. It becomes confusing to see many patients in one session. You begin to lose your keenness at observation. We'll come back again another day."

I finished the dissection of an association tract in the brain, the problem that Ranson had suggested. I was admitted to the graduate school to work for a master of science degree. Having written my thesis on the inferior longitudinal bundle, I prepared for the oral examination. At their discretion the examiners could deviate from the thesis with their questions. There were two examiners from the university's Evanston campus. One of the questions was to identify the shortest verse in the Bible. The examination lasted three hours.

I climbed the stairs to the elevated platform wearily but with a sense of satisfaction. The master of science degree wouldn't buy bread or butter and wouldn't attract patients, as Pearl often pointed out, but I had attained a scholarly goal and had established a first from the department of surgery.

I felt an increasing sense of responsibility for the care of Dr. Kanavel's patients. One morning, as I was trying to keep up with his short, rapid strides down the corridor of the hospital, I suddenly realized we were in a small laboratory that was used by the house staff on the medical service. He reached in his coat pocket and pulled out a microscope slide. Without a word the laboratory technician got up from her chair, and he took off his rimless glasses, carefully placed them on the table, put the slide under the microscope, adjusted it to his satisfaction, and stood up.

"Tell me about the symptoms of the patient from whom this slide was prepared, Doctor."

I was momentarily taken back. Dr. Kanavel's voice was stern and demanding, completely in contrast to the gentleness and feeling of professional comradeship that he had generated while we had been making the rounds of the patients. All activity stopped in the laboratory, and two interns from the medical service stood transfixed, suspecting that their turn might be next. I held up the slide to the light to see if I could get help from its gross appearance. It was stained in the customary fashion with hematoxylin and eosin. I moved it about and focused the eyepiece to my own vision. It was a section of the thyroid gland, and I could find no acini filled with colloid material. Instead there was a piling up of the columnar cells that lined those structures and were folded upon themselves. I knew it was a section from an exophthalmic goiter. I looked at the cells under higher power; I didn't want to overlook the possibility that it was an adenoma with malignant cells.

"I believe this is a section of the thyroid gland which has come from a patient with an exophthalmic goiter; statistically more apt to be a female than a male. She has prominent eyeballs, larger than

113

normal pupils, perspires easily, has a rapid pulse, and is thin. Her face is flushed and she appears anxious. She has a fine tremor of her hands and fingers when her arms are outstretched. If the test was done, she should have shown an increased basal metabolic rate, and she may well have had an immediate stormy postoperative course with a high temperature which required ice packs to bring down."

"At what temperature would you have taken the ice off?"

This was a clinical surgical question that, I was sure, wouldn't be found in a textbook of surgery as yet, and I didn't know the answer, but I suspected it might be the correct thing to remove the ice before the temperature reached normal. I decided to speak with assurance. "I would remove the ice packs when her rectal temperature reached one hundred."

"Not bad, not bad, considering you haven't had any experience with these patients. Never let it get quite that low; a hundred two is about right, and get the ice away quickly, or the temperature will plunge below normal."

Dr. Kanavel turned to the interns. "Now, that's an example of thinking. It's something you can do for yourselves as you sit here and look at slides you have stained. Work out for yourselves the symptoms you think the patient showed. Teach yourselves a little bit instead of complaining that your teachers don't tell you enough."

I was constantly amazed at the diversity of Dr. Kanavel's practice and the scope of his surgical operations. He had described a new operation for removal of a tumor of the pituitary gland. He performed abdominal operations, removed the uterus for fibroid tumors, corrected deformities of the nose, and was recognized nationally for his knowledge of the treatment of infections of the hand.

I worked every morning in the hospital and spent the afternoons at the medical school. Dr. Pollock suggested that we work on an experiment that would allow us to study the tone of muscles as it might be influenced by various reflexes of the head and neck. It would be necessary to make an animal preparation that we could examine and re-examine, and this required that it be without any voluntary control over its muscles.

I had read about the experiments upon decerebrate animals performed by the great English physiologist Charles Sherrington, but

114

Pollock was vigorously disdainful of the method of preparing animals that Sherrington had used. Cutting through the brain with a knife created so much shock, he said, that though the animal's extremities were rigid, it was an inferior experimental subject. Pollock said if the blood supply to that part of the brain between the cerebral hemispheres and the spinal cord could be shut off, the level of decerebration could be altered at will and muscle tone could be studied under ideal conditions.

I suggested that a method of removing a small piece of bone from the base of the skull in cats by using a dental burr was being used in Dr. Ranson's laboratory to afford access to the brain stem so that certain fiber tracts could be sectioned. I thought that the same surgical approach would make it possible to ligate the basilar artery which ran along the center of the brain stem. If this could be done, then the carotid arteries in the neck, which supplied the cerebral hemispheres with blood, could be ligated, leaving only that part of the brain and spinal cord below the ligature viable. The operation would have to be performed on cats and monkeys, and the artery was small and fragile. I could flatten out the end of a small right-angled hook used in eye muscle operations on humans and have a small hole drilled in it to carry the silk ligature so I could get it around the vessel. The trouble was that the vessel was about the same size as the silk ligature, but I could use one of the three fine strands that were twisted together to make the thread. Alley cats roamed the streets in the neighborhood of the medical school, and there were men who supplied the laboratory with experimental animals regularly; cats would cost fifty cents each, and the city did not run a pound as they did to destroy stray, unlicensed, and unclaimed dogs.

I explained my ideas as Pollock paced up and down the small laboratory office emitting clouds of smoke from his cigar. When I finished, there was no response as he continued to walk up and down, gazing at the floor, taking the cigar out of his mouth, and gesturing with it as he mumbled unintelligibly. I sat quietly, surrounded by cigar smoke that seeped through my clothes and into my skin.

"I think you hit on something, my boy. How soon can you show me such an animal?" Pollock was pacing and puffing faster.

After he left the laboratory, I was in a panic. I had promised more than I could produce; I had never done such an operation; the cat's basilar artery was very small, and if it tore, the experiment would be a failure. Adding to the difficulty was the problem of making a small opening in the bone of the skull without tearing through the dural covering and damaging the underlying brain stem. I had thought of using a dental foot-powered drill and burr, but in my enthusiasm I had forgotten that I would have to ask Dr. Ranson for permission to use his drill. Dr. Kanavel said that a good surgeon should think out every step of the operation he planned, and if he did, he could more easily adapt his thinking and actions to unusual situations that he had not anticipated and abnormal findings that might be present.

"Ligating the basilar artery of a cat is quite a formidable procedure, wouldn't you say?" Ranson smiled in a way that implied that he considered it a complete impossibility. "But go ahead and try. I haven't any money available from my funds to purchase cats for your experiments."

I had permission to use the old, foot-powered dental drill. I'd have to keep the drill moving fast and smoothly; it would have to do until I could go to the dental school and see if they had an outdated electric-powered motor and drill that I could borrow or buy.

Jim Skolka, the big Bohemian who worked in the physiology laboratory, could help me construct a jaw retractor, and only Jim could drill a tiny hole in an eye muscle hook. Jim greeted me with his big, friendly smile and his guttural, mixed-up English.

"How you, young Mr. Doctor? You put cats to sleep upstairs, now, not dogs, huh?" Jim guffawed. "Good thing, too. The big professor up there, he not know how to put big dogs to sleep, had to send for Jim." Jim's frankness was a legend in the school. "What I do you, young Mr. Doctor? Anything I can. You told that man Gunning and Professor Mr. Hoskins when Jim couldn't make them understand. They dumb. Now, what you want, it's something, no?"

Jim listened carefully as I told him what I needed. "Suppose you want quick, huh, like everybody?" Jim grinned. "Where's hook? No got, huh? But you can get quick from hospital, no?" Jim ushered me out the door of his little shop, which was crowded with pieces of all sizes of glass rods, Harvard tracing drums, which he was repairing for the next class of students to use, Bunsen burners, a lathe and vise, wrenches of all kinds, and in the corner, a watchmaker's bench.

I found Hazel Johnson, the operating room supervisor, in the workroom surrounded by nurses cleaning instruments and packing drums to be sterilized during the night in preparation for the next day's operating schedule. Her white uniform was spotless and starched stiffly. Her cap was slightly awry on her head, and strands of hair fell about her ears. I stood silently until she looked up from the list of nurses' names on the paper before her. She was assigning their hours for the next day, and it was probably a poor time to interrupt.

I told her about the basilar artery, how I could get at it to put a ligature around it, and how the animals would then become rigid and decerebrate. It would be a completely reflex animal responding to external stimuli without any voluntarily initiated movements of its own. She listened and so did her students. I said I needed an eye muscle hook which I could have flattened and bent into a right angle with a small hole drilled into it so a ligature could be threaded through. Without a word she gave me the hook and ignored my thanks.

Pollock and I began our series of decerebrate animal experiments and observed the reflex changes that occurred in the cats with varying levels of their central nervous system without blood supply and nonviable. Pollock thought better when he paced up and down the laboratory, filling the air with smoke, and often unconsciously gesturing with his cigar. This was good training for operating with many distractions surrounding me. At the end of each experiment, I injected methylene blue into the circulation to identify grossly and microscopically the level of the decerebration.

I continued to eat my lunches at the Greasy Spoon, but occasionally I splurged and went to a restaurant at Michigan Avenue and Twenty-second Street where I could enjoy food served by waitresses and sit at a table with clean linen. Several of the younger men just starting their practice in internal medicine ate there. The restaurant was opposite the Lexington Hotel, which we knew was the headquarters of Al Capone and his boys. The papers were full of gangland killings, the result of fights over territory in which rival mobs could peddle liquor illegally, run houses of prostitution, and own speakeasies and gambling concessions. The four deuces, 2222 South Wabash Avenue, was well known as Al's personal house.

Since my medical school days, Nick Valentine had cut my hair, first at Hammond's shop next to Jim Colosimo's cafe on Wabash Avenue and later in his own shop farther east on Twenty-second Street. I was never allowed to tip Nick and was frequently given a manicure because Nick insisted that a young surgeon should keep his fingers clean and free from hangnails. I was always aware that Nick's patrons were big fellows, but they were soft-spoken and it was the most silent barbershop I had ever been in. The barbers never started a conversation with their customer. Tips to the barbers and manicurists were lavish, and I felt embarrassed because I was allowed to spend only my quarter for a haircut.

Dr. Kanavel kept me busy reading proof on the new edition of his book on infections of the hand and made me feel completely responsible for the accuracy of the revisions. He suggested that I dissect in the anatomy laboratory and work on accurate and detailed descriptions of the surgical anatomy of the fifth cranial nerve. The sensory portion of that nerve was being sectioned, after making an opening in the skull, to relieve the terrible excruciating pain of tic douloureux. He believed the operation could be performed more easily if the exact anatomical relations within the skull were studied carefully. I went back to the gross anatomy laboratory and again helped the freshmen medical students with their dissections. At the same time, I made measurements and diagrams of a hundred skulls which showed the exact locations of bony openings through which the branches of the nerve left the skull and of the pattern of the important artery that entered the cranial cavity and had to be ligated to avoid hemorrhage.

Dr. Kanavel often discussed the problem of doctors learning surgery by doing; without teaching or training. It was dangerous to put a knife in the hands of any doctor, he said. Actually, every doctor who graduated and passed the state board examination for a license had the legal right to operate upon people, if the patient would get up on the operating table. "The patients don't know the difference; a doctor is licensed as a physician and surgeon, so they believe everyone should be able to operate upon them."

He told me the interesting story of the creation of the surgical journal by his old chief, Franklin H. Martin, who also organized an annual gathering of doctors interested in surgery so they could attend the clinics of the well-known surgeons in Chicago and be taught how to perform operations by observing surgeons like John B. Murphy, Albert J. Ochsner, Arthur Dean Bevan, and Lewis L. McArthur. This annual congress had led to the formation of the American College of Surgeons in 1913. The goal was to elevate the surgical care of patients. The college was then campaigning for an elevation of the standards of hospitals; if they were successful, this would be an important step in raising the level of the surgical care of patients.

These tales about the development of surgery, the evils of a kickback of part of the surgeon's fee to the referring physician, the immorality of operating upon a patient without prior examination and preparation, and the lack of laboratory facilities in hospitals were interspersed with fascinating stories about the Vincennes trail, the explorations of Joliet and Marquette, and the early settling of the West. Dr. Kanavel talked when he took me with him on trips to operate in hospitals in small communities when the patient couldn't be moved with safety to Wesley Hospital. Repeatedly, he said that doctors could easily make money enough to provide a decent living for themselves and their families; the trouble was that their names were on every sucker list in the country for shady investments. Over and over again, he advised me to invest my money in municipal bonds that were voted for waterworks and schools and to avoid buying speculative stocks. I was always secretly amused by this advice, because I didn't have any money to invest and it would be a long time before I did. But I was complimented because he thought I might be successful enough as a surgeon to become an investor.

He said the reputation of doctors is more sensitive than that of any other profession and the good name of a surgeon is exquisitely reactive to patients' gossip. "The most stimulating, gratifying, and at the same time, the most exasperating experiences in a surgeon's life can be the relations with patients and their families. It is easy for a doctor to become careless and assume they know as much about their illness as he does. Or he can become frustrated, after explaining carefully in simple language to have them evidence by their next question that they have comprehended nothing."

He warned against forming the habit of telling the patient nothing in explanation of a decision and rationalize that this was best for their peace of mind. "Many patients are told only that their operation will be on Friday. This is wrong." He taught me to inquire about the responsibilities of the family; their ambitions and aims; in short, to establish a personal relation similar to that of the old family doctor.

Operations for brain tumors, stomach ulcers, goiters, plastic operations for defects and injuries of the nose, drainage of pus from the chest cavity, removal of portions of the intestinal tract, repair of cut tendons of the hand, and operations for hemorrhoids ran the gamut of operations we performed; from the brain to the anus or from the sublime in surgery to the ridiculous. I was being educated in fundamental basic principles applied to the surgical treatment of every part of the body. I had to learn to think as a surgeon, Dr. Kanavel kept insisting; think logically, judiciously, and then after your decision is made, act unhurriedly and accurately. Would I wish to have the operation under consideration performed upon a member of my own family? After every operation, he said, I must sit down and think it through again to discover, if possible, how it could have been done better. How could the patient have been treated in a better way from the beginning of making the diagnosis to the postoperative convalescence?

At each operation I was asked to identify anatomical structures. I was told and shown exactly what he was trying to accomplish and was goaded into acting in anticipation of his next move. A good assistant was one who prepared the way for his surgeon, one who made the operation appear to be easy because he was a step ahead. The most ordinary, clumsy surgeon could be made to look like a master, he said, by an alert, intelligent assistant. When an assistant could lead the way, he was a surgeon himself. This was training in doing that complemented my education as a surgeon.

Dr. Kanavel's criticisms of my work were never expressed at the operating table nor in the presence of patients, interns, nurses, or my contemporaries. Often, he would go to the toilet between operations and would ask me to stand outside the door while he emphasized the errors in technique, procedures in the hospital, or relationships with patients and nurses that I had committed.

Pollock and Kanavel advised me to register for a doctor of philosophy degree in the graduate school. The thought of being examined again by a committee of the faculty, which would undoubtedly be a larger one than I had faced for the master's degree examination, made me hesitate. Dr. Kanavel pointed out that I could set a precedent for others who wanted the highest graduate degree based on work in the medical school. No one had earned a Ph.D. degree from the university majoring in surgery. This was enough challenge for me to go ahead with my experimental work and register for the degree.

Dr. Kanavel telephoned me one night after I had gone to bed and asked me to meet him in thirty minutes on the corner of Randolph Street and Michigan Avenue. I didn't ask the why or wherefore. Taxicabs were scarce, besides I couldn't afford one; the elevated trains and the streetcars didn't run as often as they did in the daytime. I dogtrotted over to the corner where the surface line ran, and I put on speed as I saw its dim headlight coming. I was in luck, and there weren't many stops before it got to the Loop. I was waiting on the curb when he drove up in his big, black Peerless touring car. He moved over in the front seat. "Drive us to Sycamore."

I knew only that Sycamore was west and a bit north, perhaps thirty or forty miles, so I drove straight ahead, keeping an eye out for a signpost that would carry the name of a town at least in the general direction of Sycamore. He was silent, smoking a cigarette. "It's obvious you have never been to Sycamore and there aren't any signposts. I'll tell you when to turn." I struggled to drive the heavy, clumsy automobile smoothly. He began to speak philosophically.

"You'll be a good surgeon; you have imagination, you're intelligent, and you're not lazy. Perhaps that's your most important asset. A man doesn't have to be brilliant, he just has to want to work at his job. You'll be faced sometimes with a choice between your dedication to advancement in your profession and other things that are important in life. Keep on trying to bring them together as long as you can, but never hug a bad bargain with a deathlike grip."

Again, there was silence as I worked hard with the wheel to keep the car in the ruts of the dirt roads. The canvas top rattled as the wind whipped under it. The wheel shimmied in my hands.

"I'm not happy about coming out here to this little hospital to operate on this patient. Dr. Spurgeon says it's a young boy with appendicitis and the appendix will rupture any minute. He just saw him a couple of hours ago for the first time. It takes a long time to educate people to call their doctors early when a child has a stomach ache. This is itinerant surgery and I don't fancy it. We'll have to leave the boy in Dr. Spurgeon's hands for his immediate postoperative care, and that's the important time. I can't come out this far every day and neither can you, but one of us will get out here within the first forty-eight hours. I couldn't insist that he move the boy into Wesley over these roads and against his advice. He's a good doctor, don't misunderstand, but he's not a surgeon. We'll have to give him detailed instructions about fluids and have him telephone us every six hours."

There was a dim light in the front entrance of the hospital, and a figure stood in the doorway. Dr. Kanavel hopped out of the car and hurried to the entrance with a quick "Bring the instruments" thrown over his shoulder. It hadn't occurred to me that the hospital wouldn't have a full set of instruments for an abdominal operation. Maybe he had brought along a few of his favorites, but as I lifted the bag I knew that all of them would have to be sterilized.

He introduced me quickly and grabbed Dr. Spurgeon by the elbow as if to propel him into action. He told me to find the surgical nurse and have her sterilize the instruments; to join him so we could examine the patient. He said I should get the anesthesia equipment together and I would give the anesthetic. He told Dr. Spurgeon he would have him assist at the operating table.

He hurried with Dr. Spurgeon down the hall. I was transfixed by my surprise at being designated the anesthetist in a manner and tone of voice that would do nothing but inspire confidence in the family doctor. But I had never given a long anesthetic; I had helped as a student in putting children to sleep for a tonsillectomy. This was a different matter. I was sure there wasn't a gas machine in the hospital, so I'd have to use a mask and drop ether. I found the operating room

122

nurse, delivered the instruments, and gave her instructions almost mechanically. They did have a water sterilizer that would be satisfactory, but it would take more time to get it up to the correct temperature.

At the bottom of the grip was a complete set of packages that I knew contained all the sterile linen and sponges we would require. There was a jar of sterile Penrose drains; so evidently the possibility of abscess formation was anticipated.

Dr. Kanavel was sitting on a chair pulled close to the side of the bed. His right hand rested on the boy's abdomen. The palm was flat, and the fingers were gently moving up and down as he patiently explored the entire abdominal wall for rigidity. I knew that during the time I had arranged for the instruments he had talked to the patient, gained his confidence, and had heard the story from both him and his parents. The boy was completely relaxed and breathing easily; his legs flexed on his abdomen to ease the pull on his abdominal muscles.

He sat back after pulling up the sheet and said musingly, "Doctor Spurgeon was called to see Bobby early this morning when he awakened, nauseated and with a queer feeling in the pit of his stomach. Then he vomited and complained of pain in his right lower quadrant. The pain has persisted all day, and he has vomited several times. Doctor Spurgeon took a blood count and found a leucocytosis. Late this afternoon, his abdominal pain became better, but his temperature rose and so did his white count. Feel his abdomen."

Dr. Kanavel remained seated, and there wasn't room to draw up another chair beside the bed. I wouldn't disobey my chief's teaching by palpating the boy's abdomen while I stood, nor would I sit on the edge of the bed, so I waited silently.

"Oh, excuse me." Dr. Kanavel rose hurriedly, grinned, and stood by while I gently explored the abdominal wall for the involuntary muscle rigidity that I suspected was present.

He led the way out of the room and turned abruptly in the hall to me. "Do you agree he has muscle rigidity over the right side, Doctor?"

I knew that he didn't need my confirmation to make up his mind, but he certainly was letting Dr. Spurgeon know that he respected my opinion, and at the same time, I was being taught. I would be the one to drive out to see the boy postoperatively, of this election I was sure, and it would help if Dr. Spurgeon's confidence in me was built up.

I took my time in putting Bobby to sleep and avoided a boisterous second stage of anesthesia. I knew Dr. Kanavel was impatient to get started and that he would move quickly after the skin incision was made. I nodded my head in agreement as he looked at me questioningly when he began to paint the abdomen with iodine, which he quickly removed with alcohol. The towel and sheet drapes went on quickly, and he was poised with his knife in his hand.

"Keep him well under for just a little while, Doctor, and we'll be through."

I gave my complete attention to the patient and found that I was perspiring and breathing almost synchronously with the boy. Fortunately, Bobby hadn't eaten for twelve hours, so I wasn't worried about his regurgitating vomitus. His color, pulse, and respirations were good.

The appendix was swollen, distended, and blue-black. Fortunately, it had not ruptured, and the apparent sudden relief from pain that Bobby had experienced was a false sign. I had only a fleeting, occasional glance at the chief's movements. Dr. Spurgeon had been given retractors to keep the abdominal incision open and thus was immobilized with his hands out of the way. Soon, I heard the appendix with a hemostat attached plunk into the sterile, small basin on the instrument table.

"All right, Doctor, stop the anesthetic and let him begin to come out. I'll be finished before he can feel any pain. We don't want this boy to have any more anesthesia than is absolutely necessary."

As I wheeled the small patient back to his bed, I passed the parents who were listening.

"Now, father and mother, your boy is going to be all right and he'll be well. Doctor Spurgeon made a fine diagnosis, and if he had not acted as promptly as he did, it might well have been a different story. You owe a great deal to him. The appendix is out and wasn't ruptured. He's a healthy young animal and he'll heal quickly. Doctor Davis, my colleague, will come out to see him day after tomorrow, and Doctor Spurgeon will call one of us on the telephone every six hours. I doubt if it will be necessary for us to come out after that; Doctor Spurgeon can take out the skin sutures. Now, you go in and see the boy but don't hover over him, mother. I'll meet you downstairs, father, and we'll discuss the fee and decide on an amount that is satisfactory to both of us. All right?"

"We can't begin . . ." The father's voice was choked.

"Don't try. We all know how we'd feel if it was our boy. Run along and let Bobby see you when he wakes." He turned away abruptly and rather gruffly said, "Tell that nurse to get some help. Let's get the instruments washed and the dirty linen back in the bag so we can get started back."

Dr. Kanavel had said many times, as we had traveled on similar trips, that the day was not far away when all roads would be paved and patients could be moved quickly and safely to a well-equipped hospital. He said that I would see the day when small communities would have fine hospitals, and qualified surgeons with experience would staff them. I doubted when he said, "A surgical practice like mine will be a thing of the past. We will educate men like you so well that patients won't be referred to city hospitals. Sort of cutting our professional practice throats, isn't it? But the care the surgical patient receives will be on a higher plane than any country in the world."

This was the third year of my program to become a surgeon. Dr. Kanavel invited me to lunch following a morning of operations, and I thought over what I might have done wrong because this was one way he taught. I wondered if I would enjoy my lunch.

"It's time you had a chance to see neurological surgery in other cities. You should visit Walter Dandy in Baltimore. He has a great imagination; the use of air to demonstrate the ventricular system is a fine example. I can't say I admire him as a person, mainly because he's arrogant and patronizing to his former teacher, Harvey Cushing. You can stop in Philadelphia and see Charles Frazier cut the root of the trigeminal nerve for tic douloureux. Philadelphia has the greatest school of neurologists in the United States. You can go on to New York and visit Charles Elsberg. He has had quite an experience operating upon spinal cord tumors. He's a fine gentleman and an excellent surgeon. You must go on to Boston and visit Harvey Cushing. You know about him already from your reading. He is the father of neurological surgery in the United States. He has told me that he considers his greatest contribution that of perfecting the technique of opening the skull and replacing the bone meticulously. I want you to spend a year with him, and this trip can serve as your introduction so he will know who you are when I write him asking a place for you. These are all men trained in general surgery; that's basic. They have become interested in the particular field of surgery of the nervous system. The danger in the future is that it will become highly specialized because there are so many unsolved problems. Education and training in basic surgical principles, which apply to all fields of surgery, will be neglected. That mustn't happen for the patient's sake. Make your plans and ask Miss Spencer to make out a check in the amount you want for your railroad fare, hotels, and other expenses. Don't skimp."

FIVE

I WALKED around the red brick buildings that sat back from the sidewalk and admired the dome of the main building of the Johns Hopkins Hospital. I stood across the street and looked at it, savoring the atmosphere of its setting and feeling some of the tradition that was building up around the institution but, in particular, its men. Halsted, Osler, Welch, and Kelly: these were the four around whom the school of medicine had been built.

Again, I experienced the distinctive odor of a city. It was a warm day, and I could smell water and fish; it was an odor of laziness and relaxation. I entered the main building and inquired how I could reach Dr. Dandy's operating room visitors' gallery. Somewhat skeptically, I thought, the young lady at the information desk accepted my statement that I was a doctor and that Dr. Dandy had written that he would welcome me as a visitor.

I quietly slipped into a seat in the small gallery that occupied one side of Dandy's operating room. There was an air of tenseness, and I could hear Dandy's orders to his assistants and nurses, punctuated with angry outbursts. I was shocked to see him put his gloved finger into the substance of the brain and roughly lift out an encapsulated brain tumor, which was caught by an assistant before it fell to the floor. There was an immediate welling up of blood from the brain, and cotton packs were quickly put into the cavity to stop the hemorrhage.

Dandy looked up and saw me in the stands. "Who're you?"

I introduced myself and said I had a letter of introduction from Dr. Allen Kanavel. Dandy nodded and began to try to get out the cotton packing so he could control the bleeding vessels. He had been Cushing's resident trained to be a neurological surgeon before Cushing left Hopkins to go to Boston. I had heard that Cushing was meticulous in his handling of brain tissue: gentle, slow, and I doubted if he approved of the finger dissection technique. Dr. Kanavel had told me that when Dandy succeeded his former chief, he had become bitterly critical of him and his methods of operating. So critical were his remarks that he had refused to join a society of surgeons whose interests were centered on the surgery of the nervous system because Cushing had organized it. He had alienated the friendship of his contemporaries by his vicious remarks about his teacher, an unforgivable sin for a surgeon to commit. Dandy's experiments upon the cause and methods of treatment of babies with water on the brain were admired for their ingenuity. They had led to his bold suggestions that air be introduced into the normal cavities of the brain after removal of the cerebrospinal fluid so that X-ray visualization of the cavities could be accomplished. Cushing had complimented his former pupil when he discussed his presentation at a surgical meeting but had expressed some reservations about the method being accepted without any qualification and its performance by individuals not adept in operations upon the brain. Dandy had become furious and, in his rebuttal, exceeded the bounds of polite disagreement so far that it was concluded that he had sought an open break with the older man. It was a challenge by the young bull moose to the old one for supremacy in the herd. Cushing's contributions to the new field of surgery had been fundamental and priceless. He did not have to take the offensive; he could let the younger men make the mistakes and maintain the dignity of his scholarship and technical brilliance.

Dandy seemed satisfied that the bleeding had been controlled and removed his rubber gloves as he stepped away from the table. His resident began to replace the bone of the osteoplastic flap and suture the scalp. Dandy came over to the railing and removed his mask. His round, moon-shaped face was covered with perspiration.

"Come around to the dressing room."

I found him sitting in a large, deep, overstuffed leather chair holding a cup of coffee. Operating room gowns, pants, and shirts were strewn over the floor and on the benches. Dandy didn't offer to shake hands.

"There's a pot of coffee over there. Help yourself. It's better to get tumors out fast than to piddle around all morning. We'll give

128

him a blood transfusion. We've got a supply of donors, and the citrate method makes it simple to replace blood loss. That one was a meningioma and I got it all out; one of the simpler ones that makes up for the disappointments in neurosurgery."

His voice was aggressive, and it complemented his short, square build and his blunt, spatulate fingers. It wouldn't be easy to organize blood donors in Chicago, and there was no way to tell whether or not there'd be a transfusion reaction. Kanavel believed in saving the patient's own blood from the peritoneal cavity, in the case of a ruptured spleen, to reinfuse it after citration rather than lose it and use a donor's blood. I wondered what Dandy's answer would be to such a question.

"How long are you going to be here? What other places are you visiting?" The questions came in a rapid, staccato, nasal voice.

I told him I was stopping in Philadelphia, New York, and then on to Boston and from there back to Chicago.

There was a snort of disgust, and the disarmingly round face was transformed by a sneer. "Frazier and Elsberg are general surgeons who just happened into neurological surgery because of the war. Frazier did do some work during the war, but Elsberg managed to stay out. Neither one of them knows enough about the physiology or anatomy of the nervous system to be real neurosurgeons. How did Kanavel ever think you could pick up any gems of wisdom from those two?" I was silent. "So you're going on to see the great man himself, are you?"

I resented his cocksureness and arrogance. Almost reflexly, I spoke.

"You were taught and trained by Doctor Cushing, weren't you, Doctor Dandy?"

"If you can call it that. Hours of torture while he picked and fiddled."

He turned abruptly and walked out of the dressing room. I did not see him again during my tour of the hospital. I was upset by Dandy's sudden reversal of attitude when I told him whom I had intended to visit. It was hard to believe the man could be that egotistical and jealous.

The medical school of the University of Pennsylvania was the oldest school of medicine in the United States, and I took the rest of the day after my arrival to visit Independence Hall and the Revolutionary days' historical landmarks. I walked through Rittenhouse Square, named after the self-taught instrument maker, astronomer, and mathematician whom I had read about as being almost a one-man bureau of standards in the early days of the federal government. I tried to visualize what the city looked like when Benjamin Rush and Physick practiced medicine. Physick had studied under the famous John Hunter in London and had a degree from the University of Edinburgh. He had refused Hunter's offer to become associated with him and had returned to Philadelphia. Dr. John Morgan had been a distinguished member of many foreign societies, and it was he who had first defined the separate confines of the physician, surgeon, and apothecary, a degree of specialization that then was considered revolutionary.

There were no surgeons as distinct from physicians in those days, although in the British Isles this distinction was a sharp one. The physicians were the scholars, they thought, and surgeons were handy men with scalpels. These early doctors in the United States had gone into the operating rooms and had delivered babies directly after treating contagious and infectious diseases. They had been general practitioners, and their long, black frock coats, their heavy gold watch chains draped across their waists, their beards, their stiffly starched linen shirts, all had added an air of dignity, infallibility, and assurance that had to make up for their ignorance about diseases and the physiology of the human body. Speed in operations was necessary because they lacked anesthesia. Lister's principles of antisepsis were unknown.

The magnificent painting hanging on the wall in the medical school depicting the surgeon standing over the patient with scalpel in hand and dressed in his street clothes, unmasked, and with the benches crowded with students, was a picture of surgery not too long before.

The stories about contemporary Philadelphia surgeons were as well known in the Midwest as they were in the East. The crippled Da Costa who met his classes in his wheel chair; the handsome Deaver, dramatic and self-assured, was considered Murphy's equal

130

as a teacher; now I would have a chance to meet Charles Frazier. Pollock had told me about the great neurologist William Spiller, who had suggested that Frazier cut the sensory root of the fifth cranial nerve back of the ganglion to relieve trigeminal neuralgia and had diagramed the place for the incision in the spinal cord which would sever the fiber tracts that carried intractable pain impulses upward to the brain. Pollock said the group of neurologists in Philadelphia, beginning with Weir Mitchell, the physician, neurologist, and poet, had constituted the first real school of neurologists in the United States. They were great teachers and clinical investigators; their neurological examinations were examples of perfection and were rivaled only by the English school. Pollock's crowning statement was that they had Old Blockley, the Philadelphia General Hospital, in which to work.

Separated by a stone wall from the university's hospital, I had heard that when interns or residents went from one hospital to the other on daily visits, it was referred to as "going through the wall." Sir William Osler had served on the attending staff of the medical wards of Old Blockley.

I went to Dr. Frazier's office and presented my letter of introduction. Perhaps it had been a mistake to appear first in the operating room gallery as I had in Baltimore; maybe I had offended Dr. Dandy by not presenting myself formally and receiving an invitation into his operating room. Dr. Frazier's secretary took my letter, and I joined the group of patients in the reception room. I had never been in a doctor's office situated in a hospital; I imagined it might also serve as his medical school office. Perhaps he ran the department of surgery of the medical school, the hospital, and practiced his profession in one office. In comparison, Dr. Kanavel had to spend a great deal of time going back and forth between his private office, the hospital, and the medical school. Did Dr. Frazier receive remuneration for being the head of the department of surgery in the medical school, I wondered. None of the teachers of the clinical subjects at Northwestern received remuneration for their services.

After half an hour, a short, squarely built doctor in whites came into the office. His nose had been broken and had healed crookedly. He didn't bother to take a battered corncob pipe from his mouth as he muttered to Dr. Frazier's secretary loudly enough for me to hear.

"Where's the visiting fireman?"

I rose quickly and went toward him, my face flushed, and I was angry. I spoke to the secretary: "Tell Doctor Frazier and his staff, I'm sorry to have bothered them."

As I turned away, I was face to face with a grinning, pixylike, rugged countenance. "Touchy, aren't you? I apologize but I thought you'd be inside with the professor and I tried to be funny with her nibs, here, the keeper of the sanctum. My name's Grant. I'm the neurosurgical resident. The professor asked me to line things up for you; he'll be busy with his office patients the rest of the afternoon. Come on, let's get a Coke." As he talked, Grant's face had become even more craggy and expressive. I couldn't help but grin and forget my momentary resentment.

The next morning as Francis Grant helped an orderly bring the patient into the operating room and put her on the table, he looked up and waved his hand casually. When the anesthetic had been started, I was surprised to see that the neck had been exposed and the patient had a goiter that was to be operated upon.

Dr. Frazier came in masked, water dripping from his elbows. He was short, had iron-gray hair, and wore glasses above his mask. Grant spoke to him, and together they came to the spectator's gallery.

"Glad to have you here, Davis. Kanavel's an old friend of mine. Fine surgeon. You're lucky. Let's get going, Francis. This is a thyroidectomy for a colloid goiter. We're surgeons here, like your chief is. We've got an angle tumor next and after lunch a tic operation."

Frazier was dexterous and worked rapidly but accurately. He left the room while Grant sutured the strap muscles and closed the wound. The tension that had been apparent while the professor was in the operating room quickly disappeared. Grant worked rapidly, and I knew that he was thinking about how quickly he could have the next patient in the operating room and ready for them to begin to operate. Frazier and Kanavel had been educated and trained in surgery in the days when speed in operating reduced the length of the anesthesia, and they still carried the dangers of anesthetics in their minds.

During the next days I saw neurosurgical operations performed

132

with a technique that was familiar. It was a direct, unhesitating approach. I saw the famous neurologists, about whom Pollock had talked, come into the operating room to learn what Frazier had found upon operation to refute or confirm their clinical diagnosis. Frazier commented proudly that he had adopted the sitting position for operations to sever the fifth cranial nerve to relieve the pain of trigeminal neuralgia that had been developed by Adson, whom he had trained.

I was accepted by Frazier, Grant, and their staff and made rounds of the patients with them. It came naturally for me to address him as "sir" and to answer "Yes, sir" and "No, sir" to his questions. I was not prepared when Frazier turned on me without warning. "Dammit, stop sir-ring me. This isn't the army. I'm not that old either." The outburst was over, and he went on discussing the problems that arose with the patient.

Grant dropped back with me as we walked together. He said out of the corner of his mouth, "Pay no attention. He has already forgotten he said it. I should have told you; it's one of his pet peeves. Why, I don't know, but maybe I'll find out sometime."

In my hotel room I made notes of what I had observed and wrote comments upon whether or not I thought what was done was an improvement over our own methods. I had never seen an operation on the spinal cord for the relief of intractable pain, and at this hospital and at Old Blockley the operation had first been performed. Grant intended, he said, to devote his own practice exclusively to neurological surgery. I wondered if I could practice in this special field of surgery in Chicago and do no other types of operation.

I thanked Dr. Frazier and Chubby Grant for their interest and kindness. "Give Cushing my regards. You'll see a fine surgeon at work; he's an artist. There's no question about the tremendous contributions he's made to this new field of surgery. He's a great lover of books, too. He's hard-nosed and egocentric. Not very lovable. Glad to have you visit us. I hope you've taken some good things away with you."

I decided to skip a visit to New York and instead to divide my time between Philadelphia and Boston. I was anxious to meet the man with whom Dr. Kanavel hoped I could work for a year.

133

After his return from the Continent, Harvey Cushing had asked William Halsted for a place on the Johns Hopkins Hospital staff to devote himself exclusively to the field of neurological surgery. Halsted was not encouraging because he could not foresee the future of such a field of surgery. Cushing persisted and spent a great deal of time in the surgical laboratory with his experiments upon removal of the pituitary glands from dogs. He was meticulous in applying the surgical principles he had been taught by Halsted to the problem of making an opening in the skull for the attack upon a brain tumor, so that the bone and scalp could be returned in place solidly, without great loss of blood and without infection. Gradually, his reputation spread for his ability to stimulate young men in surgical training to be productive in clinical and experimental research. He was called to the recently built Peter Bent Brigham Hospital to become surgeon in chief and professor of surgery at Harvard Medical School. Later, it had been due to his efforts and surgical techniques in France during World War I that had stimulated some of his contemporaries and younger men to enter the field of neurological surgery.

The streetcar line paralleled the Boston Commons, and across in the distance was the gold dome of the state capitol. Later, I would take the time to see Bunker Hill and take a conducted tour out to Lexington and Concord.

I had never seen a two-story hospital spread out over so much ground; its wards were connected by open corridors. As I walked to Dr. Cushing's office, after receiving complicated and confusing directions, I heard a signal bell ringing a code. I came to a three-story building in which I had been told the operating rooms and the chief's office were located. The secretary smiled pleasantly and read my letter of introduction.

"Doctor Cushing hasn't arrived yet. He will be doing a suboccipital craniotomy this morning. You see, he doesn't begin operating until eleven o'clock. You may sit here, or go up one flight to the operating room suite and sit in the stands to watch the preparations. Doctor Cushing considers getting ready for an operation quite important. Go out the door, turn to your right, go up one flight of stairs, and turn to your left. I'll have Adolph meet you."

I hadn't been treated initially as well anywhere on the trip. I didn't know her name, but I was sure she had been with Dr. Cushing a long time. She was slightly exophthalmic and her face was flushed, but her neck was smooth. I surmised that she knew the correspondence about my visit and had anticipated me. I also suspected that she was guiding me away from meeting Dr. Cushing before the operation.

A huge, blond, grinning man dressed in light blue cotton pants, a short-sleeved white, semistarched jacket which buttoned snugly at the neck, wearing a white, stiffly starched, square hat perched rakishly on his head, met me in the corridor. He was carrying a long scissorslike instrument with ring ends. He snapped it onto his jacket as he stuck out his hand in greeting.

"You're Doctor Davis from Chicago. I'm Adolph, the chief's man." The statements were made in a heavily accented voice and established our equal importance. Adolph was proud and confident of his talent and prerogatives. He took my coat and gave me a gown but no cap or mask. The operating rooms were separated by a scrub sink area. One room was enormous, holding two operating tables and separated only by a folding curtain screen. Dr. Cushing's operating room had an unusually high ceiling, and the customary skylight faced the north. The stand was made of pieces of pipe, and as I climbed up, I knew that a seat on the two pipes would keep me from becoming drowsy.

Adolph wore no mask, but the two surgical nurses were masked and busy draping the tables and arranging an enormous number of instruments. The operating table was much lighter in structure than those at home and could evidently be adjusted to many positions. Adolph began to wind a long gauze bandage between two supports that would apparently support the patient's chest. Then he attached an outrigger, which he bandaged with gauze and padded carefully. The patient's head would fit into it, and the back of the skull would be easily accessible. The anesthetist would have to sit under the headrest and on a stool close to the floor.

Adolph brought the slender young woman on a cart to the door of the operating room. He had draped a towel around her cleanly shaven head. He spoke to her quietly and then lifted her in his arms and carefully placed her on the operating table. I was fascinated as

Adolph arranged and rearranged her face in the headrest, put small pillows under her knees, adjusted the straps that held her arms, placed pillows under her hips, and put more padding on the crutch support so that her breasts were protected. She had excellent breathing space; she didn't have to raise her chest every time she took a breath. This was something I could take home to improve our crude methods for positioning a patient for a suboccipital craniotomy.

There was only the faint, stirring noise of people moving in the operating room. The nurses handled the instruments quietly and did not talk to each other or to Adolph. To attract each other's attention, they cleared their throats gently. I concentrated on the signs they made to see if I could anticipate which instruments or supplies they wanted.

The nurse anesthetist, Miss Garrard, put the patient to sleep and had a rubber catheter, which she had placed in one nostril, connected to a machine which, as nearly as I could figure out, blew ether vapor into the patient's upper respiratory passages. As Dr. Cushing came in, he stopped and whispered to the anesthetist, listened carefully, and looked at the chart she held up for him to see. It was a record of the pulse, respirations, and blood pressure. I had read that when he was an intern at the Massachusetts General Hospital, he had initiated the practice of keeping a record of the patient under anesthesia similar to the tracings every student made on dogs in the physiology laboratory. It was a record of the patient's vital signs which he could see at a glance.

He was dressed in a gray operating suit with a military collar on the shirt which buttoned around his neck. His Adam's apple was enormous. His surgeon's cap fitted perfectly and was firmly and securely on his head, covering his forehead to absorb perspiration on his brow. Some surgeons wore their caps like a Happy Hooligan hat perched precariously on the side or back of their head with the tie strings dangling. This cap looked as if it had been tailored.

He wore tennis sneakers, and I wondered how little support they must give him when he stood for hours operating. His mask was a large piece of folded gauze which completely covered his prominent nose as well as his mouth. He looked toward Adolph, who quickly came and tightened the mask where he had tied it over the top of his cap. Cushing held out his hand and never looked up from his regard of the patient's scalp. A ball of cotton soaked in soap and water was firmly flipped into his palm by one of the nurses. Quickly, he went on to cleanse the scalp and drape towels that he fastened with safety pins into the scalp. He made a motion with his hand, as if he were holding an object between his index finger and thumb and drawing it toward him. Surely and quickly, the handle of a scalpel was placed between the thumb and finger and with the cutting side up. Much as an artist would sketch in the outlines of the painting with a short pencil, Dr. Cushing outlined the craniotomy incision from one mastoid process to the other and with a vertical incision in the midline to bisect the crossbow. He had not drawn blood, but I could see the clear outline of the proposed incision. A large piece of wet gauze was placed over the scalp and would aid in stopping any oozing that might occur. More towels and sheet drapes isolated the incision perfectly. The sheets were gathered together so they didn't fall sloppily on the floor. There was a moment or two in which he gazed at the operative field, patted a towel more securely into place, arranged a towel clip, and then briskly turned away. As he did, he glanced up and jerked his head up and down in a greeting. I was amused at the ceremony of putting on his sterile gown and the adjustments that Adolph made to make it fit comfortably. He was even more particular to have his rubber gloves fit perfectly. He grunted disapprovingly as he made the nurse remove the first glove she had put on his hand.

A big redheaded young man came into the operating room followed closely by a small man and holding his dripping hands before his face. Suddenly, I remembered the name of the resident. I looked again and almost spoke out loud. I couldn't believe it. There was Rusty Wheeler, from that small town in Iowa, who had been in the Beta Theta Pi fraternity at Knox College with me. I had not known that Rusty had gone to medical school. Wheeler looked up, tossed his hand in greeting, and shrugged his shoulders.

I had never seen a brain operation or, in fact, any operation performed so deliberately and yet with speed that depended upon knowing just what step came next. Rusty was a good assistant, anticipating Cushing's moves well, but still getting grunts of disapproval and an elbow that sharply reminded him to keep his feet, body, and hands within his area of action.

The second assistant had to stand on a platform to reach the level of the operative field and was in trouble most of the time. He would relax his hold on a retractor and be reminded with a tap across his knuckles. He would shift his position and weight, and his foot would touch Cushing's leg. Once, Cushing deliberately raised his foot, stomped down, and pushed the assistant's feet back. I could see the expression of annoyance in the movement of Cushing's hands and shoulders. The operating room was completely quiet except for the sounds of the patient's regular breathing. Often, Cushing only held out his hand, palm up, and the correct instrument was placed in it; other times, he moved the index finger and the thumb together rapidly to denote a tissue forcep. Three hours went by, and I had forgotten all about the uncomfortable, narrow, parallel pipe seat. I leaned with my arms on the stand and my chin on the backs of my hands, completely absorbed. Cushing turned abruptly, looked at me, and asked, "Is this how Kanavel operates on posterior fossa lesions?"

"No, sir, there's a difference."

"You should know better than to speak into my wound." The reprimand was sharp and sarcastic. Cushing turned back to the operation. I became angry and started to leave the stand. It was a grossly unjust and unfair situation. Rusty Wheeler threw me a quick glance and moved his head negatively. Suddenly, I realized I had been tested and caught. I shouldn't have spoken even with a mask over my mouth and nose; it was true that particles of saliva could be projected into the wound. But I had been asked a direct question, and it had seemed to require an answer. I had learned a lesson. If I was to come there and be a voluntary worker, I'd have to learn all the customs and quirks of Adolph, the interns, residents, nurses, secretaries, right up to the chief.

Cushing's technique was the perfect example of handling tissues gently, securing hemostasis, and planning, by layer-to-layer dissection, to restore the wound to its normal relations as nearly as possible. He did spend a great deal of time sponging, inspecting, and sponging again and again before he was satisfied there was no bleeding. Finally, he began to attack the angle between the skull and the

138

cerebellum where it was suspected a tumor of the eighth cranial nerve was present.

I wondered if now he would move faster and be less inclined to putter, as midwestern surgeons would describe his movements. There was more decisiveness, and I could see the plan for removal of the benign tumor develop in his technique. He made an incision into the capsule of the tumor and then took a curette and removed portions of the tumor piecemeal. He placed black silk sutures into the capsule and used them as traction lines which helped him tilt the tumor from side to side so he could begin to see all around its circumference. I was holding my breath. I sat back for a moment; I had been projecting myself as the surgeon. There was a saying that went the rounds at home that the surgeon who held his breath in a tight situation during an operation was the most likely candidate for a coronary occlusion.

Alternately gutting out the contents of the encapsulated mass, placing sutures so he could make gentle traction, Cushing finally placed two of the silver clips, which he had devised, around the small blood vessels that ran into the base of the tumor. He lifted out the remnant and held it high before him in a gesture of triumph. Dramatically, he let it fall into the round basin that the surgical nurse had provided. Four hours had gone by. The closure should require less time, perhaps an hour and a half. Cushing continued and closed the wound layer by layer. The last suture was placed in the scalp, oblong pieces of silver foil were placed on the wound edges, and yet he did not leave. He put on the head dressing which consisted of a long roll of gauze that he shaped to the patient's head and secured with safety pins placed with the same meticulous accuracy he had exhibited throughout the operation.

Briskly, Cushing turned from the operating table. "Wheeler will bring you for dinner at my home this evening at seven o'clock."

Without a word of acknowledgment to his nurses and residents he left the operating room, drawing off his rubber gloves and stopping, it seemed to me, at a prearranged spot for Adolph to take off his operating room gown. It had been like watching a great painter work at his easel, attended by a valet.

Rusty Wheeler had a great deal of work with patients in the hospital that had to be postponed to escort me to dinner at Dr. Cushing's home. I could have gone by myself. As we rode in the streetcar, we talked about our college days and filled each other in on the fortunes of our friends. Rusty had been a hated sophomore when I was a freshman in the fraternity, and I knew that neither of us would ever be able to revive the old brothers-in-bond spirit. I wanted to ask questions about what it was like being Dr. Cushing's resident. Rusty anticipated me and settled some of the questions. "I'm going into general surgery, not neurosurgery, so I'm not really the chief's resident. I'm filling in until the man he's picked shows up in the fall. It's a great experience, but he just tolerates me. I can't shave heads or put on six-yard-roll head dressings to suit him."

The Cushing home was a large, many-gabled house which sat back from the street. It needed a coat of white paint, and the shutters should have been painted a deep forest-green. Its size alone made it impressive.

Dr. Cushing answered the doorbell. "So, you're Davis." The tone of his voice and his scrutiny made me feel that only now would he make up his mind whether or not he would offer me the hospitality of his home.

"Yes, sir. I appreciate the opportunity of visiting your hospital and watching you operate."

There was a flicker of a smile, the eyes narrowed, and something between a grunt and cough escaped. "You and Wheeler are old friends, I hear. Come in."

He led us through a living room crowded with mid-Victorian furniture. The room was somber in the dim light of the evening. We were seated at the dining room table before I realized that there would be no preliminary small talk. I risked a quick glance at my watch. We were exactly on time. Just as promptly, a white-haired maid wearing a starched, frilly uniform and apron, with a cap perched on her head, beneath which her hair seemed to fall haphazardly about her ears, neck, and eyes, began to serve the soup.

All through dinner, Dr. Cushing talked. He asked no questions and expected no comments. Almost on a clocked schedule, dishes were removed and the next course was served without a word passing between him and the maid. He told about receiving a broken finger while playing baseball at Yale; he seemed to deprecate his athletic abilities but then went on to tell how the Y club of Montclair, New Jersey, had presented him with an honorary blanket and a silver bowl. He talked about the Midwest, the explorations of Joliet, adding parenthetically that he supposed young fellows like us knew nothing about the early history of the midwestern states. He spoke interestingly, and his use of words and the grammatical construction of his sentences were hypnotizing. His hands moved gracefully all of the time, it seemed; sometimes he would lock them together just below his chin. His long nose, his dark eyes, and his large head gave him a Semitic appearance.

When coffee was served, he began to talk about Sir William Osler, whose biography he was writing. He became more animated and talked more rapidly, as if he were so filled with the subject he couldn't wait to get some of his thoughts expressed. It was as if he had been warming up with his preliminary monologue.

"Well, enough of that. I must get to work. You fellows come into the library with me and look at my books while I go to work."

The library was a small room with its walls covered from floor to ceiling with shelves of books. His desk was piled high, and yet he seemed to go to work immediately with great concentration, as if he had just risen a moment before to stretch his legs. Rusty and I moved from shelf to shelf as noiselessly as possible.

I was startled by Dr. Cushing getting up and pulling out a book, placing it in my hands, and saying, "Here's a fine copy of Vesalius. Sit down on the floor and look through it. You should know what to look at in a book as rare as this is. If you don't, make it a point to find out. Wheeler, sit down."

Half an hour passed, and I was afraid to get up; we had certainly disturbed the chief even though we had moved as quietly as possible before the book shelves. Why should I be thinking of Cushing as "the chief"? I had exhausted my limited possibilities with the Vesalius. Rusty was sitting there cross-legged and sound asleep. We should be leaving. Rusty's head jerked as I kicked his foot and got his attention. Slowly, he nodded his head in agreement with my signs suggesting that we leave. We got to our feet.

"Where you going, Wheeler?"

Rusty was saved a reply by the ringing of the telephone. Cushing let it ring several times before he took off the receiver with a snort of disgust. He cradled the telephone receiver on his shoulder, lighted a cigarette, and blew smoke through his nose. He was listening, but his impatience was growing.

"I don't care what the patient's name is, I won't operate on anybody outside my own hospital. I'm not an itinerant surgeon. I——" Evidently, whoever was on the other end could interrupt just as easily. At any rate, Cushing remained quiet but not for long.

"All right, if he wants me that badly, tell him to come to Boston." There was a brief pause. "It's ridiculous to say he can't be moved; of course, he can be moved. Well, if he says he shouldn't be moved, have Elsberg operate upon him. He's a competent surgeon. I didn't say he was a neurological surgeon. You said it. What good would it do for me to come there in consultation? You say Kennedy and Sachs have said he has an intracranial tumor. I won't operate in another hospital. No, that's final. I'm busy. Good-by."

He hung up the telephone and, without a word, went back to his writing. Rusty and I moved forward to express our thanks and say good night. Again, the telephone interrupted. Cushing let it ring, it seemed interminably. He picked up the receiver with an audible snort of anger.

"Yes?" He leaned back in his desk chair and regarded the ceiling as he listened. "All right, I'll arrange a room for him for arrival in the morning. Don't let someone be stupid enough to give him morphine so he'll sleep on the train. What? That's balderdash. Let 'em insist. I'm not going to discuss fees over the telephone. Such damned foolishness. He can't be as sick as you say if he's so interested in fees. All right, sure, I understand these Wall Street men. Tell him it'll be my own fee and I'll decide that later, plus a contribution of fifty thousand dollars for our surgical laboratory."

Cushing put his hand over the telephone mouthpiece and looked impishly at us. "Maybe that'll discourage the important Morgan partner from coming here, but if he accepts, he'll obey my orders and won't try to run his own illness." He turned back to the telephone. "He does? All right, I'll see him in the morning. Good night, Doctor." He turned to Wheeler. "One of the younger and brighter Morgan partners, Henry Davison, will get in from New York on the morning train. See that a private room, with bath, and a room nearby are ready for him and his wife on Ward A. Treat him like any other patient. I'll see him with you later in the morning. Good night. Stay around as long as you wish, Davis. Tell Kanavel he can write me about arrangements for you to come on as a voluntary assistant in September." We were dismissed as he turned back to his writing.

I thought about the supreme self-confidence and actual salesmanship that Cushing had exhibited. He had implied that his surgical fee would be less if the patient agreed to make a contribution to the surgical laboratory. But he hadn't said that. I went to bed only to be half awake and half asleep as I imagined myself in Cushing's place. I wondered if I would ever have a patient referred to me. I got to the hospital early the next morning and found Rusty, who said that later the night before, the reservation for Mr. Davison had been canceled. We conjectured what additional conditions had been insisted upon by one side or the other that were unsatisfactory.

As we reached Ward C, Rusty asked me to wait outside the chief's office and to join them on rounds. I asked Rusty if he thought Dr. Cushing would mind. The only way to find out was to wait and see.

The door opened. "You here, Davis? Well, come along then." It was said grudgingly; my presence was something to be tolerated. By the time we got to the ward, there was quite a procession. We entered in order of seniority, the medical students last. Cushing turned and with a show of irritation motioned me forward in the group. He stopped by the bed of a patient to which the nurse had taken him. "Good morning, I trust you had a comfortable night." This was the voice of a physician, sympathetic and gentle in his approach to his patient.

"I believe you have already met my resident, Doctor Wheeler. May I present Doctor Davis, a visitor with us today, who will join our staff in the fall; a Midwesterner like myself." He introduced each of his retinue in turn, calling their names and identifying them as house staff or students. I was impressed and confused at the sudden change in manner.

Dr. Cushing sat down and asked about the patient's wife—was she comfortably situated? He said he had discussed the symptoms only in part over the telephone with the family doctor. He asked the patient to tell him in detail all of his complaints starting back when he considered himself to be perfectly well. He wasn't interested at the moment, he said, in hearing what other doctors thought or what they had prescribed. He would take that up later.

The patient's story was not interrupted until he had come to the end of all he could think of to tell about himself; even his own interpretation of his symptoms was borne patiently and silently without comment. Then began a cross-examination of searching questions which slowly developed the chronology of the onset of symptoms and signs. It became obvious that the occurrence that upset the patient was the localized convulsive seizure that he had had a year previously for the first time in his life.

Pollock had taught me that when an adult had a convulsive seizure for the first time, it was the obligation of the doctor to prove he did not have a brain tumor. Cushing asked many questions about the seizure, eliciting the story of a motor aura that consisted of a slight twitching on the left side of the mouth. Then the seizure spread to involve the arm and leg on the same side. The patient insisted he did not lose consciousness with the first attack, but recently, they had lasted longer, and finally, two weeks previously he had lost consciousness.

When I saw Dr. Cushing examine the patient and test for weakness of muscles, loss of sensation, and the state of the reflexes, I was confident my examinations would not suffer in comparison. Pollock had drilled me in demonstrating the minute, fleeting changes in reflexes and had taught me the ways to bring out the slight differences in strength between opposite extremities.

"What about him, Davis?" I said I thought he might have a rather slow-growing intracranial tumor on the right side, near the motor cortex, and it could well be a meningioma.

"Anything you'd do before you would operate on him? I assume you would operate on him."

I knew a storm would break around my head if I mentioned performing an air study of the cerebral ventricles to see if they were symmetrical and not displaced. That would be Dandy's pneumoencephalogram. I had a good reason, in addition, not to do the new di-

144

agnostic test; I had no experience with it. "I would be interested in studying the plain X-ray films of the skull to see if there were any changes in the bone which would corroborate the diagnosis of a meningioma."

Cushing persisted. "I'll probably have to fight off everyone around here to avoid doing an air study. Why wouldn't you do one right away?"

I said we had no experience with the method yet and that Dr. Pollock and I were making X-ray films of the ventricles of accurately fixed brains which we filled with mercury and then X-rayed. We wanted to see what a series of normal ventricles looked like. There appeared to be differences in the shape of the ventricles between individuals and between the two sides of the same individual.

"I'll be interested in what you find."

My stay was climaxed by watching Dr. Cushing remove a meningioma from the right side of the cerebral cortex of the patient examined on rounds. It was just in front of the motor gyrus, and the dimple in the overlying dura mater, from which it originated, could be seen as soon as the bone flap had been elevated. Cushing acted as if this were an everyday occurrence. I saw masterful tilting of the baseball-sized firm mass with many black silk sutures which he had placed through the substance of the tumor, gentle dissection of the brain from the circumference of the tumor with wet cotton pledgets, and meticulous hemostasis. The mass was held up for all to see, without comment.

I understood why all of his contemporaries regarded Cushing as the master neurological surgeon. Even though I would not be his resident, I could learn by observation. I had three years of education and training in general surgery and now could watch an operation with appreciation of the different situations that arose. I was sure Dr. Kanavel felt no jealousy toward Cushing; for myself, Kanavel would remain my "chief." Now I would be lucky if Cushing would add the icing to the cake.

September was three months away. I had the examination for the doctor of philosophy degree to pass; I had to keep up the standard of work I had set as Kanavel's first assistant. He gave me more and

145

more responsibility in the care of his patients, in organizing the work of the interns, and in operations. A cake of ice in a tub in the corner of the operating room, with an electric fan blowing across it, provided a slight amount of relief from the heat that was increased by the operating room lights. Miss Johnson kept a supply of lemonade and iced tea in the surgeons' dressing room.

Patients perspired copiously during an operation and lost an enormous amount of body fluid. Added to this loss, which couldn't be measured, was the amount of blood lost in spite of the most careful efforts at hemostasis. Fluids had to be replaced by introducing normal saline solution through needles introduced under the breasts or into the thighs. The Murphy drip enema was a lifesaver, but sometimes the lower bowel rebelled and the water was expelled messily over the bed. Someday, Dr. Kanavel prophesied, pharmaceutical houses would make it possible to give fluids intravenously which contained proteins, carbohydrates, and fat.

It was difficult to replace blood loss by transfusion. A carefully prepared parafinized Kempton tube, into which blood was collected from the donor and then introduced into the recipient, was fraught with many problems, the most common of which was coagulation. Success carried with it the danger of a reaction because blood typing had not been perfected. Lillienthal's citrate method had not been accepted. Blood donors were difficult to obtain, and blood banks were beyond imagination.

Many patients in hemorrhagic shock died for lack of blood replacement. Properly prepared intravenous solutions were scarce; reactions occurred from glassware. Blood volume studies were unknown. Replacement fluids were limited to normal saline and water, and whether we gave too much or too little, we could never be sure.

One day in mid-July, the first test of my judgment and independent action occurred dramatically. That morning we had operated upon a patient who had a hard, firm, exophthalmic goiter. She had been first on the schedule, and the operation had been swiftly and anatomically performed. As was the custom, when Dr. Kanavel isolated the thyroid arteries at the upper and lower poles of the thyroid gland, I grasped each one with a hemostat and identified it aloud. I

146

was taught teamwork in operating and was proud because he spoke of "our operations"; that "we were operating."

The schedule had been finished, and Dr. Kanavel left the hospital for his downtown office. I made rounds with the junior intern, preparatory to going next door to the medical school to meet Pollock and carry on one of our experiments. As we entered her room, I heard the gasping respirations of the thyroidectomized patient. Her color was bluish, and her nostrils were dilating with each attempt to breathe. Her pulse was barely recognizable at the wrist. Her pupils were dilated, and she was unconscious.

I took off the dressing rapidly. The neck was full and tight. We did not have the dressing cart with us. I cut the center skin sutures with my bandage scissors, closed the blades, and thrust the points into the wound and then separated them. There was a gush of blood which covered the bed clothing and the patient's gown. I told the intern to have Miss Johnson get an operating room ready immediately and to ask an anesthetist to stand by. I put the dressing back and held it with compression. One of the thyroid arteries had broken loose from its ligature. It was lucky we had come by just when we did. I would open the wound widely after I had prepared and draped her for operation just as we had in the beginning. I'd look systematically at each upper pole and each lower pole. Maybe it would clot in the meantime from pressure. This would be a godsend to the patient but make it more difficult for me to find the bleeding vessel. Maybe it would be oozing slightly. I'd need some good help from the surgical nurse and the interns. I'd have to go ahead and not wait for Dr. Kanavel to get back to the hospital.

I gave her saline solution subcutaneously. I called Dr. Kanavel before I scrubbed. I told him what had happened and what I planned to do in detail. He said he would appreciate hearing how we got along and would be out to see her later. He wished me good luck. I wasn't that calm.

I couldn't repress an audible sigh as I saw the right inferior thyroid artery pumping a small squirt of blood with each pulsation of the vessel. I ligated it quickly and then carefully and methodically inspected the remainder of the surgical field. It was dry everywhere else. It didn't take long to close the wound layer by layer, replace the

147

dressing, and get the patient back to her room. As I arranged her in bed, with the back rest elevated slightly, she was breathing smoothly and regularly. She opened her eyes and looked about her. There was a faint smile of recognition, and she mumbled. I leaned down to catch what she was trying to say.

"Thank you for coming by to see me. I didn't expect you till later tonight."

I sat down on a chair beside the bed. I felt as if I had suddenly become older; perhaps not in years, but certainly in surgical experience.

I had gathered clinical data from patients who had a loss of sensation due to lesions of combinations of the cranial nerves. I added these data to my examinations for loss of sensation after operations upon the fifth cranial nerve to relieve the pain of tic douloureux. This evidence supported animal experiments. I had written my thesis several times, because I knew that at the coming examination for the doctor of philosophy degree, I would be the target for questions from many more members of the faculty than had taken part in the master's examination. I was the first candidate for the degree from a clinical department in the medical school. Again, Dr. Kanavel assured me that I would know more about my subject than anyone else in the room. But I knew that the questions on subjects corollary to my thesis would cover fields of study about which I might not have the faintest idea. The problem would be again to keep my poise, good humor, and alertness. I told myself I could ask questions any one of them couldn't answer if they wanted to play ball in my back yard. I was whistling in the dark.

The day finally arrived, and as I rode the elevated train out north to the Evanston campus where the liberal arts, engineering, speech, music, and other schools were located, I had that sinking feeling in my epigastrium. It could make my voice tremulous, and that could be interpreted as being unsure of myself. I had an almost uncontrollable urge to talk with anyone in the elevated car who might listen.

I began to watch my fellow passengers. Just what kind of work did that one do, what would their voices be like, how many children did

148

that woman have at home? I looked at their hands; long, clawlike nails with silver polish made me shudder; broken nails on broad, spadelike fingers that had been broken probably belonged to a carpenter or a bricklayer; maybe that fellow with a broken nose had been a professional boxer when he was younger. I wondered if he had the short, mincing steps of a slightly punch-drunk ex-fighter.

It was a long room with the windows on the east and south overlooking the lake. I had never seen such a long table; I gave up trying to count the chairs arranged along its sides. I took a chair as inconspicuously as possible along the wall. Several men were grouped around the room when Dr. Kanavel came in, followed by Ranson and Leslie B. Arey, a young embryologist who had recently been added to the department of anatomy. Dr. Kanavel came directly to me.

"There will be more of the faculty from the Evanston faculty here than are on your examination committee. They are here to try to protect a graduate degree which affects the amount of money they are paid according to the rank they hold on the faculty. They don't like an outsider from surgery getting a philosophy degree. Your patients won't pay fees according to the master of science and doctor of philosophy degrees you hold. So these men say why should he work for our degree? Clinicians who teach at the medical school don't receive remuneration for their teaching. I know you are excited and tense. No use telling you not to be. Think of all this like you would about an operation. That's the best advice I can give you. I know you'll give it your best. Come with me."

He moved to the head of the table and motioned me to the chair beside him.

"Gentlemen, it is one minute before three o'clock, and this examination is scheduled to begin at three o'clock. Please be seated, as you wish. My name is Kanavel, chairman of the department of surgery. The candidate for examination is Doctor Davis, a graduate of our medical school, who also holds a master of science degree. He has successfully passed the examinations in French and German required of candidates. He has written a thesis which has been handed to each of the five members of the appointed committee required by the graduate school."

He smiled and reached in his pocket for a cigarette and match. He regarded them for a moment and then said, "I and the candidate regret that we have been remiss in not providing a copy of the thesis for each of you present today. I am sure the committee welcomes you as guests, and on behalf of the candidate, I invite you to take part in the questioning."

I thought, perhaps, they would give me some clue to their questions by introducing themselves and saying to which department in the university they belonged. For a moment I was in a panic, and from afar I heard Dr. Kanavel's voice.

"That is agreeable to you, is it not, Doctor?"

There was a certain grimness in his voice which indicated that he was not in sympathy with the collective effort of the north campus faculty. He had set a few ground rules, and he wanted to beat them at their own game. I mumbled my agreement.

I looked around the table. There were fifteen men, some pipe smokers, whom I believed to be patient, slow, persistent men relying upon their pipe to keep their emotions under control. I looked toward the entrance to see a tall, stooped, angular figure enter the room. His eyes seemed to be too large for the eyeglasses he wore. His nose was long and pointed, and his lips were tightly pursed so that his mouth seemed to be a straight line that accentuated the sharpness of his chin. He wore a high starched collar which came together so closely that it left only a small space for the knot of a red string tie. There was a stir at the table as everyone rose to greet the newcomer.

"Sit down, gentlemen, please." The high-pitched, reedy voice matched the face. "Excuse me, Allen, for being late." He turned to the others. "Allen Kanavel and I were classmates at this university, and he knows my proclivity for being tardy. Please proceed."

This was the famous Walter Dill Scott, president of the university, who had a reputation as a psychologist and an unusual talent for getting gifts of money. No one could correlate this talent with his appearance and character, more suitable for portraying the cartoon character who campaigned against alcohol, tobacco, and all carnal sins. The president had a habit, almost a tic, of frequently wetting his lips with his tongue. I couldn't help but think that he was working up an appetite for the grilling.

"Doctor Davis, will you briefly outline the problem which you

150

have investigated, state your material and methods, and summarize your conclusions."

I settled down as I proceeded logically, step by step. Momentarily, I thought I was speaking down to the audience but quickly dismissed it from my mind; after all, Dr. Ranson and Dr. Kanavel were the only ones who knew the details of my work from the beginning.

"Thank you. I'm sure everyone will agree that you have given a clear, lucid, and simple statement. Now, gentlemen, your questions. Shall we go right around the table, beginning on my left?"

The questions from Ranson, Pollock, and Becht were concerned with the problem and the subjects corollary to it. They were searching and persistent. I began to wonder if they were really friendly to me; I became a bit angry with myself for having to hesitate with an answer. I should have a quick, correct response for everything they asked. I spoke my reasoning aloud when I could not give the answer promptly and was surprised at the interest that was evident around the table when these occasions arose. It seemed that these situations were far more entertaining to the audience than when I gave a quick, correct answer. There came a slight pause in Dr. Ranson's questioning.

President Scott stood up. "Allen—that is, Mr. Chairman—it is necessary for me to leave, if you will excuse me. May I say, Doctor, that I have enjoyed your responses. The faculty on this campus regards the doctor of philosophy degree seriously. This explains the presence of so many representatives of the other schools of the university. You have shown that you and the departments of the medical school, in which you have worked, also regard it as an important academic achievement. I hope you will be successful in your examination." A wry expression, a tight pursing of the lips, changed the appearance of his face as he looked around the table. "You have other hurdles to jump. Good day, gentlemen."

Ranson's final questions were perfunctory and concerned themselves with the anatomy of fiber tracts in the brain and spinal cord. "I have finished my questioning of the candidate, Mr. Chairman. May I beg the indulgence of those present and ask the candidate to explain his suggestion, which our department has adopted, to aid the teaching of these exact anatomical facts of the nervous system to young medical students?"

151

I was astonished. I had tried to interest the students by making simple practical applications to hypothetical patients. I knew the students enjoyed these mental exercises and seemed to remember fiber tracts better, but I had thought I sensed that Dr. Ranson disapproved of this mixing of clinical interest and pure anatomy. I fumbled for words.

"Just give the gentlemen a simple illustration. I consider it a real contribution to teaching." Dr. Ranson was making it appear too important; I had done nothing but apply Pollock's principles of teaching me about clinical neurology. I looked at Pollock, who smiled understandingly.

"The idea is not original; I tried to make a practical application of some facts that are difficult for the students to remember. Doctor Pollock has helped me in this way." Briefly, I explained the function of one of the simple fiber tracts in the spinal cord and told how this had been determined originally by recording the symptoms of many patients and correlating these symptoms with the gross and microscopic study of changes in the spinal cord. All I did to get the students' interest was to describe a hypothetical patient with these symptoms, and in some instances, illustrate the loss of function in gait and sensation by acting out the symptoms. Then I would question them about which fiber tracts would be destroyed under such circumstances. There was a polite silence. I wondered if some of those present thought this was a prostitution of a pure, scientific discipline.

Dr. Kanavel called upon each one of those present, reminding them to identify their departments in the university. The questioning began to spread over wide fields of interest: biographical facts about men in science; historical events in medicine that the questioner had obviously looked up before coming to the examination; questions from the English department about sentence structure, just as in my master's degree examination.

"I'm McGivern, mathematics. How many cranial nerves are there in Great Britain?"

Immediately, a slide rule floated before my eyes. I had never been able to understand a slide rule, let alone use one. How could I figure out the answer if I didn't have a slide rule? McGivern sat there with his elbows on the table glaring at me. How many people were there living in Great Britain? The multiplication in my head would be impossible. The silence was oppressive, and my hands were sweating. I reached for the pencil on the table and drew the pad of paper before me. I glanced up, frowning, and my eyes caught Pollock looking directly at me as if he were trying to convey a message telepathically. He shook his head negatively and then looked down at the pad of paper.

I must not try to figure it out with pencil and paper. Suddenly, as if a light flashed before my eyes, I realized it was a trick question. Anatomists in Great Britain named the nervus intermedius as the thirteenth cranial nerve. In the United States it was considered a part of the facial nerve that I had studied for my thesis. So in Great Britain there were thirteen cranial nerves on each side, multiplied by the population. I looked at McGivern and almost laughed aloud in my relief.

"Well, what's the answer?"

I explained the difference in terminology almost exuberantly. There was laughter around the table, and the loudest came from McGivern.

"That satisfies me about the candidate's ability to think, and now since everyone here has had a shot at this fellow, I move, Mr. Chairman, that his examination be ended."

Dr. Kanavel said almost apologetically, "You are excused, Doctor Davis. The committee will deliberate, and you will learn the results of the examination later."

If I had failed, the examination couldn't be taken again. I felt confident I had passed the ordeal, regardless of the opinions of those around the table. Besides, only the five members of the committee voted. I wondered about the attitude of the faculty on the north campus about the doctor of philosophy degree. I had respect for those things considered the best and for tradition. I might be prouder of it than of my doctor of medicine degree earned in course; just why I didn't know. It wouldn't attract patients, but the future might hold something in store that I couldn't imagine at the moment. It was the physician who was considered the scholar, the academician; the surgeon was the one who used his hands; therefore, it was said that he couldn't be a thinker, or possess any scholarly attainments. Pollock had repeatedly said that I should be a new kind of surgeon of the nervous system, not one who mechanically carried out the directions of the medical neurologist.

153

D<small>R.</small> KANAVEL'S parting advice was, "Pick their brains. Take the best of what you see and learn, put it with what you have already learned, and you'll come out with your own professional surgical philosophy. This is something every surgeon must get for himself. You'll have to be careful or you'll be mimicking Cushing's actions and attitudes. Don't do that any more than you would mimic mine. Discard the worst, keep the best for yourself to modify and improve."

Pearl and I drove in our Velie through the beautiful Mohawk Valley. The turning leaves provided a variety of brilliant colors, and the crisp early morning air ushered in the beginning of fall. We stayed in a hotel near the railroad station the first night after we arrived in Boston. The newspaper for-rent columns advertised a room with a bath and an alcove with a sink, gas burner, and dishes on Hemingway Street. When the landlady pointed out it was across from the Forsythe Dental Infirmary, near the Fenway and Mrs. Jack Gardner's house, and within walking distance of the Peter Bent Brigham Hospital, we took it. We couldn't afford to use the Velie, so we stored it in a nearby garage.

I had been given a National Research Council fellowship in 1922 with a stipend of $166 a month. It was a condition that no other remuneration could be received. I had been interviewed for the fellowship by Dean Lewis, a surgeon at Rush Medical College and Presbyterian Hospital. He was born and raised in Kewanee, Illinois, and his father was a traveling salesman for a wholesale grocery firm. Lewis and Kanavel were friends and had published a surgical paper as joint authors. My interview was a perfunctory, necessary procedure. I received the reward of a series of circumstances over which I had no influence. In the second year the stipend rose to $190 a month. It was not long after that young men engaged in postgraduate work in clinical fields of medicine, such as surgery, were excluded from receiving Research Council fellowships.

I was concerned about how Pearl would occupy her days; I hoped she wouldn't work and we could live on my fellowship income. Maybe she would become more interested in my professional education and training. I knew that Helen Raftery, whom I had met at Mrs. Cheeseman's boarding house, had married Harry Malloy, a newspaperman in Boston, who had become the public relations man for a retail shoe store owner's association. Perhaps Helen would take Pearl under her wing and keep her time occupied.

I went to the hospital the next morning. I felt more at home than I had on my previous visit and went directly to Dr. Cushing's operating room. Kenneth MacKenzie, of Toronto, had become the neurosurgical resident, and Rusty Wheeler had left to enter practice in Duluth. Again, I watched a skillful operation. Cushing never once glanced at me sitting in the stands, and when he had finished at three o'clock, again putting on the head dressing himself, I waited a moment before slipping out of the operating room. It had been a long time since breakfast, and my hunger accentuated the apprehension with which I approached the door of the surgeons' dressing room. It was slightly open, and I stood for a moment gathering my determination to enter. Perhaps I should wait outside until Dr. Cushing had changed out of his operating room clothes. On the other hand, he would then be surrounded by his house staff and would have little time to say what he expected of me during the coming year. I knocked firmly and after a pause, knocked again.

"What is it? Stop knocking and come in."

Cushing was sitting by a small table on which there was a hot plate that held a teapot covered with a cozy. He had not taken off his rubber gloves or his operating room cap. His mask had been loosened and hung below his chin. He had removed his gown, and again my attention focused on the military-type collar on his gray surgical shirt. Resting on his crossed knee was a pad, and its top was propped against the table. He was holding a cigarette and sketching on a piece of the long blue paper that was used for the surgical patients' hospital record. He never looked up but continued to sketch and absently reached for his cup of tea and took a sip. I became entranced with the deep, sucking inhalations he took from the cigarette. When he released the smoke, it seemed to come from all of the orifices of his head. I maneuvered little by little so I could watch the drawing. He was sketching with loose lines the location of the tumor that he had just removed and was recording its surface appearance. When he had dictated the story of his operation, it would be typed on this particular sheet of paper. His concentration was complete. He held the paper at arm's length, regarded it intently, and dropped it to the table as if he were washing his hands of the matter and was dismissing it with disgust.

"What're you doing here?" The question was harsh, abrupt, and the cold, blue eyes showed no recognition. My spirits sank.

I identified myself, told him I was ready to go to work, and reminded him that Dr. Kanavel had arranged for me to spend a year with him as a voluntary assistant.

"Oh, yes, Davis, isn't it?" The tone of voice was vague. He was pouring himself another cup of tea. My hope that I might be invited to sit down and enjoy a cup was fleeting. There was a grunt as he turned away. "Well, go ahead, make yourself at home."

I waited momentarily for more, but he had picked up the dictating tube to record. I mumbled a thank you and left. What did he mean by making myself at home? What good would it do to ask anyone what was meant by that indefinite order? There were private patients on Ward A and semiprivate and ward patients on Ward C for surgical patients. I wanted to examine patients and follow their course before and after operation; I would like to be taught by Dr. Cushing when he made rounds to see his patients. I knew how to get into the operating room and watch him work. I could record my own histories and physical examinations; my high school typewriting course would stand me in good stead. The question was how to start examining patients. I'd have to introduce myself to the nurse in charge of each floor on Ward C, convince her that whatever I did wouldn't upset her organization and administration of the care of her patients, and then go ahead.

I had been told that Dr. Cushing made rounds late in the afternoon. I decided to wait at the entrance to Ward C until the entourage came along. I'd have to figure out how to get something to eat be-

156

fore his operations began; I couldn't go without food from seven in the morning until evening every day.

Miss Tilton, the nurse in charge of C-2, was pleasantly buxom. Her round face and red cheeks were the proper setting for her large brown eyes. Her white uniform was always immaculate and stiffly starched. She pointed out that the neurosurgical patients' charts had a gray cover. While I waited that first day, she gave me charts to read. She saw my hesitation and said: "You'll never know how far or fast you can go until you start to do something. Indoctrination is not a feature of the chief's educational program. Of course, if you do nothing, you'll never make a mistake." Miss Tilton threw the last sentence across her shoulder as she went out into the ward. She went to each patient's bed and critically appraised the linen, straightened a cover, tucked in a corner, and arranged a pillow here and there.

I became engrossed in the story of a patient with a tumor of the auditory nerve, and the entourage was on the floor outside the nurse's station while I was sitting with the chart in my hands. There was silence, and I felt I was the cynosure of all eyes. Miss Tilton took charge of the situation. She gathered all the patients' records, and I put the one I had on top of the pile. She handed them to one of the young men who wore a short white coat, its upper left-hand pocket filled with pencils, pens, and a thermometer. He had a notebook in his hand and a stethoscope hanging from another pocket. She turned away, let him juggle the load as best he could, stepped next to Dr. Cushing, and unobtrusively steered him toward the first patient's bed.

There was a commotion as the medical student tried to pass on the bundle to one of his fellows and pick out the correct chart. He had written the record, and it was up to him to read it. I silently prayed for him. All the facts were down. I had read them, but they were not in chronological order, and this was the important fact that Cushing had emphasized in the paper he had written about the difference between this tumor and a cerebellopontine angle growth.

The student began in a clear, confident voice. Cushing looked directly at him and seemed to be giving him his entire attention; in fact, it was a stare that the boy began to feel. His color mounted,

157

his voice became weaker, and he began to stumble over his sentences.

"What's the matter? Can't you read your own writing? You men are writing more and more poorly; should teach yourself writing if you didn't learn in grade school. Never heard of the Spencerian system, I suppose. Anyway, stop. Do the whole thing over and get the subjective symptoms recorded in chronological order. You should learn to read something besides your textbooks. They're five years behind anyway."

He turned abruptly to the patient, smiled, and sat on the edge of the bed, swinging one of his legs off the side, rhythmically. He took one of the patient's hands in his.

"When did you first notice the noise in your ear and in which ear?"

"Must have been five years ago, Doctor, I had this bell start ringing in my right ear; it's never stopped."

"Trouble hearing?"

"I didn't think so, but my wife kept after me saying I didn't hear half the things she said. Never had any trouble on the telephone, I'd tell her."

"Course not, you're right-handed and hold the receiver in your left hand most of the time, don't you?"

"Yes, sir, that's right. Have to write orders telephoned in."

"Any funny feelings in the right side of your face?"

"When I shave, it doesn't feel quite right on that side."

"How long?"

"The last year, I'd say."

Dr. Cushing kept watching the patient, put out his hand without looking away, and Miss Tilton quickly grabbed the chart from the student's hands and put it firmly in the chief's. He leafed through the pages quickly, glanced at the visual field chart, the graph of the hearing tests, and the laboratory data. He held out his hand again. This time, Miss Tilton handed him an envelope of X-ray films that she had taken from a basket she carried. He began to hum softly as he removed the films from the envelope and held them up to the light. He paid particular attention to a film that showed the petrous ridges of the temporal bones. Finally, he grunted and handed the films back without turning his head. He stood up, patted the patient on the head, and ruffed his hair.

"You'll be all right. We'll take care of your trouble, and you'll be back in Cleveland good as new before you know it." He turned to his resident. "Sign him up for day after tomorrow. I'll talk to his wife tomorrow, ten-thirty, my office."

I was disappointed that he had not examined the patient. He had accepted all of his staff's findings. He hadn't discussed the symptoms with them. This same routine went on at the bedside of each patient presented to him for the first time.

He meticulously examined the dressing on each patient who had been operated upon. He removed and tightened the safety pins in the long, six-yard gauze roll bandage so that the dressing fitted snugly and smoothly. He spoke kindly and encouragingly to each patient as he hovered over them. His questions were directed to their comfort and the change in their symptoms. He showed and grunted his disapproval over a soiled dressing or piece of linen. He did not explain his opinions about the patients, did not point out the nice-ties of his brief examination of functions, gave no reasons for his de-cisions for or against an operation. The rounds consisted of policing the work of the residents, house officers, and the students. I would have liked to ask a question now and then, but I knew it would be ignored and this would be the gentlest kind of discipline. Perhaps this was an exception; I would wait for other opportunities to go on rounds before deciding that they were not as helpful as they might be. There was no question that he expected the young men to work at educating themselves; I wondered what would have happened had I been bold enough to ask questions.

I pursued the same routine each day, reading until I was well acquainted with each patient's story. I followed them to the operating room and sat unobtrusively in the stand during the operation. I soon learned that Dr. Cushing would not greet me in any way when he briskly came into the operating room to begin his work. I was con-cerned because I had encountered the chief face to face in the corri-dors between his office and the dining room three times, and my "Good morning, Doctor Cushing" was ignored completely. The first time I thought my greeting had been too subdued, or that he was pre-occupied, but the last time I knew that I had been deliberately snubbed. I tried to stop wondering what I had done to bring about being sent to Coventry. Perhaps he was trying me out. I made up my mind to greet him cheerfully whenever we met out of the operating room. I thought of ways to get him to speak or recognize my presence. He smoked Herbert Tareyton cigarettes. Perhaps he might reach for a cigarette and find his pack empty. I bought a package of cigarettes and carried it in my pocket ready for the situation to occur. I imagined how I would let him search his pockets and then would step forward dramatically and, without a word, extend a fresh, unopened package of Tareytons.

In the meantime, I examined the patients and recorded my findings. I went to the hospital early each morning and used the surgical stenographers' typewriters, following the exact typing outlines they used. They had given me their permission, and since I never interfered with their work, there was no objection. As my examinations of the patients increased, I had to spend time late in the day to complete my records. I didn't gain anything by making rounds, so I utilized the time typing my histories and examinations, making a carbon copy for myself.

One morning, the two typists hesitatingly suggested that if I would dictate my histories and examinations on one of the cylinders, they would be happy to transcribe them and put my records on the charts just as they did for the students and house officers. They were sure there could be no objections raised and I would have free time for other work. I accepted promptly and was pleased that help and interest in my efforts had come from an unexpected source.

I spent each morning visiting the patients who had been operated upon previously, before Dr. Cushing began operating. I did not attempt to accompany the new resident, Putnam, who had to make his own examinations of patients, record them, perform postoperative dressings, and shave the head of the patient scheduled for operation. Shaving had to be done with a straight razor; this was a decree from the chief, who meticulously examined the scalp for nicks in the skin as he prepared his field of operation. Adolph could make or break a new resident by being too busy to keep the razors honed and stropped.

Putnam was tense, fussy, and tended to become overwhelmed with minutiae. I wondered if he was not attempting to get Cushing's approbation by his effeminate, compulsive attention to details. Often, I thought, Dr. Cushing's surgical artistry was handicapped during long intervals when he fussed and fiddled, without advancing the steps in his operation and without accomplishing his immediate goal which an onlooker could not agree was vitally pressing. Perhaps Dandy's criticism was justifiable. On the contrary, he moved unhurriedly and purposefully throughout most of his operations; he seemed to relax and enjoy fitting the gauze bandage head dressing when the operation had been completed.

More and more often, Cushing left the opening steps in the operation, the final closing sutures of the scalp wound, and the dressing to his man Friday. This was the nickname the house staff had given Gil Horrax, a tall, cadaverously slender man who had been one of Cushing's early residents in Boston. He was an accomplished surgeon, and when I had encountered him alone, I found him pleasant, willing to answer questions and teach with a dry sense of humor. He examined the private patients who came from all over the United States to see Dr. Cushing: the wealthy women with wens in their scalp who insisted that the famous brain surgeon should operate upon their heads and those with serious brain tumors. Cushing had great confidence in Gil but arrogantly kept him from becoming the surgical individual that was his right. Gil opened and closed the scalp, the boys said around the luncheon table, but was never allowed to take out a tumor. I couldn't feel too sorry for Gil; I assumed that he could express his independence if he wanted to step outside the shadow of the great man. Besides, Gil didn't seem to be unhappy.

I listened to the small talk in the house-staff dining room. There were innuendoes that I did not understand, but I could take part when the conversation was more general, and I had developed a feeling of friendship with the assistant residents and house officers. It was a slow process, but I was being accepted into the fold. They had listened with something like respect, I thought, the afternoon I chanced by one of the general surgeons who was noted for his frankness, the most independence that anyone on the surgical staff exhibited, and a sense of humor lighted by his sputtering, moist stammer.

John Homans was demonstrating a patient who had a serious infection of the tendon sheath of his index finger which was the result of a minute needle prick. I was standing in the background of the group listening when suddenly Homans singled me out, assuming that I was a medical student.

"Mister, where can this infection spread?"

I was surprised and not sure whether or not I should identify myself; it might appear a bit immodest and could be interpreted as wanting to evade the answer.

"The radial bursa, Doctor Homans." Stem Foster tried to hide his grin.

"Now, gentlemen, that was said with assurance, and as I've said many times, you might as well be all wrong as just a teeny-weeny bit wrong. Here is one of the most important appendages of the body. The loss of function of his hand will keep this man from earning his living; make him useless. It's more important to treat this infection properly than to be able to take out brain tumors." Homans waited for the audacity of his statement to be appreciated properly. "There are more of 'em," he added with a smirk. The medical students dutifully chuckled.

"Now, young man, you don't know what you're talking about. Did you ever hear of the midpalmar space?"

"Yes, sir, I have," I said respectfully.

Foster tried to interrupt. "Doctor Homans, this man——"

"Which man, Foster? For goodness' sakes, don't interrupt me." Homans' sputter was explosive, and a fine spray of saliva shot out from between his lips. "Now, just where is the most exquisite point of tenderness when the midpalmar space is infected? Tell me that."

"It's at the level of the distal crease of the skin of the palm and between the metacarpals of the middle and ring fingers." I tried to keep my voice from being dogmatic. These questions were daily problems in Dr. Kanavel's patients. The correct answers had been drummed into me day after day.

Homans was stopped momentarily by my answer. He peered at me. Foster put the patient's chart in his hands.

"You see, Doctor Homans, the temperature graph is a septic one, and more and more streaks are developing in his upper arm."

"Yes, yes, I know, Foster. We'll get to that. Just show us, mister, with the point of your pencil on your own hand, where the most exquisite point of tenderness is."

I looked at Stem Foster. He inclined his head, slightly shrugged his shoulders, and grimaced as much as to say, "I've tried to protect him, now go ahead and give him the works."

I stepped closer to Dr. Homans and with my pen placed a mark on the small, circumscribed area that Dr. Kanavel had worked out from his clinical and anatomical studies.

"Good. Now, all of you look at that and don't forget it. I don't know where you learned it young man, but you're right. Now, tell me . . ." Homans' voice became soothing and saccharine. He'd find something to fault me on, it seemed to imply. "What would you do for this man? How'll you treat him? You seem to be an expert in this field."

I had not examined the patient, and so without answering I stepped closer to the bed and looked at the hand and arm without touching it. I saw red streaks of lymphatic involvement extending up the inner aspect of the forearm and arm. The forearm was swollen. The palm was flat, but the index finger was red, tight, and gentle passive flexion of the finger caused the patient to grimace with pain. I saw the slight puncture wound on the tip of his finger. I stepped back and faced Dr. Homans.

"I believe he has a tendon sheath infection of the index finger which is likely to be streptococcal in origin. It should not be opened, but a massive, hot, wet dressing should be applied to include the entire hand, forearm, and arm to the axilla. The arm should be elevated and kept immobile, the dressing surrounded with hot-water bags and wrapped in flannel towels. He should receive at least three quarts of liquids each twenty-four hours."

There was silence. Stem Foster spoke. "Doctor Homans, meet Doctor Davis who is a voluntary assistant with Doctor Cushing. He's had three years of general surgical training under Doctor Allen Kanavel in Chicago."

"What? What's that you say?" Homans reached out and shook my hand. "My God, why didn't you say so? Almost made a damned fool of myself, didn't I?" He grinned at Foster. "You'd enjoy that, too, wouldn't you, you old dog?"

163

Homans turned to the group of students. "Allen Kanavel knows more about the hand than anybody in this country, or in the world for that matter. A fine gentleman, too. Just shows, if you have the right kind of an inquisitive mind, some imagination, and a hell of a lot of determination to work, you can solve a lot of surgical problems that are kicking around under your hands and feet every day. Glad you're here. Now, for heaven's sake, Foster, get our friend here to help you run this treatment. I'll be following him, too, don't forget that, and I'll be reading Kanavel's book tonight. You'd all better do the same."

The story was told by Foster with glee in the dining room and embroidered as usual so that I began to doubt just what I had said and done, but it did establish me. When I think now of the handicaps that existed in the treatment of infections at that time, I shudder when I recall the deaths that today are prevented by the antibiotics. Laudable pus from a staphylococcic infection was a good prognostic sign; the thin serum that exuded from a streptococcal infection was a dangerous omen. We had to depend upon the natural resistance of the body aided by hot packs.

Dr. Cushing continued to ignore me, and I continued to examine patients and attend his operations, carrying my pack of Tareytons all the while. I stayed on the periphery of the circle when we gathered in the surgical laboratory on the ground floor at brain-cutting sessions. The chief made this a ceremony, too, and it was a delight to see the dignity with which the study was carried out. The brain, properly fixed in Formalin and suspended to prevent any asymmetry, was taken from its jar. As he stood and stared at it, turning it from side to side, clasping his gloved hands before his face, with his cigarette hanging loosely from his lips, the history and physical findings, the operative note, postoperative notations, and the laboratory findings from beginning to end were read aloud.

Then, without a word, he would make coronal slices through the brain, examining each one carefully and muttering unintelligibly. I had to guess from the expression on his face and the tonal pitch of the mutter whether he was annoyed or pleased with what he saw. There was no explanation or lecture; one could consider it a privilege and a rare treat to be allowed to be present during the ceremony and try to learn, or regard it simply as required attendance at a boring display of egotism.

It was a new experience for me, and I saw how some of the gliomas spread across the bridge of association fibers to the opposite side of the brain; how the ventricle on the side of the tumor was compressed to a mere slit and the displacement of structures that produced symptoms when their functions were impaired. Again, there was a method, a technique, an intense concentration to be evaluated and either adopted wholly, or the best features taken and molded into my own way of doing things. These sessions were examples of continuing education; self-education by Harvey Cushing.

I examined patients on Ward A where the hospital's beds for the attending staff's private patients were located. I had experience in dealing with private patients, and even though they would pay Dr. Cushing a fee for his attention, I had freely interpreted his advice to make myself at home. I had some qualms at first, but my examinations were of some help to Putnam, who had slyly indicated that they could reduce the amount of time required for him to get his findings on the record. I was careful to introduce myself and make the patient comfortable and aware of my interest in his illness. Often, the patient asked my opinion and advice, but I rigorously held to my teaching and answered that it would be far better for him to get Dr. Cushing's opinion only; that I would certainly tell Dr. Cushing what questions he wished answered. I obtained the history, recorded my findings, and signed my written opinion as to the diagnosis.

As I walked leisurely to Ward C, Miss Tilton came to meet me. She seemed disturbed, which was unusual.

"Where in the world have you been, Doctor Davis?"

"Why? What's the matter? I was down in the laboratory watching Miss Thing cut and stain tissues."

"Your bell has been ringing for over an hour. Why haven't you answered it?"

"My bell? I haven't any call rings."

"Certainly, you have. Hasn't anyone told you?"

"No one has told me."

"Oh, that man. How does he think he can run a service if he doesn't get everyone's co-operation." I didn't inquire about the object of her disgust, but I had watched Putnam treat the nurses on the floors and in the operating room with a supercilious superiority which resembled the arts and wiles of feminine competition.

"Well, you have. Now, listen for two long and three shorts. The chief's secretary has been telephoning all over the hospital trying to find you. He wants you in his office, and you'd better get down there pronto."

I went into the outer office, and Madeline Stanton looked up quickly. Her desk was covered with loose, typed pages, and by her typewriter was a handwritten manuscript of long yellow paper covered with the minute handwriting of Dr. Cushing which, it was said, she alone could decipher.

"Go right in. The chief has been trying to reach you for almost an hour." Miss Stanton's reproof carried a warning. There was no door on Dr. Cushing's private office, and the entrance to it was not visible from the reception room. I walked in and straight up to his desk.

Cushing was hunched over a book which was lying open on his desk. He had a pencil in his hand poised over a pad of his favorite yellow paper. I stood silently and watched him turn the pages and make occasional notes of single words or phrases. I resolved not to be the one to break the silence; nor would I shift my weight, or in any way call attention again to my presence. I glanced down at my wrist watch. Five minutes had passed. I could not make out what it was that Dr. Cushing was reading. The book appeared to be a bound volume of a medical journal, and it was printed in French. Finally, I could make out the running title on the top of a page; I saw the words "multiple sclerosis."

Another five minutes passed, and I suddenly felt a sense of shock as I realized that the situation was comical and I wanted to laugh. Cushing was trying to make me speak or do something to distract his attention from his reading so he could scold me. Or he was demonstrating that he could concentrate completely when he was deeply interested in what he was reading. He carefully placed pieces of paper between several pages, closed the book, and looked up.

"Bring a chair here by my side." He reached into his right-hand pocket confidently. His hand remained there as if he were searching for something. Then he reached into his left-hand pocket more abruptly. His hand came out empty. He leaned forward and pulled open the center drawer of his desk and peered into it. Then rapidly he went into each drawer on the right and left sides of his desk. He was becoming more and more irritated. Suddenly, it dawned on me that this was the moment I had been waiting for and for which I had been prepared during the weeks I had been at the hospital.

I pulled a fresh, unopened package of Herbert Tareyton cigarettes from my pocket and offered it to him. He took it without a word or look, ran his fingernail down the tax stamp, opened the foil, and tapped the end of the package so that the tip of a cigarette protruded. He lifted the package to his mouth and put the end of the cigarette between his lips. Then he put the package into his right-hand coat pocket. He took an old-fashioned wooden kitchen match from his vest pocket, flicked his thumbnail across the tip, and lighted the cigarette. The long, drawn-in breath seemed to burn the cigarette completely.

"You have been examining my private patients on Ward A. Who gave you that privilege?"

"You told me to make myself at home, Doctor Cushing. I have been attempting to learn by examining patients and recording my findings. I have had experience in meeting and taking care of private patients; I have not offended anyone to my knowledge. Nor have I discussed their condition with any private or ward patient." I was surprised how much more effective it sounded to speak quietly and firmly.

Cushing made a noise between a snort, a grunt, and a short dry cough. Slowly, he took out another cigarette, lighted it from the first, and then meticulously ground the butt into the tray with unusual vigor. He pulled the book closer to him and put his finger between the pages of the first paper bookmark.

"In that record of Mrs. Morgan, you made a diagnosis of multiple sclerosis. Completely wrong. She has a tumor in the high cervical spinal cord." There was a pause. "At least, you write your examination findings down interestingly, instead of using alphabetical short

167

cuts and drawings of pipe cleaners to represent the human body. Bad judgment in diagnosis."

I wondered what the other men who had examined the patient had written down as their diagnosis. Perhaps there was more to this than my difference of opinion, or could I have been the only one who had diagnosed multiple sclerosis?

Dr. Cushing opened the book and read a paragraph about the recrudescences and remissions of the symptoms of multiple sclerosis. He turned to one paragraph after another in which all of the manifold and shifting manifestations of the disease were described. He would intersperse the reading with his own comments which were based on his experiences with patients. He told the story of a tumor arising from the covering of the spinal cord and pressing upon it which would produce all of the symptoms Mrs. Morgan presented. It made no difference, he said, that the cerebrospinal fluid findings were not characteristic of a tumor; the tumor could be there just the same. Besides, the fluid findings didn't support the diagnosis of multiple sclerosis. The monologue went on for more than an hour. I was spellbound by the dramatic emphasis that he put upon his diagnosis as passionately as a lawyer defending his client. He closed the book slowly and almost reverently.

"Now, you see you are wrong. I'm going to operate upon that woman tomorrow and remove her spinal cord tumor. You wouldn't have given her a chance to get well. Your diagnosis doomed her to endure a disease which will progress until it is fatal. Do you realize your diagnosis was wrong?"

I was confused by the intensity of his reaction to this particular patient in comparison to his attitude when he made rounds, and by the effort and time he had spent in teaching me about multiple sclerosis, which was noted for the multiplicity and bizarre nature of its symptoms. It had been the most stimulating and profitable hour I had spent since I had been there. I had made my own diagnosis based upon my own examination, observations, and the knowledge I had acquired; I had thought I had come to a logical conclusion. It was a fact that I could be wrong.

"I appreciate the time you've spent teaching me about multiple sclerosis and the differential diagnosis between it and a spinal cord tumor. I've learned far more than I could have by reading. I can't change my diagnosis, though, until you remove the spinal cord tumor and prove the diagnosis of multiple sclerosis wrong."

Cushing turned toward me abruptly, and for a moment I thought he was going to get out of his chair and stand over me. His hands gripped the arms of his chair for a moment; he settled back and fished into his pocket for a cigarette. "Do you mean to say that I've wasted all this time on you?"

"No, sir, I'm deeply appreciative. I hope you are right about Mrs. Morgan and that you will take out her tumor and make her well. But until I see the tumor, I can't reverse my diagnosis so easily. I recognize your greater experience." There was a moment of painful silence. The subject was changed abruptly.

"Why haven't you been operating with me?"

"I have been taught to wait for the direction or invitation, if you wish, before entering an operation. It seems I've taken your statement to make myself at home a bit liberally as it is. I have had a considerable amount of work with Doctor Kanavel at the operating table, and I wanted to learn more about patients with neurosurgical diseases and your techniques of operation. I've learned a great deal."

"Starting tomorrow, you will act as second assistant at every operation on patients from Ward C's second floor. Tell Putnam I said so. We'll see how you perform at the table. That's all." He turned away and busied himself at his desk. I wanted to say more, to tell him what great respect and admiration I had for him, but I had been dismissed.

I worried about how well I could perform as one of Dr. Cushing's assistants at an operation. He was exacting and meticulous. The drapes and entire operative field were neatly arranged. He said that an operation shouldn't go wrong because of the failure to control simple, mechanical details. He didn't allow anyone to put down an instrument; it must be handed back to the surgical nurse for her table. Bloody sponges didn't clutter up the field, and the nurse didn't have to dodge a sponge tossed toward her sterile instrument table.

I arrived at the hospital early the next morning and saw the patient who was scheduled to have a suboccipital craniotomy for a cerebellar tumor. My notes were in good order, and I knew all the details of the patient's history. I sat down, closed my eyes, and imagined I was performing the operation, as I had watched Dr. Cushing do it, step by step. I would be given a cerebellar retractor to hold. I would not change its position, I would not move my feet, I would not look up from the surgical field, and I wouldn't answer any questions he might ask me. I hoped the tumor would be cystic in the right cerebellar hemisphere as I had predicted in my notes.

Dr. Cushing didn't speak to me as we were scrubbing our hands and forearms, standing at the scrub sinks side by side. I was careful not to shorten the prescribed scrub time by a second; in fact, I stayed longer. I saw him glance sideways and knew he was watching my scrubbing technique. I was careful to have all the soap off my forearms and elbows when I stepped away to enter the operation room.

"Keep your fingers in the right place and don't let this incision bleed. Don't change them once you are in position." The command was sharp and challenging.

There were large groups of hemostats to hold by tapes put through their handles and retractors to hold. Finally, after three hours, the dura mater was opened and the cerebellum exposed. Cushing carefully placed a retractor in the deep neck muscles and gave it to me to hold so that the surgical field would be easily visible. I knew that the retractor was placed in a crucial position. For two hours I held the retractor without changing its position and without tiring my forearm and hand muscles so they would go into fatigue contractions. Once, he stopped and looked at the retractor critically but did not change its position; he only grunted unintelligibly. I felt him searching, I thought, with his feet to see if he could bring down his heel onto my foot and indicate his displeasure. He would have to take a deliberate step to the side to reach my feet; I had thought of that contingency.

Cushing introduced a needle into the cerebellar hemisphere, emptied the cyst, and then methodically and artistically dissected the mural nodule of tumor and the velvety-lined cavity away from the normal cerebellar tissue. Patient observation of minute bleeding points controlled by stamps of muscle followed until I wondered why he persisted in watching for fresh bleeding. The field looked dry to me. He closed the wound step by step and put on the head dressing, shaping it carefully to the patient's head. At the same time he checked the record of the patient's blood pressure, pulse, and respirations as she recovered from the effects of the anesthetic. He helped Putnam and me take the patient from the table and put her on the cart. He stood and looked at her reflectively and quietly. He squeezed her hand and indicated to Adolph that he should take her back to her room by a nod of his head. Then he turned and put his hand on my shoulder; his mask and surgical cap dangled from his other hand; it was almost as if he were physically exhausted and was leaning on me.

"At least, Allen Kanavel has taught you how to hold a retractor." He turned and walked away.

I watched the operating schedule daily for the appearance of Mrs. Morgan's name. I decided I wouldn't discuss her symptoms with anyone; I'd wait and see what happened. I had gathered from scraps of conversation that Dr. Cushing had called Edward Taylor, a neurologist in Boston, into consultation about Mrs. Morgan. It was gossiped that he had shown his disgust and contempt for Taylor's opinion unmistakably, grumbling, after Taylor left his note on the chart, that medical neurologists were becoming a thing of the past. They couldn't cure any of the diseases that they thought they could diagnose, they were theorists only, they thought they should be in the operating room directing the surgeon where to make the incision and what to do.

After two weeks, Miss Tilton casually remarked she had been told by the supervisor on Ward A that Mrs. Morgan had left the hospital. I felt sure Dr. Cushing had not changed his mind about the diagnosis, and I felt a sense of embarrassment that everyone knew that Taylor had agreed that she had multiple sclerosis. It wasn't exactly embarrassment but perhaps sympathy for the chief, because there seemed to be a thinly hidden touch of satisfaction among all the staff that the great man had been proved to be wrong. If he had discussed the pros and cons of the diagnosis in a meeting before everyone, it would have been far better than to have intimated that he was correct, everyone else was wrong, and if Mrs. Morgan and her family wouldn't agree to an operation, he couldn't force them into it. Maybe Mrs. Morgan's symptoms would improve, but that was what happened in the course of multiple sclerosis; they would recur, and this would be repeated until the disease progressed to a fatality. What advice had he given Mrs. Morgan? I wished I knew.

I continued to assist in operations upon patients from Ward C. I had been tried once again with a retractor, which I held immobile, never shifting my feet or my weight and never looking up from the field of operation. Then came the day when Cushing firmly grasped the handle of the retractor I was holding just for a moment. I relaxed my fingers but did not move my hand and then resumed my grip, whereupon he took his hand away. I was pleased that I had met one of the chief's technical requirements, but my elation didn't last long. Suddenly, as the closure of the scalp of the craniotomy incision neared the end, he stepped away from the operating table.

"Give the sutures to Doctor Davis. Let's see if he can close the wound."

I looked up in amazement and caught the eye of Putnam, who I knew would like nothing better than to see me make a fool of myself. I realized that Dr. Cushing was going to stand there and watch. He'd be breathing right down my neck; I put out my right hand, palm upward, and felt the needle holder slap into it. I put the needle through the galea on both sides of the incision and placed the suture ends between Putnam's thumb and forefinger. I introduced six sutures and then removed the hemostats and began to tie the fine silk. There wasn't tension on the edges of the wound, but suddenly I realized I had never tied silk before. The first suture broke as I tried to hold the ends taut and complete the square knot. Successively, I broke each of the six sutures. There was complete silence in the room; even Adolph had stopped moving around. I held out my hand for the needle holder and another suture. This time the surgical nurse slapped it into my palm hard, and I looked up. She was smiling behind her mask, and her eyes gave me encouragement.

"When Doctor Davis finishes closing the wound, give him a spool of silk to take home with him. Maybe he can learn how to tie silk sutures and not break them." Dr. Cushing gave his characteristic mixture of a grunt and throat clearing and left the room. Not a word was said as I went on to tie sutures and close the wound without breaking another one. I'd show him I could put on a head dressing, too. Carefully, I supported the head with one hand and held the rolled six-yard gauze bandage in the other. It was six inches wide and not easy to handle. The surgical nurse put her fingers beneath the patient's chin, as she always did for Dr. Cushing, and with her other hand removed instruments from the table. She had safety pins ready just at the right time, and the points had been Vaselined so they would slip through the gauze easily. Carefully, I fitted the bandage and introduced the pins to make it snug. I finished and was admiring my handiwork when Dr. Cushing came back into the operating room and inspected the dressing silently. He patted it here and there, felt the edges where it might loosen. Finally, he held out his forefinger and thumb without looking up, and the nurse put a safety pin between them so accurately he didn't have to change its position to introduce it into the gauze. Quickly, he reversed its direction and locked it. He left the room without a word.

The contradictions in Dr. Cushing's personality disturbed me because I constantly compared them with Dr. Kanavel's predictable reactions to similar situations and problems. Rather abruptly one afternoon when we had gathered in the laboratory to examine and study the brain of a patient who had died with a tumor, he sat on the edge of a table with one leg swinging and with his hands clasped in front of him, a cigarette in his mouth. He appeared to be enjoying a joke privately; a smile on his lips and his head cocked, his prominent nose dominated his profile. He turned to the group who were standing quietly waiting for him to speak; all of us alert and attentive.

"You all know Gus, my chauffeur. I came out of the house this morning to find the lawn strewn with leaves, the front porch filthy dirty, the car needed washing, and Gus was standing there holding the door of the automobile open, trying his best to appear like a footman. The whole scene irritated me. I told him he should be ashamed of the way he had neglected to keep the place and the car clean and orderly." He paused and grinned broadly. "Gus listened with a patient look on his face. As he closed the door, he peered in at me and said, 'You forgot to wipe the egg off your chin, Doctor Cushing.'"

Momentarily there was silence and then a snicker, which grew into full-bellied laughter. The chief sat and chuckled, his eyes twinkling as he glanced at our faces.

As he picked up the brain knife, we gathered about the table, and

173

the moment of relaxation was gone. Again, meticulously, he dissected and described the relation of the infiltrating tumor to the white and gray matter of the brain. Miss Stanton sat at the side and recorded his dictation which was accurate anatomically but was spiced with comments of explanation or suggestions as to how the clinical symptoms developed as a result of the location of the tumor. Cushing held the last coronal section of the brain in his hand, peering at it intently; then looked far away out the window.

"You men must keep trying to find better ways of operating upon brain tumors. Undoubtedly, there will be new developments in physics and electricity which can be applied to the human being. These are not quite like other tumors in the body which are cancerous. They don't metastasize for one thing; they are massive, lawless reproductions of the embryonic or adult cells of the nervous system. Our present methods are crude; they are the best we have, but I've just learned about a high-frequency-current knife which will coagulate and cut." He gestured with the section of brain in his hand. "If you're easily discouraged, find something else of interest to you in surgery." He put down the brain section, turned quickly, and left the laboratory.

The fall weather had turned the leaves along the Fenway, mornings were crisp, and frequently my walk to the hospital was through a cold rain. The annual football game between Yale and Harvard stimulated the conversation in the dining room. It was the liberal arts college that we had attended before entering medical school that commanded the loyalty of each of us in sports and alumni gatherings. In medical school there had been day after day of work and concentration upon preparation for our professional lives; there were only sentimental attachments to individual teachers who had outstanding personalities and who had dramatically presented their subjects.

As I walked to the hospital that Saturday morning in November 1923, it was raining steadily. The Yale captain, Ducky Pond, certainly had an appropriate nickname for the day. I was scheduled to assist Dr. Cushing in an operation upon a man from Ward C, and Saturdays were not a bit different from any other day as far as the operating room schedule was concerned.

I was at the scrub sink just before eleven o'clock when Dr. Cushing came in and exchanged nods with me. I concentrated on a review of the patient's story and symptoms.

"Are you going to the Yale-Harvard game today?"

I couldn't believe what I heard. Momentarily, I was angered; even the chief was joking about my desire to see the game that had been glamourized in my mind. Here I was scrubbing in preparation for an operation; it was eleven o'clock, and he wanted to know if I was going to the game.

"No, sir. I don't rate the Yale-Harvard game; I'm from the Midwest."

"Who says so? I'm from Cleveland. What's the matter with the Midwest?"

"The boys say there are no tickets for anyone but Yale and Harvard graduates. Apparently, close check is kept on those who use the tickets the alumni buy."

"Go down and tell Miss Stanton to give you one of my tickets."

I stopped the scrub brush in mid-air. I blurted, "But I'm scheduled to assist at the operation this morning, Doctor Cushing."

"I've operated before without you. We'll manage to get along. You haven't much time to get lunch and get there for the game."

I dropped the brush and hurried to the door. Cushing's voice stopped me. "Have you got a raincoat to wear?"

"No, sir, I haven't."

"How in the world do you expect to sit through a football game on a day like this without a raincoat?" His voice was full of disgust for such an apparent lack of planning. I could find no response.

"Tell Miss Stanton to give you mine."

Again, I started through the swinging doors. "Davis, have you got rubbers?"

I turned again and with some annoyance, which I hoped didn't show on my face, remained silent.

"Perfectly ridiculous. The stadium grounds will be a sea of mud. Tell her to give you my rubbers."

I told Miss Stanton that the chief had sent me to get one of his football tickets, his raincoat, and his rubbers to use at the game. She looked at me in amazement and shook her head in disbelief. She reminded me that I would be surrounded by members of Dr. Cushing's class at Yale.

I followed the crowd after I left the subway in Cambridge. Bad weather or no, there would be a capacity crowd, all of them prepared to sit through the rain. Miss Stanton was correct; I was surrounded by men of Dr. Cushing's age, their wives and children. They glanced at me and evidently expected me to introduce myself and satisfy their curiosity as to how I came to be sitting among them. I became embarrassed and devoted my attention to the program; maybe as the game progressed, there'd be enough excitement to make it easier to get acquainted, and then I could break the ice.

I was not disappointed in the thrill of seeing the teams line up for the kickoff. The field was wet, and the rain was a constant drizzle which wasn't going to stop. The ball would be slippery, the footing bad, and Yale's Ducky Pond, their fleet halfback, would be handicapped. It looked like the slow-footed, heavier Harvard team might bull their way to win. The first half was a thriller, and just as it neared its end, Ducky got away on an end run, was tackled, and slid with his tackler hanging on, across the goal line for a touchdown. I was on my feet yelling and was being pounded on the back by a gray-haired gentleman who was old enough to be my father.

As the excitement subsided, so did the spirit of camaraderie. I was ignored as my neighbors replayed the slide through the mud. I saw men passing down the aisles collecting objects. I had thought the boys had been joking, but this was the collection of the ticket stubs. An impatient voice shouted in my ear, "Come on, sign your ticket stub and pass it along." Everybody about me was writing his name on the stubs. I fumbled inside my coat for my fountain pen. Should I sign my own name, or should I sign Dr. Cushing's? I would be a forger if I did the latter, but if I signed my own, perhaps they did check the seat numbers against lists and then Dr. Cushing would have to write and explain how I got one of his tickets. This was what the boys had meant when they talked about how carefully records were kept to prevent ticket scalping and to keep this game purely a student and alumni spectator event.

"Come on, hurry up." The man was waiting for me. I tried to visualize Dr. Cushing's signature; his writing was small, but the capital letters of his name were large. Painfully and laboriously, I signed "Harvey Cushing," joining the upstroke of the *y* with the *C*. Reluctantly, I gave up the stub. I had committed forgery, and it would have been better to let Dr. Cushing write letters of explanation. Perhaps they would refuse the professor seats in the future because he had given one away. They might accuse him of selling the ticket.

The second half of the game began, but I couldn't keep my attention on the field. It was raining harder, and the chance for any other score became slimmer. I wanted to get up and leave and get home where I could think about what Cushing's reaction might be. I'd have to tell him, but was it a stupid thing I had done? If I got up to leave, when everyone else was staying to the bitter end, I'd be conspicuous. I sat vaguely aware of mud-covered figures whose uniforms were indistinguishable. The rain made me miserable, but I had been barely aware of it during the first half. Finally, I heard a cheer from each team on the field as they huddled together; it was for their opponents. Yale had justified all the Frank Merriwell stories I had ever read, with a victory. On the subway home, I thought of returning to the hospital and telling Cushing about the ticket stub. It would be too late to find him there. I'd have to return the rubbers and raincoat; I'd better not keep them over the weekend. The outer room of his office was empty. Miss Stanton had left, and there was no light in the inner office. I cleaned off the rubbers with a piece of paper I found in the wastebasket. I hung the wet raincoat on the coat rack. I'd rehearse a speech that I'd give the first thing Monday morning to Cushing. Why should I be worrying anyway about what Cushing would think about the ticket stub? I had used my best judgment, and I had saved him from bothersome correspondence. But I had forged his name. I certainly had not enjoyed the last half of the football game.

I decided on the way to the hospital Monday to wait and time my approach just as the chief left his office for the operating room. I wasn't scheduled to assist. I'd have to make it appear casual and not a deliberately planned encounter. I'd have to start talking immediately because Cushing would rush by; I'd have to take the chance of irritating him by initiating a discussion. I met him just as he came into his outer office.

"Good morning, Doctor Cushing. Thank you for giving me the chance to go to the football game. I enjoyed watching Yale win." He kept on walking, and I stayed by his side. "I'm afraid I did something which you may not approve." He stopped short and waited. "I signed your name on the back of the ticket stub which the usher collected between halves."

"What did you do that for?"

"To keep you from having to write letters explaining why I had the ticket, if I had signed my name. There are strict rules about allowing the tickets to get out of the possession of the alumnus who requests them."

"That's all poppycock. Now you've spoiled the fun I was going to have answering their letters. Don't think too much, Davis; just do what comes naturally once in a while." He put his hand on my shoulder. "We won, didn't we?"

The days passed rapidly, and again I was learning surgery by being taught at the operating table. As Dr. Kanavel had taught me, I soon learned how to work right along with Dr. Cushing. I was amazed how he could tell by the color, size, and flattening of the convolutions of the brain that a tumor lay beneath the cortex. I would think where I would make the incision in the cortex and how I would protect the surrounding brain. It became a silent game with the more experienced surgeon winning the close decisions. I had to learn to see what he saw. The careful attention to every detail was repeated in the preparation of each patient for operation and during the long, unhurried procedure. In the days following operation, Cushing fussed over disarrangements of the head dressing, bed linens, and bedside tables.

The chief had assigned me the task of reviewing the records of all the patients who had been found to have a tumor of the cauliflowerlike, delicate structure in the ventricles of the brain that manufactured the cerebrospinal fluid. They were benign tumors of the choroid plexus which often grew to large size. The filing system that he had instituted when he began to practice surgery made it easy to pick out the patients' records and follow their progress. I spent time at the hospital and at the medical school library nearby, and at the

Boston Medical Society library, reading all of the books and articles I could find on the subject. There were single patient reports but no definite descriptions of the tumor. I carefully wrote the manuscript describing the clinical course of the patients and the gross and microscopic appearance of the tumor after I had made fresh stains · f the tumor tissue. I was certain I had avoided split infinitives, but I was not sure that I had written an interesting paper. Once again, my high school typewriting classes stood me in good stead; Miss Stanton complimented me on the neatness of the typing and thanked me for saving her time and work.

A week later Miss Stanton gave me my beautifully typed manuscript covered with red pencil notes in the margins and red gashes through words and phrases. "Loosen this sentence," "There's a better word to use, find it," "Rearrange these paragraphs so they follow logically, you made the transition but the reader can't," Cushing had written. Miss Stanton recognized the look of dismay when I had hurriedly flipped the pages.

"Everyone has found it good practice, Doctor Davis. I'm sure you'll be no exception. Above all, don't become discouraged."

I remembered Miss Stanton's advice when the fifth rewrite came back. I compared it with the first and exulted because there were comparatively few red gouges. "Consult a thesaurus and learn word values," "Your vocabulary needs to be increased," "Stop using unnecessary words," and a final "More power to your elbow" was like receiving a decoration. I knew that the sixth draft was acceptable when she showed me the title page with my name as the first of an author partnership with Dr. Cushing.

I busied myself with a project of my own when I discovered a child with a brain tumor in a location that had produced the physical signs of decerebration. I had found in a human being the counterpart of the animals I had operated on and studied with Pollock. The child was blind and severely emaciated when he was brought to Dr. Cushing for attention. I had never been so engrossed in a patient before and enthusiastically talked about how the reflexes of an experimental decerebrate animal could be elicited in the patient. I demonstrated the signs of decerebration to the students and house officers. After persisting day after day, I finally got Miss Thing to consent to photograph the patient so I could record the reflex changes that followed movements of the head.

Miss Alice Thing was a quiet, tall woman of indeterminate age who stained sections of tumors for microscopic study, took photographs of patients, brain sections, and tumor specimens. She added them to the patients' records. Miss Thing couldn't understand why I would have to bring the patient to her room in the laboratory, put him on a comfortable mattress on the floor so he could be photographed directly from above. I drew her diagrams, took her to the ward to see the patient and how I brought out the reflexes. I saw the first sign that her resistance was breaking down when I told her that such a patient had never been described before in the way I proposed. I assured her that photographing the child would not be harmful; that there was nothing Dr. Cushing nor anyone else could do to cure the child; that I had permission from the parents to record the reflexes. No, I hadn't asked Dr. Cushing because he had been out of town, but the child was to be released from the hospital at the parents' request and there was no time to waste. She knew very well, I told her, from her long experience working for Dr. Cushing, how interested he was in getting every kind of a record on every patient. If it was a question of using Dr. Cushing's supplies, I would buy film for the camera. I wooed Miss Thing.

I borrowed a clean, unsterile, drape sheet to cover the mattress so there would be a good background; I carefully fastened a breech cloth about the child and tried my best to hurry Miss Thing's movements as she placed her tripod and camera above the child and mounted a stool to focus upon the full length of the child's body. I restrained my impatience; I knew that one exposure for each position was all that Miss Thing had agreed to take. I couldn't afford to have her make a mistake, so I must be patient. I knelt at the head of the child and, as I had done before, slowly turned the child's head in one direction and then the other. When Miss Thing finally got organized, she was efficient. I rose from my sore and aching knees and extended my hand to help Miss Thing from her high perch.

"Demonstrate those reflexes for me, Davis. Don't you think I'd be interested, too?" Miss Thing's face became crimson, and hurriedly she gathered her tripod and camera, knocking over the stool in her haste. Dr. Cushing looked at her disdainfully.

"Relax, Miss Thing. I doubted that Davis could persuade you to do something out of the ordinary and, particularly, without a written order. I congratulate both of you; now, show me."

Each reflex appeared promptly and better than I had ever elicited them. Without thinking I began to describe the physiological and anatomical reasons for their presence. Dr. Cushing asked questions and, finally, was on the floor on his knees clucking and grunting as he repeated what he had watched me do. He got to his feet. "Alice, develop these films right away. Keep the patient here until Miss Thing is satisfied she doesn't want to repeat an exposure. See to it that you write this up for a paper. Maybe you can write it better than the one you just finished. Perfectly horrible. No style at all." He turned on his heels, reaching in his pocket for a cigarette, and left the room.

Dr. Cushing was sitting at the adjoining table in the dining room the next day with the professor of physiology from the medical school and the professor of medicine. I overheard him say, "We have an interesting patient on the ward, Henry. A decerebrate lad with all of the reflexes of Magnus-deKleijn. Has a craniopharyngioma. He's cut off in the midbrain, just below the seventh cranial nerve nucleus. He has corneal reflexes. It'd be worth your while to see him; you, too, Walter. Tell the nurse to get a young fellow by the name of Davis to demonstrate the signs for you. Better not put it off or the patient won't be here. We can't fail to verify that lesion by a post-mortem."

I was impressed by Dr. Cushing's intent to obtain an autopsy upon every patient who died on his service. He made the request personally if the house staff or Gil Horrax failed. I had heard the story of how he had tried to persuade a father and mother to permit a post-mortem examination upon their fourteen-year-old daughter who had been brought to the hospital blind and in coma due to a brain tumor. Cushing had no opportunity to operate upon the child because she had died so quickly after her admission. He explained, argued, cajoled; pointing out the contribution their child could make to other children who might suffer from the same condition; that

181

they should know what had caused their child's death so they, too, could help other parents. The parents had sat stubbornly and unresponsively to his arguments, saying that they didn't want Lois "cut up." Silently, Cushing took his checkbook from the drawer of his desk and wrote a check for fifty dollars. He pushed it across the desk for them to see and with it a permit to be signed for the autopsy. The mother took the check, and the father signed the permission.

Dr. Cushing was more vocal on the subject of verifying brain tumors by careful description of the gross lesion and by accurate studies of many stains of the microscopic sections than on any other subject. He was able, he emphasized, to correlate preoperative symptoms and the findings at operation, as well as the postoperative course of the patient with the kind of brain tumor that he encountered at operation. Thus, progress could be made in studying new ways of treating brain tumors, using all of the newer methods that would be developed. He said in disgust that surgeons who called themselves neurological surgeons and who didn't or wouldn't consider brain tumors their primary concern did not deserve the name.

The entire staff was anticipating with interest how the chief would obtain an autopsy permit on the small, old, misshapen woman on Ward D. He had given strict instructions that she was not to be discharged for any reason and was to be considered as a special exception to the efforts of the hospital administration to shorten the stay of patients and keep the beds active, particularly the free beds. He visited her each time he made rounds. Her entire bony skeleton had become deformed by Paget's disease. She had come to consult him because of a tumor mass which had grown from the skull through the scalp and presented as a fungating, bleeding mass because a surgeon elsewhere thought he could remove it and had encountered almost fatal bleeding. Cushing had lectured the staff repeatedly about Paget's disease and the error of considering a presenting lesion on any patient lightly.

The house staff had speculated as to how much of an autopsy examination the chief proposed to make. That he had the permit there was no doubt; in fact, it was understood that he had agreed with the spinster's brothers and sisters that he would bear all of the burial expenses, including her last trip back to the small town in New Hampshire from which she came. There would be no hospital bill or doctors' bills. In return, Cushing had insisted there would be no restrictions upon the thoroughness of the post-mortem examination.

When I first heard the story, I wondered if the patient had been consulted, or were her relatives and Cushing hovering around her bed like vultures? However, there was no question that she had been a principal negotiator. She was a burden at home to her sisters and brothers, all of whom were married and had their own families to support. She had a private room which she had been encouraged to decorate as she chose. She was a special guest of the hospital and received special consideration. She knew that she could not recover from her widespread disease.

I heard the news as soon as I came to the hospital the morning she was found dead in bed. I was not prepared for a summons to Dr. Cushing's office where I found the chief pathologist and his staff, with the neurosurgical house staff. It was soon clear that Cushing had relegated the pathology department to a subordinate role in carrying out the autopsy, after they had washed out all the blood in her vessels and had injected Formalin solution. Duties were being delegated in detail, and I looked from face to face to be sure I was coming to the correct conclusion. The entire skeleton was to be removed for preservation, as well as carrying out a thorough gross and microscopic study of every tissue of her body. It was difficult to understand just how this could be done and still provide an object to bury. Suddenly, I heard Dr. Cushing's voice addressing me. "Davis, you will be responsible for making a plaster cast of the face, so that it can be inserted beneath the soft tissues of the face and head and fit perfectly. I understand you have had experiences making molds and casts of the face for Kanavel."

I nodded my head in agreement and muttered, "Yes, sir."

"It's essential that the head and face be firm, and a plaster cast of the face and back of the skull will do. The skin of the extremities, fingers, and toes can be stuffed firmly with cotton waste. I want this job done without interruption and waste of time. All of the incisions have been planned accurately, and with drawings to follow, you will have no difficulty. Every incision is to be closed neatly and with the finest dermal sutures. There is to be no levity of any kind and no smoking." In a respectful voice he added, "She was set against the use of tobacco."

I carefully put a thin layer of Vaseline on the face and back of the head. Then I made a plaster mold which was removed easily so that the dissection could proceed and her entire skull could be removed. The casts fitted well, and I helped introduce a running subcuticular suture in the hairline which couldn't be seen. At seven o'clock that evening the shell of the patient was ready for transport. Dr. Cushing made a minute examination of every suture line and felt every extremity, finger and toe. The thorax and abdomen had been packed tightly with cotton waste, and he muttered and grumbled over the asymmetry due to the absence of the bony chest wall. He stepped back.

"An excellent job, gentlemen. I congratulate you, and I want you to stand at attention for a moment in a silent salute to a patient who has made a contribution to medical science which no one in this room will ever match. We will be the agents who try to make the hidden secrets of her terrible disease known so all men may benefit."

It was a solemn, dignified moment which no one present would experience again; it was a requiem. Without another word Cushing strode, almost with a military carriage, from the room.

Cushing spent hours with his old books and his writing. We could tell just where he was in the writing of the biography of Sir William Osler, the great physician and teacher, because we could hear him holding forth in a monologue in the staff dining room on the occasions when he took lunch there. He practiced getting his thoughts in order by recounting important episodes that he was about to write. Some of his older colleagues maintained that Cushing patterned his life after the subject of his book but lacked the equanimity of that physician. It was agreed he was driven by an inner compulsive force to regard an unemployed moment as a total waste. The boys said that his efforts to be one of the party on the rare occasions when cocktails were served were laughable. He would invariably claim to be "drunk as a fiddler's bitch" after sipping part of his first and only cocktail.

One balmy afternoon in the spring, I was called to the chief's office and found him standing by Miss Stanton's desk dressed in operating room trousers and shirt, in tennis shoes, holding two tennis rackets. "Hurry along and get into an operating suit, put on the tennis shoes you'll find in my locker. Come out to the court. We may need a fourth for doubles."

Miss Stanton shrugged her shoulders after he left. "He isn't sure that Doctor Foster will be there; you're the substitute."

As I changed my clothes, I prayed that Stem Foster would be there. I had been given an old, battered tennis racket by a neighbor when I was in high school and knocked an old tennis ball against the side of the garage until I was able to hit it squarely. In college I played a few games, but poorly. I tried to remember where I should stand when my partner served. I certainly hoped Foster could play.

The game had started with the two chiefs of service playing against their senior residents. Cushing gave orders to Henry Christian on every ball that came to him. Christian appeared not to hear him, or paid no attention to him, methodically and gently hitting the ball back each time to keep it in play.

"My God, Henry, hit it where they can't return it. You put it right at them. Those young fellows will wear us out. Use some strategy, man."

I was the only audience, and I was on the bench in reserve. Cushing finally could not stand the trouncing he and his colleague were getting. He didn't propose that they change partners; he decreed it. He played with his resident, and the medical side played against them. The match was more even, and Cushing grinned and hollered in glee when they would score a point and win a game.

Abruptly, after they had won a set, Cushing said, "That's all for today. We'll have to do it again. Foster, play a set with Davis. He's been here patiently waiting to fill in if necessary. You must be sure to keep in good physical shape, Davis."

Stem Foster came over the sidelines. "What about it? Anyone for tennis?" There was derision in his voice. "Physical condition, my eye. He does this once a year and never sets foot on a court until the next time. He's pretty well co-ordinated, isn't he? This is a kind of act he must go through with once a year to be sure he has im-

185

pressed us with his ideas about keeping in shape if we are to be surgeons. He can't stand losing, so we let him win. What I need is sleep, not exercise. See you later."

Harvey Cushing must have set his course to be recognized by posterity early in his life. He began to keep a diary in which he still religiously wrote day by day. He rigidly disciplined himself and was unsparing in demands upon his energy and talents. It is difficult to find fault with him when he drove his residents and nurses relentlessly, because he asked even more of himself. I agree with the opinion that H.C. couldn't bear to be defeated at anything he undertook. It was said that he didn't speak to a colleague on the medical side who jokingly reminded him that he had tripped over the low board that divided the running track from the baseball diamond at Harvard, had fallen ignominiously, and the fly ball that he missed scored two runs against Yale. He could not help trying to direct the lives of everyone around him, trying to make them discipline themselves so they would be working at their greatest possible efficiency. There had to be a happy medium; I wondered how he could exist alone on the reluctant admission of his contemporaries that he was brilliant and clever, but not have their affectionate friendship.

When Harvey Cushing went to the Johns Hopkins Hospital at the age of twenty-seven, Osler was forty-seven and Halsted forty-five years of age. Both men then in their prime influenced him; the one in scholarly pursuits, with complete acceptance; the other professionally, but with critical reservations.

While Cushing profited from the operating surgeons at Massachusetts General Hospital, who were scornful of the Johns Hopkins surgeons and their inartistic rubber-gloved, slow surgical techniques, his dedicated interest in patients and their surgical care did not come solely from either group. His inheritance from the three generations of physicians in his family who preceded him characterized his operating skill, his surgical teaching, and his research, all directed primarily toward the care of the patient. He valued the contributions of the surgical research laboratory but far more if there appeared to be a direct application to the care of the patient.

In retrospect, one can appreciate the teaching method that he used to test the convictions and knowledge of the young men about him. His philosophy was that those who did not like the work well enough to stay in spite of his treatment were not suitable to stand the rigors of a surgical practice in later years. This was at least an attempt to rationalize a pedagogic method that was often difficult to understand.

Cushing repeatedly emphasized that one should become proficient in general surgery before specializing in neurological surgery. The surgical specialists, he said, should be as much at home in the abdominal cavity as in the field of their particular interest. He admonished his followers not to let neurological surgery get too far away from general surgery; its roots should lie in the fertile soil of general surgery.

His belief that every patient he operated upon deserved his undivided attention from the beginning to the end and his habit of holding the patient's hand as he stood by the bed considering the story of complaints and the presenting symptoms were evidence of an intimate and confidential relation with his patients. His teaching was flexible; it was not formalized; it did not provide patients for neurosurgical residents to operate upon in the hope that they would learn by the mistakes they made, or qualify by sheer numbers. He demanded the same degree of concentration from his assistants as he gave the surgical problem.

Harvey Cushing's dedication to improvement in the care of patients, his ability to stimulate his students to learn at the bedside, his continued interest in experimentation and correlation of the results with the patient, his superb technical skill, his scholarly attainments gained by concentrated effort, and his defense of his surgical beliefs and principles are characteristics that made him a great clinical surgeon.

SEVEN

"WE'RE glad you're back. I'm sure you had a good, profitable year, but if you don't mind my saying so, I think it's just about the right time for you to have left Boston. Just a bit longer and you'd have been spoiled."

I wasn't sure just what Dr. Kanavel referred to, but that it wasn't an idle statement I was positive. Maybe I had shown early symptoms of acquiring some of Cushing's personality traits of which Allen Kanavel didn't approve.

"What immediate plans have you in mind?"

I told him my thoughts about earning money helping teach in the anatomy department at the medical school. I hoped he would support my request to Mr. Gilmore, superintendent of Wesley Hospital, for permission to admit patients. I could help teach the nurses. He said that Gilmore volunteered the information that he liked me and that was rare for that cagey, tight-lipped gentleman. He thought Dr. Ranson had something for me. I could keep busy with his patients, and he'd like my help when he operated upon neurosurgical patients. Allen Kanavel put his arm around my shoulder affectionately. His cigarette bobbed up and down between his lips as he talked, and the smoke curled around his face. "You can teach me all the new techniques you learned from Cushing."

Kanavel left me in his customary, quick manner, and I felt I was back home again as I watched him walk down the corridor with his characteristic rapid gait, swinging his hips from side to side. I had a warm feeling of pride that I was his pupil in surgery, as Dr. Schroeder's comment about Dr. Kanavel's walk flashed through my mind. Schroeder had pulled me around unceremoniously as we were standing waiting for the elevator and said, "Kid, look at Allen Kanavel walking down that hall. If he isn't careful, he's going to saw himself in two one of these days."

I knew that the aggressive, extroverted, blustering, profane William Schroeder was openly critical of Dr. Kanavel's opinion that there was something to be said on both sides of the intramural jealousies and fight that had been going on for several years between the medical school and its faculty and the hospital and its staff, which Schroeder led with bare-knuckled methods. Schroeder had shown an interest in me, and I knew how strong an ally or an enemy he could be in my desire to become a member of the staff of the hospital. By my silence, I couldn't let Schroeder assume that I shared in his criticism of my chief. I knew that sooner or later, Schroeder would test my loyalty with his satirical humor and probably before a group of doctors.

I didn't know whether or not I could hold my temper and respond in kind to Schroeder's vicious, sarcastic tongue. I had been present in the surgeons' dressing room when John Gill had brought his son to meet Schroeder. Gill was a small man with a squeaky voice who wore a Vandyke beard to bolster his stature as a doctor. He came to the hospital on Schroeder's operating days and donned operating room clothes so he could watch operations and hope that he would be invited to scrub and act as an extra assistant. Schroeder made him the butt of a repeated joke about putting him on stilts so he could get up to the level of the operating field. Yet Gill continued to be servile and obsequious, and, as a student, I remembered how he had bragged in the outpatient surgical clinic about how he "worked under Schroeder."

Schroeder was sitting on a chair, bent over his big, protruding abdomen, puffing and tying his shoelaces that day when Gill came into the dressing room with a tall, muscular, fine-looking young man eighteen or nineteen years of age. They stopped in front of Schroeder.

"Doctor Schroeder, I want to introduce my son."

Schroeder never rose from his seat, but raised his eyes and head as he stared at the boy's feet and surveyed him deliberately and carefully to his head. Then he turned his attention to his shoelaces and said, "Don't you believe it, kid."

I had not forgotten the shocked expression on Gill's face and the indecision between expressing deep anger at the insult, or laughingly accepting it as a joke. There was no indecision on the part of his son. He grabbed his father's arm and without a word took him from the room.

Schroeder rose from his chair, chuckled, and with a devilish grin, said, "By God, the kid's got gumption even if his old man hasn't."

Thus far I had been able to meet Schroeder's quips, but I realized they had always been preceded by an indication that he seemed to be interested in me and my career. I remembered that when I had first come to work with Dr. Kanavel, Schroeder had stopped me as I came into the dressing room to change my clothes, had turned me around and said, "Kid, keep on dressing neatly and making yourself look as prosperous as you can no matter how cheap your clothes are; it's important to look like a surgeon." This had been followed repetitiously by the question, whenever we chanced to meet in the mornings in the dressing room, "Are you on your second million yet, kid?" It was hard for me to judge Dr. Schroeder's surgical ability fairly when he exhibited vulgarity, bravado, and meanness. I could understand how he had become the center of the controversy between the medical school faculty and the hospital. He was a formidable opponent and could be a helpful proponent.

It seemed that Dr. Ranson had not moved from behind his desk during my absence. The collar of his white gown was securely fixed high above his shirt collar; his rimless spectacles glistened, and he smiled shyly as he rose, quite formally, to shake my hand.

"Ah, andt, it's nice to see you back, Doctor Davis, andt, ah, did you enjoy the year with Doctor Cushing? I've had an interesting correspondence with him for many years about the pituitary body and the hypothalamus. For a surgeon he exhibits a surprising knowledge about the anatomy of the nervous system."

Ranson grinned more broadly and looked over his glasses. He had not been able to resist a sly poke at the clinician who dared to add to scientific knowledge by employing research methods in observing a patient. Men like Ranson really envy the clinician, but finding that they are unsuited to care for patients, they never miss the opportunity to emphasize the differences between their pure academic approach to the sciences of medical practice and the clinicians' ability to use the facts of the basic sciences in the art of the practice of medicine.

"Andt, now, Davis, you have come back at a time when you can be of considerable assistance to us in the department. We are short-handed at the moment, and I would like to offer you a position of assisting me teach neurological anatomy. I wish you to take charge of the laboratory sections, and I will give the lectures. Occasionally, I must ask you to take over a lecture." He paused and pursed his lips in the familiar grimace that made me think he was tasting something bitter. He continued to look down at his desk. "Ah, andt, I hope the time you will need to spend with the students will not interfere with your practice. Your acceptance will be a great help to us and allow me the opportunity of conducting a thorough search for a young man who wishes to devote himself exclusively to a teaching career in anatomy."

I was touched by Dr. Ranson's attempts to make me feel that I was needed and that it was I who was making the sacrifice to be of help, knowing, as he must, that the money I would receive would be an anchor on which I could build my plans for a practice.

"I hasten to accept, Dr. Ranson. I am sure my teaching duties will not interfere at this time with my practice. I appreciate the opportunity." I wondered if Ranson viewed the practice of neurological surgery with skepticism.

"Ah, andt, it's nothing at all, Davis; quite the contrary, I assure you. Come back and take your old room for your research work. We'll go over the laboratory assignments together." He had become embarrassed and began to shuffle his papers, a sure sign. I thanked him again and walked toward the door. "You haven't asked about your remuneration. Ah, andt, I suppose you thought that such a position doesn't admit of bargaining and you're right. The budget calls for three hundred a month." My face must have reflected the thought that quickly passed through my mind: What would I do for money during the months when the course was not taught? Ranson added, "Ah, andt, that is three hundred a month for twelve months. You can help us in other teaching duties." This was a different experience from what I had had when I worked for Mr. Falk that hot August afternoon knocking bugs off his potato plants.

I had received a letter from my mother in which she wrote that my father had "layed off for a trip or two" because he had a pain in his chest. At first, she thought it was pleurisy, but it didn't hurt when he breathed, and it came suddenly and felt like a vise being tightened around his breast. Unknowingly, my mother had described the pain of spasm of the coronary arteries that feed the heart muscle. The pain, she said, came suddenly and was very bad because "it makes tears come to your father's eyes and then it goes away as fast as it comes." Dad might have an attack while he was on his engine, and anything might happen. I concluded that my father shouldn't continue his work. The pension system on the railroad had just been put into effect; Dad had been an engineer for thirty-five years, and whether or not he was eligible, I didn't know. Would he agree to stop work? Perhaps if I pointed out that it might be endangering other people's lives for him to continue, he would accept retirement. This would be a brutal way to put the proposition, and I hoped it wouldn't be necessary.

Given some time to get started with my practice, I would send some money home each month to supplement whatever pension he would receive. The home was paid for, but the taxes would have to be paid. I'd get my father and mother to come up, at least for the day, and I'd ask my old teacher of medicine, James Carr, to examine him and get an electrocardiogram. More often than not, an electrocardiogram would show no evidence that might be used to support a request to the railroad company to have my father pensioned. I was confident that if I advised retirement, my decision would be accepted without question by my parents. It was this complete faith they had in me that gave me great concern, but for this reason I had to be sure that I had given my best thought to the problem.

I made rounds with Dr. Kanavel to see his neurosurgical patients, examine them, and operated with him just as I had when I was in my residency program. From the beginning I was pleased and a bit embarrassed when he introduced me to patients as "my associate who is a specialist in your trouble." More and more, he asked me to start and finish operations while he devoted his efforts to the body

192

of the operation. I prepared and draped the fields of operation using the newer techniques I had learned in Boston. I noticed the look of amusement on his face the first time he became aware of the changes, but he made no comment until he was leaving the operation when he said, so that everyone in the operating room could hear, that Dr. Davis' advancements in technique certainly made the operation go more smoothly.

Dr. Kanavel set fees on his patients and collected them without offering me any part of the fee or paying me as an assistant. I was only too happy to be working in the operating room putting my new ideas to the test, and it never occurred to me that payment for what I was doing should be considered until Schroeder made it his business. Dr. Kanavel had dressed and left, but Schroeder, other attending men, and several interns crowded the small dressing room.

"Kanavel's getting a lotta work out of you, kid, for nothing. You'll never get far on that second million if you keep working for him. He's playing you like he'd play a flute." He turned to include the rest of the audience. "The kid's a babe in the woods; he's been told that it's sinful to split a patient's fee. Hell's bells, you'll starve to death. Did ya ever watch Kanavel's walk? The son of a bitch will saw himself in two someday."

My anger burst. "Dr. Schroeder, I won't stand by while you talk about my chief. What you think you might say to his face is your business, but my guess is you'd never have the guts. What I do in association with him and trying to be a better surgeon is my business and his. I haven't asked you for help nor money, and I never will. You go on splitting patients' fees if that's what you do or think is ethical and honest; I don't and won't, but it's none of your business."

Schroeder heard me through, and I was ashamed that my voice had risen almost to a shout. Then the older, squat, grotesque figure came toward me, laughing, and clapped me on the back.

"Dammit to hell, that's what I like about the kid; he's got spirit and isn't afraid to speak up. He's got loyalty, too, and some of you ought to learn what that is. We know where we stand, don't we, boy? Don't you worry, I'll never go behind your back to knock your brains out. Keep your nose clean round the hospital, hear? I wish I could claim you as one of my students." He gave me another pat on the back and waddled out of the room. I knew that Schroeder had paid me his highest compliment, expressing himself the only way he knew.

A day or two later, Dr. Kanavel invited me to lunch.

"I heard about what happened in the dressing room the other day. I'm sorry Schroeder drew you into an argument, but I'm proud and complimented by what they tell me you said. He's unpredictable, and it may well turn out that he'll be your staunchest supporter, but he's too much of an egotist to like what happened in front of all his satellites. He has power in Wesley Hospital because he has a large surgical practice. Think about your future relations here in the hospital with him. Remember this: If he's correct and I *am* a son of a bitch, you can't defend me. If he's not correct, there's no need for you to defend me."

I had the responsibility of teaching the course in neuroanatomy except for the lectures, and I spent time in organizing the laboratory work, searching the outpatient clinic in neurology for patients whose symptoms would illustrate the importance of learning and remembering fiber tracts in the central nervous system. I had discussed my ideas of teaching the students many times with Pollock and had been particularly careful to emphasize that I was simply carrying out the method of teaching to which he had introduced me when I followed him on rounds at the Cook County Hospital. I knew that he was pleased, because he helped me choose patients to appear before the class of sophomores.

There was a sense of the dramatic as I brought the patients to the classroom, demonstrated their symptoms, and saw the interest that was aroused in the students. They were understanding that all of the drudgery of learning about complicated nerve and muscle mechanisms was useful practically, and they were learning that some facts were more important for them to understand perfectly than others. I felt a sense of responsibility for these men who were just a few years younger than I, and a great sense of satisfaction that I was making a contribution to each of their desires to become a doctor. Often, I felt embarrassed when they showed that they appreciated my enthusiasm for teaching and working with them.

There was time to continue to work with Lewis Pollock on problems in the experimental laboratory, and I had to make new contacts for a supply of alley cats upon which we could study the effects on the tone of muscles, and on convulsive seizures produced by experimental injuries to parts of the brain and spinal cord. The supply was scarce, and I had to find the money to pay fifty cents for each animal to the suppliers. It was necessary that every experiment be planned beforehand down to the last detail and that the anesthetic be controlled carefully so that the animal was not lost before we got started on the experiment. My relations with Pollock began again as if there had been no interruption.

It was difficult not to be impatient with the slowness with which I was developing a practice. Pollock had not had a patient who needed an operation or I would have been consulted. I kept busy at the medical school and in the laboratory when I was not occupied at the hospital with Dr. Kanavel's patients. I was not going to loaf around the doctors' lounge and dressing room; at least, I could appear to be busy. I'd made up my mind not to complain or appear poor-mouthed.

My first opportunity to be consulted about a patient came from Dr. Paul Magnuson. The big, tall bone-and-joint surgeon called my name with his strong, raspy voice. "Doctor Davis, wait a minute." Magnuson was far in advance of his coterie of interns. "I want you to examine a patient of mine and tell me and him what's wrong. He's got a bad pain, he says, in his arm. Says his thumb and index finger get numb. Can't sleep lying down, has to sit up in a chair. Can you give him an appointment?"

I thought for a moment that Magnuson was joking. Could I give him an appointment? There was no smile on Magnuson's face, and he hadn't been sarcastic.

"I'll be glad to see him at ten o'clock tomorrow morning here in the hospital. Tell him to ask Mrs. Williams at the reception desk for me. I'll call you as soon as I examine him. Thank you for asking me to see him."

Magnuson paused while he looked at me. "That's the way to do it, young fella. Doesn't seem so long since you were pulling on that leg for me at St. Mary's Hospital in Galesburg, does it?"

I sought Dr. Magnuson when I had finished examining his patient and told him in detail about my findings and opinion that there was irritation of the nerve roots by compression from an injury to the cervical vertebrae which he received as a boy when he dove into shallow water. I told the patient that exercises would improve his posture, and massage, which he could receive in the physical therapy department after intermittent traction on his neck, would relieve him.

"You don't want to operate on him right now, huh?"

"I think he should have good conservative treatment, but he'll have to come to physical therapy daily for a while. I'll be glad to check his condition occasionally on his visits."

"You told him all this?" I nodded. "All right, I'll tell him the same, and I congratulate you on not being too anxious and fast to operate. Next time come and tell me what you think before you tell the patient. You see, I might have told him that I thought he should be operated upon. If I had said that, then we'd have the chance to argue it out before you told the patient." My face flushed as I realized I had made a mistake. I had become too absorbed in the patient and his questions, which I tried to answer, and had forgotten a courteous, ethical custom. Magnuson put his hand on my shoulder. "Forget it, don't be upset. You have to learn some of these things by practice. Now, what do you intend to charge him?"

"Will ten dollars be all right?" I asked hesitantly.

"For God's sake! I can see you need a lot of education. What about Carl Leigh's ability to pay? He's a rich man who has a tremendous business manufacturing banana crates and onion bags. That's the first thing to know: his ability to pay. Next, you have sacrificed and worked hard to know more than the average doctor about his condition. Get some confidence. If you don't respect your own ability and knowledge, no one else will. Send him a bill for examination and consultation for fifty dollars." Magnuson stopped and grinned when he saw the look of astonishment on my face. "You probably haven't got any billhead stationery. Make it out on a blank piece of paper; type it and put your name at the top. Your office is here at the hospital; put that down. You'll see plenty of patients who can't afford to pay in consultation for me, so don't fret. You're worth it." Magnuson started down the corridor and then turned back. "I heard about your run-in with Schroeder. I like the old man. He's rough and he's crude, but I've always got along with him, and for the same reason you'll get along with him. I speak what I believe, and he respects people like that, particularly if they don't carry a grudge."

The next week I had another experience with Dr. Schroeder. He was the only attending surgeon who had his professional office in Wesley Hospital. As I was walking down the corridor, he popped out of his office.

"C'mon in here, kid." He had hold of my arm. I wondered what I had done to displease him, because he was angry.

"See that typewriter." He didn't wait for my affirmative nod. "A young whippersnapper got in here and gave me a fast sales talk to sell me a new typewriter. I told him I had a typewriter, but he kept on. I couldn't get rid of him. So I told him to take off his coat, let down his pants, and get up on my examining table. I felt his belly and told him he had to have an appendectomy. He struggled up and said, 'I've had my appendix taken out.' I said, 'I've got a typewriter, too, goddammit.'" Schroeder roared with laughter until the tears streamed down his face. I left him uncertain as to whether I should laugh at or cry for the embarrassment of the ambitious young salesman.

Dr. Kanavel had patients come to him suffering with tic douloureux, and I helped with the operations, which were difficult, long, and exhausting, though they were based upon a strictly anatomical dissection. On my trip east, I had watched Charles Frazier have the patient in a sitting position during the operation, which was initiated by Alfred Adson, a former student of Frazier's, who was then at the Mayo Clinic and head of the section of neurological surgery. I had asked Dr. Cushing why he persisted in having the patient lying down for the operation, but I was cut short.

"What if the patient vomits during the anesthetic? What about the blood pressure in the sitting position? Think before you ask questions like that," was his reply.

I thought it might be better for the patient to be sitting up if he vomited rather than be in a position that favored aspiration. The blood pressure was a factor, but Frazier didn't use morphine to prepare the patient for the anesthetic and more often than not used a local anesthetic agent. I knew that there must be a crucial step in the operation that made it go smoothly, or failing in that step, it could be a difficult, bloody procedure. I had stood for five hours with Cushing while he used the suction apparatus, sponged, retracted the temporal lobe of the brain, and looked for the root of the fifth cranial nerve to section. Dr. Kanavel had been forced to introduce a gauze pack in one patient to stop bleeding from the middle meningeal artery, which he was not able to isolate and control before it ruptured.

I helped the freshmen medical students dissect out the trigeminal nerve and its branches on each side of the skull of their specimens and then made accurate diagrams of the relations of the bony openings in the skull through which the three branches left and the other opening through which the middle meningeal artery entered the skull. I measured the size of the Gasserian ganglion and concluded that the key to a smooth operation was to control the artery first. It entered the intracranial cavity through its foramen, which I found always to be situated in the lowest portion of the middle fossa of the skull. The next step was to find the exact plane of dissection between the covering of the brain and the covering of the ganglion. I was anxious to put into practice what I learned in the anatomical laboratory.

The opportunity came sooner than I thought. I had examined Dr. Kanavel's patient carefully and discussed her symptoms and the findings with him. When she agreed to the operation, I spent a great deal of time getting the operating table adjusted to the proper sitting position and checking all of the necessary attachments to hold the patient's head securely in the correct position. I went to the hospital early on the morning of the operation and quickly rehearsed the interns and anesthetist in their roles. When Dr. Kanavel arrived and told me to get the operation started, I had the patient put to sleep, scrubbed and draped the field of operation, and made the skin incision. Momentarily, I expected him to come into the operating room, but by the time I was ready to make the opening in the bone of the skull, he had not arrived. So I went on without haste but methodically and carefully followed step by step each stage in the operation I had worked out in the anatomical laboratory. Finally, without difficulty I exposed the sensory root to be sectioned. Should I wait for Dr. Kanavel, since I had taken over the operation completely and, perhaps, had gone along too rapidly? I could easily put a blunt hook around the nerve, pull it gently toward me, separate it from its motor division, and cut it. The operation would be over except for suturing the wound. Just then, Kanavel came into the operating room, took a sterile towel from the nurse, and, drying his hands, walked behind me and looked over my shoulder.

"Show me the field so I'll know how to do it that well if sometime I have to operate on these patients in this position without you."

I was not sure whether or not there was a note of sarcasm in the chief's voice. He had told me to go ahead and the operation had gone well, but were these acceptable excuses for taking the operation away from him? Step by step, I retraced the steps of the operation, demonstrating each of the important anatomical landmarks which, I believed, made the operation simpler providing they were accomplished before going on to the next maneuver. He was silent but attentive. All that remained was to sever the sensory root.

"It's a beautiful demonstration. Go ahead and sever the root. You've done the rest of the operation and shouldn't be deprived of the most definitive step."

There was no indecision in my mind, or in my movements, as I severed the nerve that would relieve the patient's pain permanently. I began to close the wound, layer by layer, using silk sutures, as was Cushing's custom.

"You're sure you should bury those silk sutures in the subcutaneous tissue instead of using fine catgut, are you?"

"Yes, sir, I'm sure."

"That's what counts; you must always be as sure as is humanly possible. Now, why don't you write up what you've learned in the dissecting room about the anatomy of this operation, and I'll sponsor you for its presentation at the Chicago Surgical Society."

It was a great feeling to have put into good effect the results of all the repetitious measurements and descriptions of the dissections. Even if it wasn't a great contribution to surgery, I had learned a great deal and had gained confidence. In the dressing room later, Dr. Kanavel said, "A fine operation. I don't think I should do it any more; I'll see to it that those patients will be yours in the future; they deserve the best."

Before I could interrupt and express my thanks, he went on. "When you present the work at the Surgical Society, remember you will be the only one who has done the study and knows about it. Speak with assurance but not aggressively; answer any questions politely but not condescendingly."

There had been longer and longer lapses between communications with Bob Gunning. He still lived with my parents, who treated him like a son, though it required all of my father's persistence to have my mother not become too concerned over Bob's coming and going. It was difficult because she answered telephone calls from patients who wanted him to come to their homes to care for them. Bob was not exact about telling her how she could reach him, and her imagination pictured patients in extremis who would die before Dr. Gunning had arrived. She fussed and fumed.

It had not been difficult to make arrangements with the Burlington through their medical director for Dad's retirement. He was assured of a pension that would be sufficient, with help from me and Bob Gunning's contribution for his board, room, and laundry, to allow my parents to live comfortably.

I enjoyed the automobile trip down home on the old Cannonball trail, so named when the dirt road had first been graded. Now there were stretches of concrete pavement running through the beautiful farmland with its black soil which was so fertile. The small villages gave me a feeling of tranquillity, but I knew that I could never have settled in even one of the larger villages and practiced medicine. There were challenges to be met in the city, at the medical school and hospital, which were exhilarating and were not present in these small towns. But as I neared home, I became nostalgic and decided to drive around the neighborhood where I was born, raised, and went to Weston grade school.

Weston School had shrunk in size; it had seemed to me to be an enormous building. I stopped the car and looked at the windows of Ella Hammond's room where she had us prepare perfect papers to be exhibited at the World's Fair in St. Louis. Again, I could smell the fresh odor of her cleanliness.

As I drove down Cottage Avenue, it was hard to realize that number 206 was such a small house. I tried to picture the rooms and understand actually how small they were. The room we had used the most should have been the dining room, but we always ate in the kitchen. The parlor was used only when company called; it never did have a stove in it, and so the folding doors were kept closed during the cold winter months. I tried to remember where we stored the stove that supplied heat for the two bedrooms and the living room when my father took it down in the summer. Then I remembered we took it apart, put Vaseline upon each leg and the shiny metal of the belly, wrapped the parts in old rags, and stored them in the cellar. We had bought the first hard-coal stove on the avenue. There was the coal shed; it wasn't really so high as it had seemed when I fell from its roof when I was flying my Japanese bird kite; another occasion when my father called me a "gummy." It didn't seem large enough either to house an outdoor privy, a box stall for my pony, and store the winter coal.

There was the corner of Mulberry and Chambers streets bordering the railroad tracks where I had waved to my father in his engine on his trips to Chicago; the corner where Mr. Tucker's candy store was located and where I tended it while he went to lunch and dinner on Saturdays, for which I received twenty-five cents.

When Bob Gunning came home to supper, he greeted me as though we had parted only a day or so previously.

"How goes it, Gypper? What about riding around after supper with me while I make rounds at the hospital? We've got a lot of interesting patients; did a partial gastrectomy this morning for an intractable, bleeding ulcer."

Dad caught my eye and gave a small wink as Bob continued to tell about how many patients they had in the hospital, how busy he was, and how Ben left all the preoperative diagnoses and care to him. He was doing more and more operations, Bob said, even though he would rather devote himself to diagnosis and X-ray work. I listened politely, knowing that Bob had always nursed a secret desire to be a surgeon even when he protested the strongest that it required more intelligence and knowledge of medicine to be a diagnostician. He was trying to tell me that he would be just as good a surgeon, learning by doing for the first time on patients, without teaching and disciplined training from an experienced surgeon in a progressive educational program. I was sure of it when he told me how much their income had been the past year. Bob talked without pause about patients, the hospitals, nurses, how he really had to direct the work in their office because Ben Baird wouldn't keep up with new procedures.

I was pleased to see some of the sisters at St. Mary's Hospital, and the subdued light in the corridors of the Cottage Hospital brought back the memory of my experiences when I had first come home to practice. Once again, I recalled the mystery and drama of the sick patient at night.

Driving home, we passed Joe Jarls's men's clothing store on Main Street, and Bob called attention to the new front that had been added. He continued, answering my unspoken question: "He hasn't changed one bit. He's been griping about how much the remodeling cost him for the past six months. Everybody's been kidding him about his latest. You know there's been a poker game out at the golf club on Wednesday nights for years. About two weeks ago, the boys drove by Joe's house to pick him up and he hadn't finished his supper. They waited and he went right on eating. They got sore and drove off. Joe had to hire a taxi to get out to the club and when he got there bellyached and screamed about the fifty cents he had to pay. He wanted them to pay his cab fare. Boy, did they give him a razzing, and to make it worse they took his money during the game. He's tighter than the bark on a tree."

It was typical of the gossip stories that could be told about almost anyone in Galesburg; there was no escaping the revelation of personal traits and characteristics. There was Art Landes who ran the moving picture theater machine, belonged to the Soangetaha golf club, played a good game, liked to hunt, and was a sucker for practical jokes. Once, his pals had put a wire on the foot accelerator of his car and brought it beneath and into the back seat where they elected to ride while he drove them down Main Street in style. They would pull on the accelerator, and poor Art had a terrible time controlling his automobile as it sped up and slowed down spasmodically all the way through town. Then there was "Bigfoot" Clyde Bandy who worked in the city clerk's office, who always walked the line between his golf ball and the hole while he scrutinized the roll and texture of the grass and at the same time made a pathway with his splayed feet. Everyone knew everybody's personal business, and they never failed to concern themselves with it, but it seemed never in a helpful way.

As I visited with my parents, I brought the conversation back to their future. They found it easier to talk about it in snatches. I wanted to be as sure as I could that they would not worry; particularly Mother needed assurance. Dad had expressed, in his own way, his complete confidence in the plan for his retirement, and I knew that he felt there was nothing more to be said. I was grateful that they didn't tell me not to worry about them, that they were getting old and shouldn't be my concern, or that they had sacrificed for me but didn't expect my care in return. These were things not to be said. It was to be understood that I was to be leaned upon for their security the rest of their lives; it was my responsibility to see to it that their happiness was insured.

As we sat on the front porch that Sunday afternoon, a feeling of calmness and quiet came over me. There were long periods of silence while the wooden porch swing in which we sat moved gently back and forth. Years ago, I had steadied the stepladder on which my father stood while he screwed the rings into the ceiling of the porch. Dad always made a game out of work we did together; the idea was to have pleasure and enjoy everything we did. Mother kept her attention riveted on the hoop of embroidery she was working on; she never failed to be pleased when Dad called attention to the beautiful needlework she could do.

A Model T Ford stopped in front of the house, and a man and woman whom I didn't recognize got out. My mother started to get up and go into the house.

"Sit still, Laura, you look all right. Looks like Dan Sills. He's a switchman. I had him on a switch engine when he was a kid, just starting."

My father moved to the top of the porch steps. "H'yar you, Dan. C'mon up." Dan Sills and his wife approached shyly and hesitatingly.

My father's introductions had never changed. It embarrassed him to introduce people, and he never failed to be incomplete and casual; defending himself always by saying that everybody knew everybody else in town anyway.

The Sills were ill at ease. "How are you, Mr. Sills? I've heard my father tell stories about old one eighteen, the switch engine in the yards. You started to railroad on it, didn't you?"

Sills did not answer my question directly; often railroad men never did.

"Those were the days, Al. I learned a lot from your father—mostly not to play at railroading. Know what I mean? No fooling around an engine; I was pretty clumsy at first catching the front step when he was coming toward me." Sills was now at ease, and my mother was showing Mrs. Sills her embroidery. Then there was silence again while Sills was apparently trying to say why they had come so unexpectedly.

"Sorry, just to bust in like this, Doctor. Mary's sister's learning to be a nurse at Cottage Hospital and she told us you were in town. You took care of our neighbor's boy when you practiced here. Sewed up the bottom of his foot when he cut it on a milk bottle."

Mary Sills blurted out the story. "Little Dan's sick, Doctor, and we want to bring him up for you to take care of. He's only six, and all of a sudden he wakes up in the morning with a bad headache and vomits right away. Sometimes it shoots right out of his mouth. He walks like he's drunk and he don't want to go out and play."

Dan Sills clasped his big hands together and nodded his agreement. "Yeah, that's right, and he's downright peaked-looking. Hope you'll help him, Doctor."

"I'm sorry to hear about Danny. Who is your doctor, Mrs. Sills?"

"Doc Morris had us bring him down to his office and gave him some pills, but they haven't done any good."

I heard a snort of disgust from my mother and saw Dad warn her with a glance before she could say what she thought about the talents of "old Doc Morris."

"You haven't any doctor looking after him regularly, I take it."

"No, it has happened so sudden. Till Ann saw him last night, we thought he just had a stomach upset and was weak, that's why he walked so funny. Ann said that there's something else the matter, she thinks. Dan worked with your father and so we thought . . ." Mary Sills's voice trailed off.

"Of course. Don't worry, I'll help you any way I can. I'm starting back to Chicago later this afternoon. Why don't I go out to your house now and just take a look at Danny. If it's necessary, you can bring him to Chicago for us to look after."

Mary Sills nodded agreement vigorously, and as they rose to leave, Dan Sills said, "Hate to take you away from your folks, like this." He looked appealingly at my father and mother. "Al, c'mon. You and Laurie take a ride out to the house with us. After the doctor looks at Danny, we can have some coffee before he has to start back."

I caught my mother's eye and nodded slightly. The grim line of her mouth relaxed; she didn't like to be called Laurie, not even by my father. I'd have to improvise my examination and do as well as I could without the proper instruments.

We rode down Main Street, Tompkins, Cherry, Brooks, and then across the tracks into the Seventh Ward, the "Bloody Seventh." These were all familiar neighborhoods. In the house my mother and Mary Sills remained silent, suffering with their own thoughts, finding it unnecessary to bolster themselves with idle and meaningless talk. Men have to talk or take action when they are worried; they are afraid to display their emotions. If I had asked Father and Mother to stay out in the car, it would have been an affront to Mary Sills's sense of propriety. I was firm when I told them to wait in the kitchen of the small house while I went with Mary and Dan Sills into the small living room where I found Danny lying in the lap of a younger woman who was rocking back and forth slowly, and softly humming a song to him. She had to be his aunt, the nurse in training, who had suggested that I examine the child. She looked up, smiled a greeting, and rose with the boy in her arms and gently placed him on the couch.

"Doctor Davis is here to see you, Danny boy. He won't hurt you and he wants to make you well."

Sick little boys have always made me feel sorry for them. Little girls can be just as sick, but somehow they appeal to me as more self-sufficient and less sad and helpless. Perhaps they are constructed to bear pain with more fortitude. Sometimes I have had to leave the room for a moment to recover my composure when I examined a child. I always had to stay out of earshot when any child is first given the anesthetic; I couldn't stand their cries.

I tried to overcome this feeling by being brusquely cheerful with Danny Sills. I patted him on the shoulder and sat down on the edge of the couch. The boy had large brown eyes and a shock of dark hair. He was peaked, as his father said. He was lying curled up on his right side, and I noticed that he had quickly turned when his aunt had put him down on the couch on his back. His lips and tongue were dry, and he had lost weight. Just the faintest smile came as he looked up as I began gently to rub his back and pretend to ask questions in a way that never demanded an answer.

"Your dad and mother tell me you're a whiz in school. That's great. You know your dad and mine worked together on a switch engine for a long time and so you and I should know each other better. Now, Danny, I want to have you do a few little things for me, won't hurt you a bit, and then maybe your father and mother will bring you up where I live and we'll be together every day for a while." The child looked up quickly at his parents, and his lips trembled. Then he quickly grabbed for his aunt's hand.

"Your aunt, too, can come, if you'd like, Danny." Immediately, the boy relaxed and silently implied his consent.

Slowly and gently, I flexed and extended the child's hands, arms, feet, and legs. There was a characteristic flaccidity and absence of muscle tone that was an indication of disease of the small brain, the cerebellum, which was physiologically like the governor of a stationary engine. I could bring the sole of his foot back flat against his buttocks on both sides, and the palms of his hands could be placed against the front of his shoulders. I didn't have a reflex hammer and it was just as well; the child might be frightened by instruments. I could try to get the tendon reflexes with my hands and examine them later more carefully. After repeating the passive movements of the extremities several times carefully and gently, I knew I had his confidence. I was most anxious to see the posture of his head when he sat up, to look at the movements of his eyes when I asked him to follow my moving finger, and to tap on his skull.

There was no doubt that the boy carried his head tilted to the right when he sat up; his eyes flickered back and forth in a rapid, horizontal nystagmus as I asked him to follow the movements of my fingers. His pupils were large; I didn't have an ophthalmoscope to look at his optic nerve heads, so that would have to wait. As I helped Danny lie down, I waited a moment.

"Danny, I'll bet you've gone to the grocery store and watched your mom tap a watermelon to see if it was ripe, haven't you?"

He grinned and looked at his mother. "Sure he has, Doctor. Danny and I both tap them, and we always take the one Danny thinks is the ripe one."

"Good. Now, listen while I tap my head." I rapped my knuckles against my own skull and opened my mouth so that there would be a more hollow sound, something near to that which I suspected I would hear when I percussed Danny's skull. The boy almost laughed aloud.

"Now, be real quiet everybody. I'm going to tap Danny's head and see if he's as ripe as I am." With the tip of my finger I tapped the boy's skull and heard the tympanitic note that indicated the presence of a thin skull and the probable presence of enlargement of the brain ventricles produced by an obstruction to the flow of cerebrospinal fluid.

"Do it again." Danny was won over and afraid no more.

"Will you try to get up and stand on the floor by the bed, Danny, and maybe walk a bit for me?" This would be helpful in strengthening the diagnosis of which I was almost certain. "Aunt Ann and I will want you to walk from one of us to the other, turn around, and come back. Just once, Danny, can you do that for me?"

The boy put his feet off the couch and bravely began to lift his trunk and head. His rumpled, soiled, cotton flannel nightgown reached just below his knees, and his skinny, pipestem legs didn't appear strong enough to support his body and his larger than normal head. Even when his eyes were open, he had great difficulty walking back and forth between us. He staggered and wobbled from side to side but was able to catch his balance when it seemed he was about to fall to the floor. I was convinced that most likely the child had a tumor in the posterior fossa of the cranial cavity which had been growing steadily until now it was larger than the available intracranial space and demanded attention. There was little to be accomplished by explaining to the parents that it could be a midline tumor made up of embryonic cells which had obstructed the flow of cerebrospinal fluid, or a cystic tumor of one of the cerebellar hemispheres. I could explain all of that if and when they brought the child to me for care.

As I left the room, followed by Dan and Mary Sills, I remembered the story of the famous internist and professor of medicine at Johns Hopkins, Sir William Osler, who was severely criticized because he whistled as he walked down the hospital corridor after leaving the room of a fatally sick child on his way to tell the parents. His reply was that the silly little whistle which was almost inaudible had kept him from breaking down and crying like a baby. I sat down with Dan and Mary Sills and Mary's sister Ann to discuss Danny's condition.

Ann's training as a nurse asserted itself in spite of her obvious emotion. "Danny has a brain tumor, hasn't he, Doctor?"

It was an abrupt and shocking beginning for an explanation that I had planned to be a smoother and more progressive approach to the child's problem, but there it was. I couldn't deny her statement, but I wanted to give the parents some opportunity to adjust themselves to the fact that, undoubtedly, after study my advice would be that an operation should be performed.

"A tumor is one of the things that would cause Danny's symptoms, but there are several kinds of tumors, some good and some bad, if a tumor can ever be said to be a good one. He should have a more complete examination and study with X-ray films and other tests which I can't do here. I think those steps should be taken, and then I can tell you definitely and accurately all about his trouble. I do think he may have to be operated upon to give him help. You think about it and let me know. If you can bring him up to Chicago, we can get all of the tests done as soon as possible and then we can discuss the problem more intelligently."

"Brain operations are always fatal, aren't they, Doctor?"

This was the layman's usual response to any suggestion of an operation upon the brain, but I didn't expect it from a nurse, who might be expected to know better. But could she know better? She had never seen a brain operation during her training, of that I was sure, and she knew that such an operation on her nephew couldn't be done at either hospital in Galesburg. I looked at her with a smile as understanding as I could muster.

"No, they aren't. Brain surgery has come a long way in the last few years. There are many things to be learned, but many things have been learned. I'm sure you realize that Danny can't get well continuing this way, and medicine will not help him."

She lowered her head and nodded; her voice was almost inaudible. "Yes, I know."

Mary Sills had listened with complete concentration. Her face was pale and strained, but I knew that she, alone, was the one who could face the difficulties of decision and suffer quietly. Dan's thoughts were lost in anticipation, in deep emotion, and in his wish that in some way the whole business would disappear into the thin air.

"We'll bring Danny to Chicago tomorrow. Will that give you time to get a bed for him? Can I stay at the hospital with him?"

The mother's decisiveness would be invaluable in the care of the boy, and it was satisfying to know that she knew by intuition that her child was seriously ill and that his care would be hazardous and problematical. I might have expected the child's aunt, trained as a nurse, to be the one to influence the decisions of the parents, but she had obviously taken possession of the boy emotionally. It might be difficult for Mary Sills, because I knew that most of her neighbors would gossip and be critical of her direct approach to her son's illness. It would never occur to them how deeply she was suffering; they could only understand the false dramatics of sorrow and worry, not the quiet calmness of her emotion. More often than not the hysteria that replaces deep feeling and judgment gets in the way of the best surgical care of patients.

The boy would have to be operated upon; there was no question about that in my mind. I went over the operating table attachments, checking each of them in my mind. I'd have to put enough padding on the shoulder rests to make them fit the child's chest comfortably and give plenty of room beneath so he wouldn't be lying right on his chest. The wrist cuffs would have to go over cotton and gauze pads around the small wrists so his hands wouldn't get free. I'd have the co-operation of Dr. Christopher, I was sure of that, and it would be comfortable to know that she would sit on a stool on the floor in the most uncomfortable position anyone could imagine, without complaint, and give the ether anesthetic.

The anesthetic was what bothered me the most. If I was correct about the location of the tumor, it could embarrass the child's respiratory center in the medulla. Just how much reserve function was there, and was it enough to compensate for the demands that the anesthetic agent would make? It would have to be ether and by the open drip method, which would necessarily mean the escape of much of the vapor around the face mask and up into the surgical field. Dr. Christopher had proposed that she investigate the possibilities of introducing a tube down the trachea in patients, but also pointed out that proper equipment for blowing in the anesthetic agent was not yet perfected. I had told her about the machine that Miss Garrard used at the Brigham, but she thought we should wait for the newer machines to come onto the market. I wished we could use an endotracheal tube on Danny Sills; I would be more sure of a patent respiratory tract all through the procedure. But I would have to use what was available and depend upon Dr. Christopher's help. I knew I could control any possible hemorrhage; it was the danger of anoxia from the anesthetic that concerned me.

I had considered reserving a bed for Danny Sills in the children's ward but dismissed the idea. I had promised Mary that she could stay in her boy's room. A comfortable cot that would be rolled beneath Danny's bed and a large, bright, cheerful room with a high ceiling pleased her. As I went about completing my examination of the child, I was actually gathering an inner strength from this calm, brown-eyed woman who spoke so quietly and with the suggestion of an accent handed down from her Irish ancestors. There was no question that the boy's condition, and what I knew had to be done, was concerning me more than perhaps it should. Danny Sills was my first patient with an intracranial tumor; he had been brought to me directly; he came from my home town, the son of a railroad switchman who had followed my education and training to become a surgeon. It seemed a bit unfair that these people should believe that I had powers and abilities that were almost superhuman. Perhaps they were only expressing their confidence in me; maybe I was building up a dramatic situation in my imagination. Why would it be worse if Danny Sills could not be cured or did not survive the operation? He was no different from any other patient, or was he? It would be necessary to detach my mind from these disturbing thoughts. Danny Sills was a surgical problem that I must try to solve with the best of my abilities and skill without allowing emotion to influence the accuracy and dispatch with which I was educated and trained to perform my acts as a surgeon.

I asked Lewis Pollock to examine the boy and consult about the diagnosis and proposal to operate. I had decided before I left to work with Cushing that patients could best be served by a co-operative study of their symptoms between the medical neurologist and the neurological surgeon. Each was equally important to the patient, and for the surgeon to disregard the opinions of the physician or for the latter to look upon the surgeon as a mechanic instructed to carry out his orders were both wrong concepts which could only react to the detriment of the patient.

As usual, Pollock was meticulous and repetitive in his examination of the boy. I had brought the interns with me to observe again the signs and findings that each of us had elicited previously, now confirmed, and perhaps added to by a newcomer to the problem. Pollock grunted occasionally as he worked with Danny, encouraging him, instructing and cajoling him. He finished his examination and began to replace his instruments in the combination brief case and medicine bag that he carried. He began to hum a tune softly. Patting Danny gently on the head, he rather formally thanked him for his help and co-operation in the examination. He talked to the child as he would to an adult.

"I trust that I have not tired you, Danny, with all these examinations I've made. You were splendid, and I thank you for your help. You have a fine doctor who will look after you well. You're a good patient, Danny."

Pollock was quiet and grave as we walked into the nearby alcove off the corridor. He took a cigar from his vest pocket, which always seemed to be filled, and again went through the same ceremony of lighting. He walked up and down the small area that had been furnished with three easy chairs for use of the patients' relatives who could sit and wait for an operation to be finished. The cigar was tilted up and down as smoke billowed about him. He used the cigar as a pointer emphasizing some obscure point in his mind.

"Well, no doubt about it. The boy has a tumor in the posterior fossa, you know that as well as I do." He was addressing me quite formally on the occasion of our consultation over my first patient and in the presence of the interns. "The child has a phenomenal loss of muscle tone, hasn't he? High-grade choking of optic nerve heads, coarse ataxic nystagmus, the Babinski-Weil test is positive—everything." He turned quickly upon the interns. "I suppose Doctor Davis has already told you that the child has either a cystic glioma of the cerebellar hemisphere, or a midline medulloblastoma. I would hope the former so you could evacuate the cyst and take out the mural tumor. Shall we talk to the mother now?"

Mary Sills sat on the edge of the large, red mahogany, leather-upholstered chair with her hands clasped and listened attentively while Dr. Pollock told her that he agreed in the diagnosis and that he believed that the decision to operate upon her son was correct. She nodded her head.

"Doctor Davis has explained everything to us, Doctor, and we have every confidence in him. It was his idea to ask your opinion, not because we didn't trust him."

Pollock smiled and grasped her hands. "Yes, yes, we understand. I told Danny he is in good hands."

"We'll plan the operation for day after tomorrow, Mary. Will you tell Dan so he can come up tomorrow and I'll have a chance to sit down and talk with both of you about the operation." Mary Sills smiled, squeezed my hand, and walked back to her son's room.

I had been taught that good surgeons always have fear; true, the fears common to them all were both rational and irrational. Rational fears, Dr. Kanavel had said repeatedly, were necessary tools of the responsible surgeon, and irrational fears were often unnecessary and dangerous burdens to the mind. I had to be realistic and recognize all of the potential dangers to Danny Sills; the physiological changes that could occur when he was first put to sleep, even before I could start the operation. To be alert to details made the surgeon responsive to slight changes in the patient's condition and sharpened his reactions so he might avoid catastrophe.

These were just a few of the factors that resulted in surgical judgment, that attribute of the good surgeon that could not be defined in a sentence; in fact, perhaps it could not be described satisfactorily at all. All surgeons knew what it was and were aware of all of its ramifications but couldn't explain it simply. Was Danny Sills's operation advisable, and if so, was it feasible in terms of Danny Sills as an individual? Should the accepted method of operation be modified in any way to better fit the specific problem that Danny Sills presented? I knew that the manner in which I used my personal endowments, my training, and my education in surgery for each patient's good would define me as a surgeon among my colleagues. This was the recognition that every surgeon, in his own heart, sought.

It was my problem and mine alone to wrestle with until I was satisfied that I had answered to the best of my abilities all of the questions that Danny Sills's tumor posed. Then I could discuss my plan of action logically and confidently with his parents. I must avoid confusion in the conference and answer every question that entered their minds.

I took the interns with me when I went to the vacant patient's room to which I had directed the Sills family. It would be more quiet than in the alcove, and Ma Brookhart who supervised the sixth floor said that she wouldn't need the room for two hours.

"Good morning, Doctor." Mary Sills's greeting was an affectionate one. "Dan and Ann came up on fifty-six this morning."

"Morning, Dan. How are you, Ann? I suppose you've had your breakfast, but can we get you a cup of coffee?"

"No thanks, Doctor." Ann Marshall spoke for Dan, who just nodded his head in agreement. I wondered if there was a feeling of antagonism toward me, or did I just imagine that Dan Sills and his sister-in-law were regarding me as an enemy? I concluded that they were thinking wishfully and were unable, as was Mary, to face the problem without erecting an imaginary foe. They hoped desperately that they could wish away what they anticipated I was about to say. In spite of themselves, this attitude expressed itself in their demeanors.

I began slowly. "As I told you we would do, we have examined Danny repeatedly and have X-ray films of his skull. We have made all of the tests that are necessary to come to a conclusion. Finally, I took the liberty of calling Doctor Pollock into consultation with Mary's permission, and we have discussed Danny's problem. If you will listen carefully and won't interrupt, I will tell you all we know

213

and what we think should be done. Then, when I've finished, I want you to ask every question that comes to your minds, and I will answer to the best of my knowledge. Danny has a growth within the skull, in the back part of the brain, which is increasing in size. It is a tumor situated in one of two locations, just a fraction of an inch distant from each other. This growth may have originated in the left half of the cerebellum, the small brain which controls the smoothness and accuracy of our muscle movements. Remember, I said it was like the governor on a stationary engine? If so, then we believe the tumor may be partly cystic and is located on the wall of the cystic cavity. The cells that make up this kind of tumor are more mature in character, and the tumor can be removed more completely after the cyst is drained. Sometimes it is good surgical judgment just to drain the fluid from the cyst and at a second operation remove the tumor. This depends on the condition of the patient, and, naturally, one always hopes to do the complete job in one operation. Or the tumor may sit right in the middle between the two halves of the cerebellum and originate from the cells of the structure which makes the roof of a small ventricle, or cavity. These tumor cells are young, immature, and if they had behaved correctly, would have grown up to be normal nerve cells of one kind or another. They are baby cells, and they multiply rapidly. Both of these tumors are called gliomas, but these are the malignant kind of brain tumors. They are different from what you know of, in your way, as cancers, because they do not go by way of the blood stream to other parts of the body. But they are not like the benign tumors that come from the coverings of the brain. The tumors made up of the young, immature cells may spread by way of the cerebrospinal fluid down around the spinal cord. Because they are immature cells, they respond better to deep X-ray treatment. We know these things because we put together all of his symptoms and the signs we brought out on examination. The X-ray films of the skull do not show these tumors, but they do show the effects of the increasing pressure within the cranial cavity on the bones of the skull. They are thin, and the lines that join the separate bones of the skull together are widened and separated. This is why we heard the sound of the ripe melon when I tapped Danny's head with my finger. Something has to give to accommodate the increasing growth of the tumor which doesn't belong within the skull normally and so occupies space that other structures should have. Doctor Pollock agrees with all of the findings and with this diagnosis.

"Danny must be operated upon to have a chance to get well. We must not treat him with X-rays before we know what and exactly where the tumor is located. Danny has a little body which has lost weight and water from the tissues. To wait until we think he might feel better would seriously affect his chances for recovery. He will not be in better condition for operation than he is now. He was in better condition some weeks ago, of course. We will put him to sleep, and I can tell you that Doctor Christopher is an excellent anesthetist. I would want her to give me an anesthetic. We must shave off all of his hair, but it will grow back quickly. We must make a cut through the scalp across the back of his head and down the middle and carefully take off the muscles of the neck which are attached to the bone so they can be sewed back in their original place and heal firmly. We must take out that portion of the skull, and we will not put it back, nor will we put in a plate to cover the bony defect. This will be protected quite well by the strong muscles, and besides, we want to make room in the bony box which is now too small.

"I don't need to say that all of us, as well as you, want Danny to be well; that none of us would suggest operating upon him unless we believed deeply that this is the only way in which he can be made well and that the operation can be successful." I had said everything as simply as I could, and completely truthfully. There was silence.

"Have I made all of this clear to you? I have tried to tell you about Danny in language you can understand. I'll answer any questions you have, so don't think they might be ridiculous. Ask anyway."

I was surprised when Dan Sills was the first to speak. He was twisting his hands as he had at home, but somehow he was more sure of himself.

"I can't say I understand every word you used, Doctor, but I know that Danny has a brain tumor and what has to be done. Mary and I want you to go ahead. Danny's a good boy . . ." His voice broke, and he looked down at the floor.

Mary reached over and took his hand. She smiled gently. "Thank

215

you so much for explaining everything in detail. It helps so much to know what we are all trying to do for Danny. We have faith in God and in you, Doctor. When will you start the operation in the morning?"

"Early. We'll take Danny to the operating room a little after seven o'clock. I hope that when he leaves his room to come upstairs, you all will act as casual as possible. Understand?"

"Yes, I do. When are you going to tell Danny about the operation, Doctor?"

"Right now. You and I will tell him."

Dan Sills was perfectly satisfied to leave matters in the hands of his wife. Mary sat beside her son and held his hand, after she arranged his pillows so he could be more upright and comfortably look at me while I talked. It is a psychological disadvantage, I have always thought, to be flat on your back while someone stands over you and talks. It could be even more frightening for a small boy.

"Danny, you're a smart boy, and I know that you don't have to be told that you have trouble which makes you feel sick and unable to do the things you want to do. You've been a fine patient and have helped us in every way to find out how we can help you get well. Now, I have to ask you to help us again. Tomorrow morning we want you to come upstairs, riding on a cart, take some deep breaths and blow up a balloon, which will make you go to sleep. Then we have to make you comfortable on a table, and I'll have to do some things to your head. For one thing, I'll have to shave off all of your hair. What about that?"

The boy looked at his mother questioningly. She nodded her head in agreement.

"Now, I tell you what I'll do. If you want your hair to grow back, as it will quickly, a different color than it is now, or curly, I'll arrange it."

He smiled and I knew that he appreciated my feeble attempt to be humorous. "I don't want curls," he mumbled.

"All right, that's the way it'll be. Now, when we're through, we'll put a big, soft bandage on your head and you'll look like a football player with his helmet on. Mother will come along upstairs with you,

216

and she'll be waiting when you come back here to your room. All right?" Danny nodded his head.

We had prepared the table, with a bandaged rest that fitted the child's head and crutch supports for his chest. Dr. Christopher greeted the boy as he came through the doors into the operating room suite and kept his mother near him even as she adjusted the gas mask over his nose and mouth.

"Now, Danny, just as I told you, breathe naturally and blow out your breath hard. See if you can break this red rubber balloon. That's it, you're doing fine."

The induction was smooth, and I breathed a sigh of relief. I scrubbed my hands and arms before Danny came up to the operating room, and the interns had followed my actions. We could spend less time later in completing our scrubs before going into the operating room. It would help shorten the time the boy had to be under an anesthetic.

Quickly, we placed him prone on the table and adjusted his head and shoulders. Pillows were placed under his pelvis, and we made sure that his knees and toes were not resting directly on the padded table. Small pillows under the feet kept his toes free; it can be more uncomfortable than the pain of a wound to have toes and feet resting flat on the table.

I scrubbed the child's scalp meticulously but without wasted motions after I had cut off his hair with scissors and then closely shaved the scalp. I had waited to shave off his hair until he was asleep because it would be less upsetting than to go through the procedure in his room the night before, or even early that morning. It did lengthen the time of his anesthetic, but this was a judgment that I had made. The child was breathing smoothly and quietly. The skin of the scalp was soft and pliable; it was young, thin skin, and I had gathered all the small mosquito-sized hemostats in the hospital so that the galea would not be injured in the jaws of larger hemostats.

The new gray-colored surgical drapes that the nurses had cut out and sewed after my pattern fitted the child's head perfectly. I checked the field of operation carefully. The ends of the sheet drapes were not dragging on the floor; they were tucked into a floor bucket. The

217

nurses' surgical instrument table was in the right place so that I could hold out my hand and they could easily take an instrument from me or give me one I needed. We had rehearsed the signals for instruments, and Jeannette Jones was letter-perfect. I hoped that she would be assigned to my operations regularly so we could work up a perfectly co-ordinated team technique.

There was silence in the room, broken only by the soft, rhythmical respirations of the child, as I put on my gown, gloves, the wristlets that kept the sleeves of the gown from pulling out of the gloves as I worked, and the sterile vest that we were using at Wesley for the first time, which covered the unsterile ties on the back of the surgical gowns. Miss Jones nodded her head, and I held out my hand into which she firmly put the surgical knife.

"We're ready to start the incision, Doctor Christopher."

There was no answer, but the boy's head was moved forcibly.

"He just stopped breathing, Doctor. I have his jaw up and his tongue out. I can just barely get his pulse. I must change the position of his head."

We took away the instrument table quickly and the drapes off, turned him over on his back, and started artificial respiration. His lips were blue, and his face was pale and clammy. Dr. Christopher held the child's jaw up and kept his tongue from obstructing his airway. As I rhythmically compressed his chest and allowed it to expand, she held an oxygen mask over his face and alternately put her face close to his and breathed into his mouth. No words were spoken, and no confused action occurred. Dr. Christopher suggested that a solution of Adrenalin be injected directly into the heart.

"There's no use to keep on, Doctor Davis; we've been at this for two hours."

I had known for a long time, it seemed, before Dr. Christopher spoke that the battle to keep Danny Sills alive was lost. I could mechanically produce an exchange of air in the child's lungs as long as the heart continued to beat rapidly but regularly. In spite of allowing carbon dioxide to build up in the blood stream by stopping my movements, the respiratory center would not respond to the stimulation, and normal inspirations and expirations never began. The heartbeats had become more rapid, irregular, and fainter. Still,

218

I kept on compressing the chest wall and allowing it to expand. Toward the last, injections of Adrenalin directly into the heart elicited no response.

I had no chance to take out the tumor that I knew was there and was the cause of the child's death. But I knew I would have to know that fact for certain. I could conjecture that the change in intracranial pressure produced by the anesthetic had caused the cerebellum to change position and be forced into the bony ring of the foramen magnum of the skull which put pressure on the medullary centers which controlled respiration, but unless I could see for myself, I would wonder if there was something I might have done to prevent it. Now the task was to face Mary and Dan Sills and tell them of their boy's death. Would they understand what I would try to say as gently as I could?

I felt exhausted and drained of blood as I began to walk to the room where they were waiting. I could feel the pallor of my face, and my hands were white. I was only partly aware of those around me. I heard, as if from a distance, Hazel Johnson say that she would take care of the child's body and send it to the hospital morgue. It seemed as if every activity in the operation rooms had suddenly stopped. The first neurosurgical operation on my own patient had ended in a dramatic operating room death, for which I, alone, must accept the responsibility. It could have been avoided had I not decided to give Danny Sills the only chance he had to get well. It was my surgical judgment alone that was responsible, and no one in the world could share that decision with me.

Mary Sills got up quickly from her chair as I entered the door. She came toward me, holding out her hand.

"You have bad news, haven't you, Doctor?"

I nodded my head. "Yes, it's bad news. He died before we could even make the skin incision. We've been working to restore his breathing all of this time. His heart continued to beat well, but his breathing never returned. I'm positive that the change in pressure that followed the anesthetic caused the tumor to dislocate downward onto the respiratory center. It happened suddenly and without warning."

There was silence as Mary Sills sat down heavily in her chair. I stood for a moment and then sat and waited for their emotional reaction. It came with a long intake of breath and a sob from Dan Sills. Quickly, Mary went to his side and put her arms around his shoulders and drew his head to her breast. She was dry-eyed, and her inner strength shone in her face.

As the silence increased, I wondered how I could ask their permission to have an autopsy. It was so necessary to determine the exact mechanism of the child's death and the nature and location of the tumor so that some contribution could be made to the progress of knowledge in operations upon similar tumors in children in the future.

Mary Sills broke the silence. "Dan and I talked about what we would want done if this happened, Doctor. We trusted you with our boy's life, and we know that every possible chance for him to get well was given him. We could not have sat by and watched him suffer as he has done. We want you to examine Danny's brain and find out where the tumor was, how it caused his trouble, and what happened. We want Danny's suffering to help some other boy or girl, if it can. Then, he won't have been here on earth without helping others."

I could not express my thoughts; I would have betrayed my deeply felt emotions. I could only grasp her hand tightly and pat Dan Sills's shoulder before I turned to leave them alone. More words were useless.

EIGHT

EARLY in my practice, patients were referred to me from Kanavel, Pollock, Hugh T. Patrick, and Peter Bassoe, nationally known neurologists; progress was slow but steady. I was the only surgeon in Chicago limiting his practice to neurological surgery. Our son, Richard Allen, was born on June 15, 1925, and the next day Dr. Kanavel insisted upon going to the nursery to see if he had any congenital defects. He wanted to be sure that a child who bore his name was a healthy specimen; he was completely satisfied. Our apartment was small, and we moved to another, farther north, so the baby could have a separate room. Pearl's girl friends, her sister, and Willa, a black housemaid, helped her take care of our son.

I received an appointment as a clinical assistant in the department of surgery and attended the outpatient department. My fear that I would not have enough to do was quickly dispelled by my teaching in neurological anatomy, continuing research with Lewis Pollock, examining and caring for my patients. I began immediately to have my patients' hospital records copied for my own personal file, and I continued to do this throughout my professional life, ending up with almost ten thousand records of patients operated upon.

I suffered for weeks over the loss of Danny Sills. I was not able to talk it out at home, and I could not bring myself to discuss it with Pollock or Dr. Kanavel. Although I was sure they appreciated my feeling, they did not initiate a discussion. I had to apply Kanavel's dictum: Sit down, review every operation, step by step, and think how you might have improved the care of your patient.

An appointment to the attending staff at Wesley Memorial Hospital came, and I continued to woo Miss Johnson's and her nurses' interest in my operating techniques, drapes, and procedures. She assigned Jeannette Jones to me as my surgical nurse, and this relationship lasted after her graduation for twenty-five years. She was faithful, loyal, and ran her part of our team with precision, discipline, and a dedicated desire to help educate the young nurses assigned to my operating room, my interns, and residents.

Hale Haven, a six-foot-five graduate of the medical school, an Iowan by birth who moonlighted as a taxi driver to help pay his way through medical school, was my first neurosurgical resident. He asked to work with me, as did every other resident who followed him in neurosurgery or general surgery.

Hale Haven was followed by thirty neurosurgical and surgical residents all of whom worked for and received the master of science degree, and some of them earned the doctor of philosophy degree in surgery. I believe that professors of surgery should choose the men to come into their residency programs with care and discrimination; that they should take a personal interest in their education and training to be carried to the point where they should be helpful in providing opportunities for beginning their professional careers. I believe that men should be discouraged in their attempts to become surgeons, and their progress discontinued if after careful observation, discussion with and observation by his associates, the professor believes that the candidate's energies should be directed elsewhere. I believe in preceptorial teaching for surgical students.

In 1926 the medical school moved to the McKinlock campus on Chicago Avenue into the Montgomery Ward Building. Dr. Irving S. Cutter, a graduate of the University of Nebraska Medical School, a teacher of chemistry who had become dean of his medical school, accepted the deanship at Northwestern. By the terms of the merger agreement between the Chicago Medical College of Lind University and Northwestern, the dean of the medical school became a trustee of Northwestern University. Cutter was an excellent administrator, decisive, fair in his judgments, and dedicated to the improvement of the reputation of Northwestern University Medical School. He used his position as a trustee to oppose the plan of President Scott and Dean Black of the dental school to allot a disproportionate share of the new building to the dental school. He was successful and as a result of this first skirmish became an influential power in the board of trustees.

Cutter recognized the need for a hospital adjacent to the medical school and interested Russell Tyson and Mrs. Joseph Coleman, leaders of the board of governors of the defunct Passavant Memorial Hospital, to reactivate their board, raise money, and build a new hospital on ground provided by the university across Superior Street from the medical school. Cutter assumed the directorship of the new hospital; effected the closest relationship to the university of its affiliated hospitals; convinced the living members of the family of James Patten, the famous wheat king, who held the 6 per cent mortgage bonds on the hospital to accept 3 per cent interest; and almost singlehandedly saw the hospital through its initial struggles for existence.

Irving Cutter listened to my appeal through Dr. Kanavel, who had become the chairman of the department of surgery, for space in the new building for an experimental research surgical laboratory. One half of the fourteenth floor was allotted, and the laboratory began without a formal budget. My surgical nurse, Jeannette Jones, acted as secretary and assisted in experimental procedures. We continued to pay fifty cents for stray cats; we could obtain an occasional dog for an experiment from the supply obtained from the pound for the teaching of students in the physiology department. Finally, Dr. Cutter provided money for two dieners, George Smith and James Brooks, black men who were faithful and loyal workers who made substantial contributions to the initial success of the laboratory. I asked for money for essential supplies and equipment to pursue experimental problems which I proposed to the dean; I was never refused, but from where the money came, I was never informed. Neither did I account for its expenditure; he always knew, however, what we had succeeded in accomplishing and whether or not the manuscripts describing our work had been accepted for publication.

Dr. Kanavel decided to resign as chairman of the department of surgery and asked that his long-time friend and colleague at Wesley Memorial Hospital, Harry M. Richter, succeed him. Cutter specified that Richter agree that I should be his executive officer and administer the department. Richter was an excellent technical surgeon; an idealist, absentminded, uninterested in his financial relation with his patients, and not a particularly acute diagnostician compared with Kanavel. Loyal and faithful to the medical school and his friends, he was not ambitious to become chairman of the department and accepted the provision willingly. At no time did he impose his ideas or will upon my activities, which I assumed, with the clear understanding that the position would not exclude me from consideration as Richter's successor, providing I did a good job.

The next few years were occupied with an organization of the staff at Passavant Memorial Hospital which had been reactivated. Dr. Paul Starr, a colleague in the department of medicine, and I wrote the constitution and bylaws for the attending staff which were adopted. They provided for a medical board to consist of the chiefs of the divisions of surgery, medicine, obstetrics, and gynecology, the director of the hospital, the dean of the medical school without vote, and a president and secretary to be elected by the attending staff. The principle was established that the doctors should be responsible for all matters concerning the care of patients and the director and board of governors for the financial affairs of the hospital. We provided that the president of the attending staff should be invited to attend meetings of the board of governors, but not be a member, and for the opposite arrangement. All members of the attending staff were required to be members of the faculty of the medical school and if removed for cause from the medical school faculty could not be retained on the hospital staff, a condition that had contributed to the division of the staff at Wesley Memorial Hospital. This arrangement worked well from the time the hospital opened in June 1929 until the last few years when the philosophies of the care of patients and teaching of interns and residents in the divisions of medicine and surgery changed so radically that bylaws had to be adopted for the protection of the members of the attending staff who practiced medicine and surgery and voluntarily gave their teaching talents and abilities without remuneration. It was erroneously stated and acted upon that those doctors who were not remunerated by the hospital and/or the medical school, but who practiced medicine and surgery for their livelihood, were not good teachers. Discriminatory administrative acts were instituted that divided the loyalties of the staff. Unfortunately, the board of governors of Passavant Memorial Hospital have never been sufficiently aware of the fact that patients enter their voluntarily supported hospital because of their doctors who care for their illnesses and not because the building stands as a hospital. This divisive philosophy exists elsewhere between medical school salaried, administrative and teaching doctors and doctors engaged in professional practice. It exists also between teachers of the preclinical sciences in medical schools and the voluntary teaching clinical faculty. The result is a lack of understanding and communication that is evidenced in an inefficient curriculum which should be directed wholly toward teaching young men and women how to care for sick patients. A medical school has no other primary function. If two or three students in each class are inspired and directed toward teaching and research in nonclinical fields such as anatomy, physiology, chemistry, and pathology, it would constitute a good yield.

Pollock and I continued our joint research investigations, and he obtained an invitation for us to present our studies in decerebrate rigidity to a combined meeting of the American Neurological Association and British neurologists in London. Our son was two years old, and I proposed that Pearl make the trip, thinking that her mother could come to Chicago and with Willa look after Richard. Perhaps I did not insist strongly enough, but at any rate I, alone, went to England with the Pollocks on the S.S. *New York*.

Dr. John Favill, a Chicago neurologist, and I shared a cabin. He insisted that he could teach me to swim before we sailed. There was no pool at the YMCA in Galesburg, and I was not allowed to go to the artificial lake at Highland Park to learn to swim. My medical school classmates had tried to give me lessons in Lake Michigan at the foot of Twenty-ninth Street. Howie Goodsmith saved me from drowning in the Wilson Avenue YMCA pool when I saw a youngster going down for the third time and jumped in feet first after him. Howie plunged across the pool and rescued both of us. John Favill tied a rope around my chest, shouted instructions from the edge of the pool, and succeeded only in blistering my skin as the wet rope tightened.

On shipboard, I acquired a skin infection from an athletic supporter I used while exercising. When we landed and were on the train from Southampton, my temperature rose, and my colleagues wondered if I had an anthrax infection. This was not conducive to my peace of mind. Alfred Taylor, an older neurological surgeon from New York, came to the Mayfair Hotel, examined me, and treated me with the directness and confidence characteristic of a good general surgeon, who had directed his interests to surgery of the nervous system. He obtained carbolic acid from the nearest chemist's shop, some large straight needles that he dipped into the phenol, and then punctured each pustule in several places. The rapidity and dexterity of the procedure recalled Dr. Horrell's treatment of my childhood injury. The pain didn't last long.

The evening before our presentation the Pollocks and I were invited to dinner at the Covenant Club within walking distance of the hotel. They had accepted an invitation for cocktails, and I walked to the club still a trifle septic and feverish. I found myself at a round table covered with silverware and goblets out of which projected a gleaming white napkin. For some reason that defied the rules of protocol I was seated next to the tall, gaunt wife of the president of the British Medical Association, Lady Berry. I was embarrassed, ill at ease, and at a loss to know how to begin a conversation with her. She had a slight impediment in her speech due to an ill-fitting upper denture. I opened by asking her how far it was from the Mayfair Hotel to the club. Before she could answer I grasped the edge of the napkin and pulled it from the goblet. Whereupon, a hard roll popped out, rose, and descended among the silverware with a clatter. She watched this performance and then quietly replied, "Just a biscuit's throw." I sat silently the rest of the dinner trying to make no mistakes in choosing my silver from that of my crowded-together dinner partners.

Following the meeting, at which our original research work was received favorably, if not enthusiastically, I went with the Pollocks to St. Raphael in France where we enjoyed the Mediterranean blue sky and the beach for a week, and then spent three days in Paris before sailing from Le Havre.

In retrospect, I am sure that my desire to excel in my profession contributed as much as, if not more than, Pearl's disinterest in my professional life, ambitions, and friends to the slowly progressive and ultimate disintegration of our marital relations. I accept the onus of not having insisted strongly upon her accompanying me on our trip to England. In an effort to try to save the situation, I agreed to move to Evanston, Illinois, to a larger, nicer apartment. Still, Pearl's use of and reliance upon her girl friends and Willa in the care of our son became more pronounced. Suddenly, she made the decision to take Richard and visit friends in Los Angeles. It was but a week or so later that she informed me that she was going to Reno, Nevada, to seek a divorce.

I had never discussed my domestic affairs with Dr. Kanavel, but one day he took me into a patient's vacant room at Wesley Hospital and without preamble said that he had been aware of the difficulty I was experiencing in my marriage and said, "Never hug a bad bargain to your breast." The opposite advice came from Lewis Pollock, also without solicitation. It was that a divorce would react unfavorably upon my professional career, and every effort should be made to avoid it. I did not contest the divorce. Typically, my father and mother did not ask questions, entered into no discussion with me about the situation, and were most concerned about the opportunities they might have for a close relationship with their grandson, which proved to be a close and affectionate one through the years.

I met Edith Luckett Robbins on shipboard on our trip to England. She had worked in the theater from the time she was fifteen years of age, introduced into her profession by her brother Joe, the eldest of a family of seven children, three of whom were living. Her father worked for the Adams Express Company in Washington, D.C., having moved his family there from Petersburg, Virginia, where her mother returned to have each child delivered so they could claim to be a Virginian by birth. Joe began to earn his living as a youngster and became the manager of a theater in Washington which billed stock companies and played John Mason, Charlotte Walker, John Drew, and many other stars of the theatrical world.

At one evening performance the child in the play became ill, and Joe substituted his baby sister. She had no lines, but the climax of the play came when the child died. There were audible cries of sympathy from the women in the audience. As the curtain fell and rose again for the cast to be applauded, Edith raised up from the bed and waved to the gallery to assure them that she had not died.

This beginning was followed by a career in the theater associated with Chauncey Olcott, George M. Cohan, Alla Nazimova, Grant Mitchell, Walter Huston, and Spencer Tracy, among others. She had been the leading lady of stock companies in Pittsfield, Massachusetts; Atlanta; Dallas; and Trenton, New Jersey. She had married, retired from the theater, had a daughter, and after a divorce returned to the theater to support her child and herself. She came to Chicago in *The Baby Cyclone,* written, produced, and directed by Mr. Cohan, starring Grant Mitchell and staged at the Blackstone Theater. Later, she returned to Chicago with Walter Huston in *Elmer the Great.* I invited Dr. and Mrs. Kanavel and Dr. and Mrs. Pollock to have dinner with Edith and me and attend the performance.

Dr. Kanavel invited himself to her apartment for her to cook dinner to make certain, he told her, whether it was right for us to be married. The outcome was that he was our best man, and Nancy was her mother's bridesmaid. My father and mother were devoted to Edith, as she was to them, and my professional and personal life became calm and happy. She taught me to change my asocial tendencies and habits, to develop a sense of humor, to retain my desire and energy to succeed but to relax and enjoy the association of friends.

With Nancy and Dick we spent a vacation in the summer with Walter and Nan Huston at their home in the mountains near Running Springs and Lake Arrowhead. It was a beautifully built and arranged house without a telephone but every other modern convenience: a swimming pool, a tennis court, and an outdoor dining platform on a point of the mountain that overlooked Riverside.

Walter and Nan had played *Othello,* the costumes and stage setting for which had been designed by Robert Edmond Jones who had married Walter's sister Margaret, who had aspired to an operatic career but had become a speech coach for actors. Her most famous and prize pupil was John Barrymore. We built and flew kites, worked on the water supply pipes, and visited Crovenay House, a tree house that Walter had built himself. He challenged me to build two bedside tables for our apartment in Chicago in his shop which was outfitted with lathes, electrically driven saws, planes, and other carpenter's tools. I finished them with Walter supervising the job, stained, varnished, and packed them for shipment to Chicago.

I was intrigued by the name—Crovenay House—believing it to be named after the inscription, "Alastair, duc de Crovenay," on the small brass plate on the oil portrait of an eighteenth-century man which hung, properly lighted, in our bedroom. Edith, characteristically, accepted my surmise that perhaps he was an ancestor of Walter's, who was born in Toronto. Finally, I asked about Alastair.

When Walter began to work in the theater, he played a single act in which he sang songs that he composed and did a soft-shoe tap dance. One of the songs was "I Haven't Got the Do-Re-Mi"; another was "Why Speak of It Now?" One night he and a fellow vaudevillian returned after their three-a-day performances to their inexpensive hotel. Sitting in the lobby was an old man, with a beard, smoking a pipe and spitting into the convenient spittoon. Lying beside him was a mongrel dog. Walter approached him and said to his fellow performer, "I'll bet you ten dollars that's a purebred Crovenay." Quickly, the cue was taken up, and they argued pro and con calling attention to the dog's tail, his head, body, and legs, as they approached the man. Finally, Walter said, "You've heard us arguing about your dog. Tell me, isn't he a purebred Crovenay?"

The old man took his pipe out of his mouth, spat, and said, "No, he isn't, but his mother was."

The following day they were on the train going to their next engagement. The brakeman was officious, talkative, and an obvious target for their simple humor. They saw ducks flying in the sky, and as the brakeman came near, they started a heated argument. Walter claimed they were Crovenays; his friend strongly insisted that they were just plain mallards. They asked the brakeman, who had stopped by and was looking out the window, to settle the argument. Pompously, after giving the question serious consideration, he said, "Crovenays don't fly this far north."

This was the beginning of the Crovenay story. Margaret Jones searched the antique stores of New York, found the portrait, had it refurbished, and affixed the brass plate, naming him Alastair, duc de Crovenay. Upon Walter's death, I inherited the portrait and recounted the story to Dr. Daniel Collier Elkin, a fine surgeon and a dear friend, born in Lancaster, Kentucky, professor of surgery and chairman of the department at Emory University. Dan had a great sense of humor, a fine judicial sense of what was and was not important, and took great delight in the story. So we founded the Crovenay Society. We chose those qualified for membership, but they had to establish their qualifications by getting a stuffed-shirt, know-it-all individual who was never able to admit that he didn't know an answer, to accept the Crovenay legend.

One of Dan's friends in Atlanta became a member by taking a subject to lunch and telling how much he had enjoyed a visit to Dan's farm in Kentucky. He said that Dan had a few acres of tobacco, cotton, some pigs, and a cow or two, but his real hobby was raising grass. The luncheon guest considered himself an authority on grass and particularly the grass planted on golf fairways and greens. Dan's friend described a new grass, bluer than blue grass, better than fescue, hardier than rye. The subject asked what it was named.

"Crovenay."

"Oh, yes, I know, but it won't grow in Georgia."

Dan's friend was elected to membership and became the third member of the Crovenay Society. Alastair's portrait and the correspondence between members of the Crovenay Society, which included Ty Cobb, are now in the Daniel C. Elkin Memorial Room in the University of Kentucky in Lexington.

Walter read Polonius' speech to Laertes, directing it particularly to Richard. When he had finished, he asked him what it meant. The boy summarized the speech pretty well, but Walter was not satisfied. So he read it as an Italian father, a Swedish father, a Negro father would have read it, emphasizing its philosophy accompanied by humor and laughter. The following morning Dick paced up and down the tennis court, with the copy of *Hamlet* held behind his back, memorizing the speech. This was a great example of teaching by an inherently, naturally gifted teacher.

Later during that visit, he asked me to tell him about the episode that occurred in Milwaukee when Theodore Roosevelt campaigning on the Bull Moose ticket had been shot. I had finished the manuscript of the life of Dr. John B. Murphy under whose care Roosevelt was placed when he was brought by train to Chicago. Walter had read the manuscript, and I said that he had read it. "I know, but tell me." When I had finished, Walter said, "Now, go right in the house and write it down exactly the way you just told me. What you have on paper now reads like the description of an experiment; it's not loose and easy." The result was that I wrote the entire manuscript over again.

The greatest lesson I learned from this natural actor, who instinctively knew how to portray a character but could not read aloud intelligibly, occurred on a subsequent visit to the mountain retreat. In the meantime, Nancy had taken the initiative and consulted Orville Taylor, an attorney who lived in the same apartment building, about the steps necessary for me to adopt her. I wished it very much but was somewhat hesitant to institute the proceeding because her father and paternal grandmother were alive. After she was advised by her attorney, she made a trip east, met them at the Waldorf Astoria Hotel, obtained her father's signed agreement, and upon her return I soon had my daughter legally.

Edith and Nan drove down the mountain to Los Angeles on a shopping trip and were to be gone overnight. Nancy, Walter, and I had our dinner and were sitting in chairs in the sunken area around the large fireplace, engaged with our own thoughts. For days I had been occupied by the knowledge that this man had just received $75,000 for making the motion picture of his stage success, *Dodsworth*. I had more education than he; I could read aloud better than he, but a $500 fee for a brain operation and all my care was exceptional. I convinced myself that by applying myself, given the opportunity, I could be Sam Dodsworth just as effectively as Walter had been and demand the same salary. I found myself looking at him critically, watching him to see what he had that I didn't.

Suddenly, Walter said, "I've got a machine over there that we can make a record on and play it back. Let's do a radio broadcast and surprise the girls when they come back. I'll be the announcer, and you and Nancy play the parts. It'll be sponsored by the Crovenay Bear Rug Company and star Nancy Pantsy Davis." I leaped at the invitation. Here was my chance to show how well I could act. When he and Nan had played *Dodsworth* in Chicago, they stayed in our

231

apartment, and many nights I would drive down to the theater to bring them home while Edith prepared a bedtime snack. Often, I arrived early and stood in the wings while they played the last scenes. Particularly, I had watched the scene in the bedroom in Paris when Sam and Fran had such an argument that the hotel clerk called their room because of a complaint. I had almost memorized Sam's lines.

"Have you got a script of *Dodsworth* around?" He had and I read Sam's lines, and Nancy read the lines of the role originally played in New York by Fay Bainter.

Walter was effusive in his praise of my reading. "That was great, kid, marvelous. Won't the girls be surprised? Let's do another."

I was ready for anything, convinced that I was a natural and with the opportunity could get $75,000 for acting in a film.

"What about a scene from *Othello?*" said Walter. "Nancy, you play Desdemona; your father can do Iago, and I'll do Othello."

We started, and Desdemona and Iago spoke. I read with assurance against Nancy's young, childish voice. Suddenly, Othello spoke. I looked up, and there Walter was in a pair of tennis shoes, swimming trunks, and a T-shirt sitting in a chair. As I listened, his hair became darker and curly; his face became black, and I could see the earrings in his ears. There before me was Othello in the flesh. I was late in picking up my cue, and as I read on I became worse and worse. I was trying to match that expressive voice and face. I failed miserably and knew it, but true to his personality, Walter laughed heartily and made Nancy and me feel that we had done a good job and that the girls would be properly impressed.

The next evening after supper we sat about the fireplace, and Walter announced his surprise and played the *Dodsworth* segment. Edith and Nan congratulated Nancy but were effusive in their praise of my performance. "No doubt about it, the kid was great. Now, we've got another one for you." As he played the *Othello* segment and I spoke against him, Edith looked at me in surprise and disbelief. Nan shook her head. When it had finished, Edith said she couldn't believe that I could have read it so badly after having heard the *Dodsworth* record. "You became hammier and hammier. I bet you were even making faces as you read the lines." I had learned by now not to take offense, to see the humor in a situation at my own expense. Edith had taught me that. We went to bed enjoying the fun we had provided for ourselves.

Several days later Walter and I were sitting at the edge of the pool looking out over the mountains at peace and without the necessity for conversation. Suddenly, he put his hand on my knee and said, "Kid, the first time I sat in the stands and saw you operate, I thought I could do it, too." We chuckled together both recognizing the basic truth exemplified in the entire episode. This remained an understanding shared with no one until his sudden death in 1950 from a ruptured abdominal aneurysm. His friendship, his talents, his natural understanding of people, and his gentleness made a great contribution to my life. He was an actors' actor, just as Dr. E. Starr Judd at the Mayo Clinic was the surgeons' surgeon.

I had been elected a member of the small Society of Neurological Surgeons and had invited them to spend a day with me at Wesley Hospital on their way to Rochester where we would spend two days with Alfred Adson. The purpose of the society was to watch the host member operate and listen to presentations of interesting patients and research work. I sectioned the sensory root of the fifth cranial nerve in a patient with trigeminal neuralgia and removed an intradural spinal cord tumor which was benign and came out completely. As I left the operating room, Dr. Cushing walked beside me, put his arm around my shoulders, and said, "Excellent, and you know enough not to talk while you're operating."

We went on to Rochester and had been invited to go directly from registering at the hotel to Dr. William Mayo's home for breakfast. Dr. Franklin Martin and Dr. Mayo had been on a trip to Australia and returned home full of enthusiasm for an operation performed by R. D. Royle, an orthopedic surgeon, and based upon anatomical studies of John Hunter, which consisted of removing parts of the sympathetic nervous system for the relief of spastic paralysis. Drs. Kanavel, Pollock, and I had questioned the soundness of the operation and had performed a series of animal experiments that did not support Royle and Hunter's claims. Dr. Mayo had directed that the operation be performed at the clinic and regarded our criticisms of his acclaim for the operation as unfriendly. Dr. Martin told me of Mayo's characteristics. "He's like an Indian; he's a good hater and a good supporter. Watch yourself on your trip to Rochester."

As we came out of the hotel, Dr. Cushing invited me to ride in the taxicab with him. I was tense and fearful that I might not be greeted favorably by Dr. Mayo and hoped that he wouldn't know who I was. He was on the porch welcoming his guests. Cushing and Will Mayo greeted each other warmly and affectionately. Dr. Cushing said, "Will, this is Loyal Davis." I shall never forget the appraising look from Mayo's steely blue eyes nor the moment when I wondered if I was to be allowed to enter. Finally, he said, "So you're Loyal Davis." He shook my hand and said, "Come in and enjoy your breakfast." I feel sure Franklin Martin had told Harvey Cushing of the situation that might develop if Mayo wished to show his displeasure. Cushing had taken me under his wing.

Franklin H. Martin was a graduate of the Chicago Medical College, later to become Northwestern University's medical school. He had married Isabelle Hollister, the daughter of Dr. John Hollister, one of the founders of the medical school. He quickly developed a large practice in gynecological surgery and had carried out one of the first experimental studies upon implantation of a severed renal ureter into the bowel.

He had become impatient with the editors of the journals to which he had submitted his papers describing his clinical experiences and experimental work; particularly, those devoted to gynecology and obstetrics which were published and owned by commercial publishing companies. Thomas E. Donnelley, a fellow Midlothian Golf Club member and a favorite golf partner, was a son of R. R. Donnelley and an important figure in the affairs of the rapidly growing printing company. Martin asked many questions and proposed convincingly that there was a golden opportunity to publish the finest possible surgical journal which would be successful. It should have editors who were practicing their profession and not full-time laymen or "hack" physicians. The quality of the paper should be the finest so that illustrations would reproduce with clear definition what the author wished to show. There should be no skimping on the number of illustrations used because the story told by a drawing or picture often saved the use of hundreds of words. The typography should be up-to-date and the copy expertly proofread. Above all, the magazine should appear on the first of each month without fail. Such a surgical periodical, he said, would have an appeal to the reader and provide an opportunity to stimulate the doctors in small communities to continue their medical education.

Martin proposed that the four young men who were associated with him in his clinical practice and experimental work, William Cubbins, Frederick Besley, John Hollister, and Allen Kanavel, join him in establishing a new surgical journal. Each of them was to contribute $500, and he would contribute $2,000. The first article in the first number of the first volume of *Surgery, Gynecology & Obstetrics* was written by the chief of the voluntary editorial staff, Dr. Nicholas Senn, under the title "Iodine in Surgery, With Special Reference to Its Use as an Antiseptic." This issue appeared July 1, 1905, and contained 112 pages, 30 of which were devoted to advertising material. Subscriptions numbered six hundred at the price of five dollars per year. In a signed editorial in the first issue, Martin wrote that the editors "realize that there is no call for another ordinary surgical journal, and that if they do not succeed in making this journal far beyond the ordinary, there is no reason for its existence."

There were many moments in the beginning when the life of the newborn magazine hung in the balance. Not enough manuscripts had been submitted to fill the third number. The associate editor, Kanavel, dug deep and with misgivings as to the propriety of the action, included his own manuscript on his study of acute infections of the hand. Slowly, the journal progressed. There was a financial deficit of $3,000 incurred after taxes had been paid in publishing the first twelve issues. The capital stock was increased from $25 to $50,000, and the Surgical Publishing Company was formed. From its beginning until his death in 1938, Allen Kanavel supervised the acceptance, rejection, and editing of the manuscripts submitted for publication.

Kanavel proposed that I become interested in the editorial functions of the journal. I accepted because it would provide an interesting review of the work being done in the entire field of surgery and I would be less likely to view surgery through the keyhole of neurological surgery. My chief began to teach me step by step, as he had during my surgical education and training. I read every manuscript submitted and then summarized it and defended to him my decision for its acceptance or rejection.

Eventually, Dr. Martin owned all of the stock of the Surgical Publishing Company, after remunerating his four young partners generously based upon their original investment. He purchased the servants' quarters and carriage house of the McCormick home on the northwest corner of Rush and Erie streets adjacent to the American College of Surgeons and the John B. Murphy Memorial Building, for the new headquarters of his surgical journal. He accepted me upon Kanavel's recommendation as a new member of his group upon the condition that I would see my patients in the professional offices he had provided in the building.

In the September 1910 issue of *Surgery, Gynecology & Obstetrics,* Martin invited the subscribers of the journal, numbering 3,500, and all other physicians interested to visit the surgical clinics of Chicago, without dues or contributions of any kind. The journal would organize the clinics in the hospitals, invite the prominent surgeons of Chicago to participate, and ask the hotels to furnish space for a headquarters. The meeting was to be called the Clinical Congress of Surgeons of North America and was to last for two weeks. The program would consist of operative surgical clinics from 8 A.M. to 5 P.M. each day. Six evenings of the two weeks were given over to literary programs of surgical subjects conducted by the established medical societies of Chicago. All of the expenses were borne completely by *Surgery, Gynecology & Obstetrics,* and the staff of the journal manned the registration headquarters, listed the clinics and operations for each day, issued tickets of admission, and suggested points of interest to visit for the wives who accompanied their husbands. It had been forecast that if two hundred visitors attended, it would be a success. The booths for registration in the La Salle Hotel were overrun by thirteen hundred doctors. John B. Murphy's amphitheater at Mercy Hospital, which held five hundred, overflowed at every clinic he held.

Martin didn't believe in doing things by halves. He offered a full two weeks' program when a less confident entrepreneur might have been happily satisfied to have whetted his visitors' appetites with a week of activity rather than run the gamble of surfeiting even the most eager seeker after learning. There was no flagging of interest or enthusiasm on the part of either the visitors or the hosts. The Clinical Congress was repeated in 1911, 1912, and at the meeting in 1913, Martin succeeded in establishing and organizing the American College of Surgeons.

During my office hours three days a week, I read manuscripts and learned how to make up the manuscripts for the printer, how to determine the size of the reduction of illustrations and their placement, and most importantly, how to use judgment in choosing manuscripts for publication. Kanavel emphasized over and over again that the journal was a forum for the presentation of the clinical and experimental investigations of surgeons dedicated to the improvement of the care of surgical patients. The editors were not and could not be "poobahs" who took upon themselves the arrogant attitude of saying whether the author was right or wrong in his conclusions. We should be as positive as we could that he carried out his studies in a scientific and honest manner. We should not fail to provide space for manuscripts that expressed contrary views based upon good evidence. All editorials were to be signed and express the opinions of the authors, though these might differ greatly with those held by the editors. Finally, the material published should be kept as well balanced as possible between all fields of surgery and should be chosen to attract the interest of and aid the practitioner of surgery in communities not connected with a medical school to improve the care of his surgical patients.

I have had great pleasure in my association with *Surgery, Gynecology & Obstetrics* over the years, thirty-four of which I have been the editor in succession to Allen Kanavel. I trust that I have helped encourage young surgeons to express the results of their investigations and their opinions clearly and succinctly without arrogantly imposing my personal views and opinions upon them. I am convinced that Franklin Martin was completely correct when he insisted that the editors of his new journal should be engaged in the practice of surgery. *Surgery, Gynecology & Obstetrics* is the only surgical journal in which all of the steps in the production of each issue, except for the actual printing, is actively carried out and supervised by the general manager, the editors, and their staff. Upon the death of Franklin Martin in 1935, he left the 238 shares of stock in the Surgical Publishing Company to his wife with the provision that upon her death the stock was to become the property of the American College of Surgeons.

Franklin Martin described himself when he told me about the characteristics of William Mayo. He was energetic, full of ideas, imaginative, and intolerant of procrastination, indecision, or softly spoken evasive answers. He belonged to the Chicago South Side Social and Medical Society, a group of young men in the practice of medicine and surgery who were his contemporaries. Admission to membership required a unanimous vote. Meetings were held once a month from September through May; after dinner, at which formal evening dress was required, one of the members presented his latest clinical or experimental observations. Discussions were free, and the presenter could be interrupted at any point in his presentation. Frank Billings, Arthur Dean Bevan, Lewis L. McArthur, Edmund Andrews, James Herrick, and Edmund Doering were some of Martin's fellow members. On many occasions Martin attempted to have John B. Murphy elected to membership, but each time he failed the necessary unanimous consent.

In 1932, sixteen years after Murphy's death, the society met, and Bevan occupied the president's chair, which rotated through each member in turn, for the third time. Bevan's address evaluated the professors of surgery at Rush Medical College, and he concluded that the best had been John B. Murphy, although he had voted against him each time, and although Murphy had insisted that he act jointly with him in administering the affairs of the department of surgery. This precipitated a spirited discussion among the dwindling membership about Murphy, and again a vote was taken with the same result that had occurred during his lifetime.

The day after this meeting in the University Club, Dr. Martin called me into his office and told the story of the society and his efforts to have Murphy elected a member. He summarized by saying, "Young man, if sixteen years after your death, your contemporaries sit up until after midnight arguing about your good and bad qualities, you will have made it." Then, in his characteristic way, he said he expected me to deliver the John B. Murphy Oration at the next annual Congress of the American College of Surgeons which was to be held in the fall in Chicago and I should concern my oration with the man and not present a scientific contribution. One didn't lightly disagree with Franklin Martin, and I was challenged to find out everything I could about this surgeon about whom so many stories were in circulation.

I had gone to Mercy Hospital one Saturday morning in my first year of medical school and quietly and as unobtrusively as possible sat down in the last row high in his surgical amphitheater. I saw him in the pit with a patient on a cart and heard him questioning the senior medical students. He skipped from one row to another with his questions, and suddenly, illogically, I became panic-stricken with the thought that he might mistake me for one of the senior students and quickly left. He died the summer I entered my third year, and I had not had him as a teacher.

I went to Appleton, Wisconsin, visited the farm where he was raised and discovered the log cabin in which he was born. It had been sided and was being used as a tool and machine shed. The original tamarack logs could be seen on the inside, as well as the ladder leading to the loft where it could be imagined the children slept. I interviewed a few people who had grown up with J.B., one of whom had become the chief of police. I obtained a few items of interest from the eldest of his three daughters, but all of his office patient records had been ordered destroyed by his widow.

Searching for the facts regarding the Theodore Roosevelt shooting in Milwaukee and his subsequent treatment proved to be interesting and illustrated the personal prejudices that often color and distort the facts. Roosevelt's speech, which he carried in the inner pocket of his jacket, deflected the bullet, and it lodged within the pleural cavity without injuring the lung. He insisted upon giving his speech, dramatically pulling the manuscript from his pocket and indicating how it had saved his life. Immediately following his speech he was examined by a Milwaukee surgeon who agreed that he should be moved to Chicago. In the meantime, several laymen from Chicago who were prominent in the Bull Moose party called their personal surgeons, indicating that they would see that the famous patient would be placed under their care. As a result, A. J. Ochsner, Arthur Dean Bevan, and Murphy were called. Bevan made all preparations for his admission to Presbyterian Hospital; Murphy had an ambulance meet the train that was bringing Roosevelt to Chicago at the Clybourne Avenue junction, and he was removed to Mercy Hospital. In the audience was Dr. Joseph C. Bloodgood, of Baltimore, who was visiting relatives in Milwaukee. In a letter that Dr. Bloodgood wrote to me he said that he was the one who gave the final advice to have Roosevelt placed in Murphy's care.

When he arrived at Mercy Hospital, an X-ray plate was made which identified the position of the bullet. Murphy called Bevan in consultation, and it was decided not to attempt to remove the bullet. Every bulletin issued about the patient's condition was signed jointly by Murphy and Bevan. Armed with Bloodgood's letter, I interviewed Dr. Bevan, asking him just what had happened. He was bitter about the experience, saying that Murphy stole the patient from him. I told him that I had a letter from Joseph Bloodgood that contradicted that opinion. Bevan read the letter, tossed it back to me, saying, "Anyone who knows Joe Bloodgood knows that he is flighty and embellishes the facts to his own advantage." With that remark he dismissed me.

The oration was met with the same reception that any discussion of Murphy received. The personal reaction of members of the audience to the man's characteristics governed their acceptance or rejection of what I had written. This same reaction followed publication of my book, which was published in 1933 by the G. P. Putnam Company under the title *J. B. Murphy, the Stormy Petrel of Surgery,* and in England by Harrap under the title *Surgeon Extraordinary.* Adolph Kroch, the nationally known proprietor of Kroch's Bookstore on Michigan Avenue, was largely instrumental in promoting the sale of the book. He filled his window with display copies after convincing Melville Minton of the Putnam Company to publish it, guaranteeing that he would purchase 1,000 copies. Kroch's confidence was supported by the fact that the book sold 25,000 copies in the United States and Great Britain.

I was in the position of being able to write the account of Murphy's life as an unprejudiced observer, trying to record the story as it had unfolded from my research. I suppose I should not have expected his daughters to have liked the book, and his second daughter, Mildred, was particularly vehement in her comments. It was clear that their mother dominated the family life, and the daughters saw little of their father and were never close to him. One of them confided to a friend that she could not remember ever having sat upon her father's lap. Harvey Cushing, to whom I had sent an autographed copy, thanked me and said, "You did the best job that could have been done; he was hardly a one-volume man." Perhaps the one incident that was so characteristic of the clever, ambitious, skillful, and confident teacher and surgeon occurred when he stood with the referring physician and the patient's parents, looking at the X-ray plate of a complicated fracture of the femur. After a long pause, he said, "This is a serious fracture which will require an operation by a master surgeon." The reply that came from the physician was, "That's why we are here, Doctor Murphy."

Murphy supported Martin's adventure in publishing a surgical journal and later agreed to become chief of the editorial consulting group. He vigorously backed the clinical congresses and was the deciding voice that convinced Martin to propose and organize the American College of Surgeons. Martin did not accept criticisms of Murphy lightly and intimated that, perhaps, I might have been a bit more complimentary.

Upon Dr. Kanavel's recommendation, I was offered and accepted a post as consultant in neurological surgery to the Veterans Administration Hospital at Hines, Illinois. I visited the hospital once a week, examined, and dictated my notes upon the patients. It was not long before patients with definite indications for neurosurgical diagnostic and operative procedures were being referred to the hospital. I did not relish the thought of operating upon patients there. There were no neurosurgical instruments, no nurse or doctor anesthesiologists, and no interns or residents. I took my own instruments, Miss Jones, and my resident to the hospital each week. It required several years before the bureaucracy of the Veterans Administration provided a set of proper instruments. I encouraged one of the full-time employed doctors on the neurological wards to assist us at the operations and take charge of the postoperative care of the patients. The operations were all performed under local anesthesia, and this was a trial for both the patient and the surgeons, but it afforded the safest—in fact, the only—way that anesthesia could be provided.

The neurosurgical service grew, and by the end of World War II we had three neurosurgical wards in addition to wards designed, supplied, and decorated exclusively for spinal cord injury patients, over twelve hundred of whom were examined and rehabilitated by three neurosurgical residents and two attending neurological surgeons. The neurosurgical residents who had their education and training during this period have had more experience without question in the treatment of patients with spinal cord injuries than the majority of neurological surgeons. When the new Veterans Administration Research Hospital was built upon the campus of Northwestern University's medical school, our efforts were concentrated at that institution, and the residency program was discontinued because the Hines Hospital was no longer the only center to which neurosurgical patients were referred. My relation as a consultant to the Veterans Administration lasted thirty-six years. I am particularly proud of the fact that I was instrumental in convincing Paul R. Hawley, the medical director of the Veterans Administration, who assumed that position following his military service as chief surgeon of the European theater of operations, that his idea to place the Veterans Administration Hospital medical care under the supervision of medical schools would elevate the medical and surgical care of veterans and make these hospitals prestige places for education and training. Northwestern University's medical school was the first to assume such a responsibility.

I was attending a meeting of the Society of Neurological Surgeons in Boston and was at dinner when I received a telephone call from Edith saying that I had been appointed chairman of the department of surgery to succeed Dr. Richter. Dr. Richter had called Edith to tell her after the appointment had been confirmed and announced at a meeting of the medical council. I learned later that the only objection that was raised was my age of thirty-six, which Dean Cutter promptly answered by saying that time would take care of that objection.

242

MANY of the older members of the surgical faculty had been my teachers for whom I had respect. The problem was to get their co-operation in administering the department of surgery. There were changes I thought would improve the teaching of surgery at the medical school and in the hospitals affiliated with the university. Northwestern University did not have its own teaching hospital; it was dependent upon three voluntarily supported hospitals and their staffs for teaching the clinical years of medicine. The chairman of the department of surgery could not arbitrarily appoint a chief of the surgical service at Wesley Memorial or Evanston hospitals. It was not difficult for me to assume that position at Passavant Memorial Hospital. I knew I would have the co-operation of Frederick Christopher who was the chief of the surgical service at Evanston Hospital; I was uncertain about Raymond McNealy, whom Dr. Kanavel and I had persuaded to come to Wesley Hospital from St. Luke's Hospital to be the chief of surgery, when a large number of surgeons had transferred their practices to Passavant Hospital when it opened. I could not blame any of the older men for being ambitious and having a subconscious, if not an open, desire to make it difficult for me.

I planned to have the surgical clinical clerks, who were junior students, assigned to the three hospitals equally and to have the surgical teaching carried on in each hospital by the surgical faculty attending men. I wanted to discontinue surgical classes that met early in the morning three times a week in a classroom in the medical school that was completely removed from immediate contact with patients. I hoped to have the students assigned to the different surgical services in each hospital; to examine patients, to take part in operations, and to follow their postoperative course; in fact, to have them become an integral part of each service and be supervised and taught by the intern, resident, and attending faculty men on the service.

I wished to have the same teaching curriculum carried out at each hospital and specifically to make each student responsible for coming to the seminar classes prepared to ask questions and discuss the subject matter. I had suffered through the question-and-answer type of classroom teaching in surgery. I expected to outline the subject matter for each seminar and cover the principles of surgery in every field within the three months of the surgical clerkship. I planned to abolish surgical clinics and lectures. I had never been able to see what was being done at an operation, sitting in a gallery, while the surgeon mumbled his teaching pearls as he was struggling to identify the common bile duct. I was quite sure that there was no one on the faculty, including myself, who could keep the attention of students for an hour unless he was showman enough to divert them every ten minutes by relating an entertaining story or performing some acrobatic stunt. I had learned through my association with Walter Huston and Edith's friends of the theater how difficult it is to hold the attention of an audience. I have never had reason to change this opinion based upon my own experiences and observing the performances of naturally talented speakers. I had no idea how difficult it would be to effect my plans and how long it would take to bring them into being.

I invited the members of the surgical faculty of professorial rank to luncheon at the University Club, including a special invitation to Dr. Kanavel. Edith had helped me order the meal, and the only defense I have for not serving cocktails is that in 1932 it was not the custom. Perhaps it would have been better had I ignored custom. There were no refusals of the invitation, and I hoped to present my ideas modestly and have a constructive discussion that would lend support for my plans. I knew enough not to begin talking while my guests were eating, but when they had finished, I suggestively proposed some of my ideas.

There was silence; not opposition, not approval, just silence. This was my first lesson in how damning and effective silence can be. I tried other approaches; questions evoked evasive, noncommittal answers. Compliments about their past performances, loyalty to the medical school and to my predecessors were accepted, I thought, as a matter of course. Time was passing, and I felt guilty at keeping them from their office hours or operating schedules. Finally, I took the bit in my teeth and in exasperation briefly outlined my plans and said they would become effective when classes began in the fall. No one thanked me for the luncheon; I suppose they may have thought the department footed the bill, not knowing that there was no departmental budget, or that giving luncheons and dinners was one of the fringe benefits of being the chairman.

Dr. Kanavel left the club with me, and we walked up Michigan Avenue to go to our office. Suddenly, as we came to the Spaulding Gorham jewelry store, he stopped me and said, "What have you got on the end of your watch chain?" I had learned not to search through my pockets looking for a match if he asked me for one; I should know whether or not I had a match and if so, in which pocket it was. So, I didn't look at my watch chain.

"I have a small locket with my mother's, father's, Edith's, Nancy's, and Dick's pictures reproduced on the metal leaves."

"Come on, it isn't heavy enough."

For just a moment I thought he was buying me a present to commemorate my assuming the chair of surgery. It was only for a moment because I knew this would be entirely out of character for him. Just what he had in mind I couldn't imagine. In the jewelry store he asked to see small silver knives that could be attached to a watch chain. He chose one, hooked it on, and we left the store. I tried to find the reason for his generosity; it was a beautiful knife and I haltingly thanked him for it.

"You don't know why I gave it to you. The next time you are in a position such as you were this noon, take out your watch chain, open and close the knife, or twirl it around in your hand but remain silent. Sit them out until one of them will have to speak. You made some enemies today by your impatience and exasperation which I must say were completely justified. It's better to let them come to their own conclusions that you expect to run things rather than to tell them you are."

I admired and respected Dr. Kanavel's judicial sense; he always had definite opinions and expressed them but never in a manner of confrontation. He believed that time cured many unpleasant and illogical situations and was patient enough to await the result. His methods proved effective in his relations with Franklin Martin, whose imagination and aggressiveness, if not tempered by sound appraisal of the situation offered by Kanavel and his wife, led to decisive acts from which he had to be extricated. Although I have remembered Dr. Kanavel's teachings and have tried to put them into practice, I have not always been successful. I twirled my knife many times and eventually substituted a cigarette, which I imagined was less obvious.

Dr. Kanavel continued to teach me until shortly before his death. Walter and Nan Huston and Edith and I were playing bridge on a rainy Sunday afternoon in our apartment when a knock came on the door. It was Dr. Kanavel who insisted that we continue playing the hand that had been dealt. The bidding went on, and I got the bid and played the hand. When the hand was completed, Dr. Kanavel asked if we had any objection if he redealt the cards and he reviewed my bidding. This he did perfectly and without effort showed that I should have bid more and that I could have made the bid. Then, just as suddenly as he had come, he left. Nan Huston angrily attacked me saying how could I submit to such an insult and she added, "in your own house, too." When she had finished, Walter said quietly, "You don't understand. Don't you know that Loyal will always be his boy and that he will always try to make him do things better? Loyal and Edith understand, and I would lose my respect for him if he resented it in the slightest way."

As I had anticipated, Frederick Christopher, who was a fellow member of the Billings Medical Club, which had been modeled after the old Chicago South Side Medical and Social Society, helped carry out our plans at Evanston Hospital. There was little difficulty with Raymond McNealy until Wesley Memorial Hospital moved into its new home across the street from the medical school and Passavant Hospital. McNealy succeeded in being appointed superintendent of the hospital which, by the terms of the affiliation between the hospital and the university, made him a member of the board of trustees of the university. I thought it was anomalous for an associate professor of the department of surgery to be a trustee of the university and asked him to resign from the faculty with the provision that if, at any time, he wished to relinquish his position as superintendent, I would welcome him back on the faculty at the same rank. This he refused to do and took the matter to the president of the university, Franklin Bliss Snyder. I defended my position to Snyder who didn't know that the appointments of associate professors in the medical school were for a term of five years and McNealy's appointment ended in June. I didn't reappoint him, but at the end of a year McNealy was requested to resign as superintendent by the trustees of the hospital, whereupon I reappointed him at the same rank to the faculty.

I decided that I had been in the practice of neurological surgery long enough to qualify for admission to the American College of Surgeons as a Fellow. It was necessary to submit the records of fifty patients upon whom a variety of operations had been performed for scrutiny by a credentials committee, in addition to a curriculum vitae. I had had my patients' records typed, and all of the data were in each folder including in every instance a record of my own examination and my dictated, descriptive operative note. I had the files moved from my office in the medical school, where I also kept gross specimens and microscopic slides of the tissues removed at operation, to the college and presented them as evidence of my qualifications. Martin was generous in his praise and immediately established a prize consisting of a life fellowship without dues for the candidate who presented the best histories. It was not retroactive, he said, and besides I was one of the family and he wouldn't practice nepotism.

The American College of Surgeons had been founded in 1913 by Martin and his contemporaries for the sole purpose of elevating the standards of the care of surgical patients. There was no other purpose then, and the goal has remained the same. In addition to annual gatherings at which knowledge, talents, skills, individual characteristic traits, and mannerisms were exchanged, the problem of establishing minimum standards for hospitals was attacked. Some of the founders insisted that the initial reports of the investigation of hospitals was so damning that, if published, the ultimate goal would be defeated. So the papers were burned in the furnace of a New York hotel. However, there was a minority led by Martin who, because they held so deeply that indifference becomes a crime, believed that it was a mistake to be moderate in condemning. This activity was later shared with the American Medical Association, the American

247

Hospital Association, and the American College of Physicians under the aegis of the Joint Commission for the Accreditation of Hospitals.

It was in 1913 that the college created the first opportunity for a discussion of cancer before a public audience, enlisted the help and interest of a popular author to write about the disease in lay magazines, and encouraged some of the Fellows to form the American Society for the Control of Cancer, later to become the American Cancer Society.

Rapid strides were being made by industrialization of the United States, and great changes were occurring in the speed of transportation. Recognizing these advances, the college instituted panel discussions on the problems of the patient injured accidentally. The contributions made to the improvement of the immediate and definite treatment of the injured patient and to the education of the medical profession and the public about the surgical, social, and economic problems of trauma through the activities of the Committee on Trauma and its regional divisions, have been monumental.

Immediately less successful, its eventual implementation shared, the original and imaginative suggestion was made that a progressive educational and training program be instituted by medical schools for graduates who aspired to become surgeons. The fundamentally important principle included in the proposal was that medical school faculties should prescribe the postgraduate curriculum and determine its fulfillment. That medical school faculties did not accept the challenge has been forgotten among the confusing claims of priority and the multiplicity of examining bodies for each surgical specialty which, it is ironically charged, resulted because the American College of Surgeons did not grasp its opportunity.

I learned that the first meeting of the board of regents, the policy-making body of the college whose members are elected by the board of governors, was devoted primarily to discussion of the principles of ethical and financial relations among patient, the surgeon, and the family doctor. There was no division of opinion, only differences about how to express themselves forcibly and unmistakably. Those among them, noted for their showmanship and facility of expression in their operating amphitheaters, were more conservative in describing rules of ethical conduct. Those of mild manner, quiet in speech, and affectionately regarded by their colleagues were vociferous in their demands to protect patients from being referred to the highest bidder.

The majority of the medical profession at the time held that doctors were not subject to the temptations of average human beings and would resist the lure of money. There were some among these who argued that although God did reveal the Ten Commandments to Moses, it requires thousands of laws to try to have them followed unsuccessfully, and therefore, it would be futile to prescribe disciplinary measures to enforce ethical principles of financial relations between the surgeon and the referring physician.

The times, occasions, and crises are innumerable upon which the college has emphasized the dignity of the family doctor and insisted that he be accorded his rightful share in the material and esoteric credit for restoring the patient's health. It has persisted in the belief that the physician must always display his self-respect and professional independence, and the surgeon must aid him in declaring his equality in responsibility and importance. The regents were fully aware more than fifty years ago that the time was passing rapidly when a doctor could maintain that he was both physician and surgeon and provide the best possible care for the patient.

In 1936 I was elected to fellowship in the American Surgical Association, the most prestigious surgical society in the United States. Shortly thereafter, at the instigation of Franklin Martin and Charles Mayo, I was elected to the Southern Surgical Association, one of tradition, high scientific standards, characterized by friendliness, frankness, and social graces. It was a long-observed custom that wives were an important part of each meeting. On the first morning of my first meeting at The Homestead in Hot Springs, Virginia, I went down to the dining room, and Edith had her customary light breakfast in our room. I sat down at an unoccupied round table but was soon joined by members who introduced themselves, and with their typical southern politeness and first-name friendliness, welcomed me. At last, Charles Green, a Texan, suddenly said, "Loyal, I suppose you think you were elected to the Southern Surgical Association because you're a good surgeon." It was a question, and I replied that I thought that was true. "You couldn't be farther from the truth," said

Green. "You were elected because your wife was born in Petersburg, Virginia." The laughter was general, and I appreciated fully the tribute to Edith and the not too subtle attempt to put me in my place.

At the end of my five-year tenure as chairman of the department of surgery, I read a report addressed to the dean, the members of the medical council, and the president of the university. I outlined the organization of the department and called attention to the fact that there was no specific budget for the department. I pointed out that the teaching of junior and senior students was carried on through the voluntary efforts of the 103 members of the surgical faculty who were engaged in the practice of surgery. Of 55 class-A medical schools from which information was gathered, Northwestern University Medical School was the only one that did not have a budget for its clinical faculty and curriculum. The situation seemed to me to be illogical and was a continuation of the practice that was necessary when the Chicago Medical College was founded. No other faculty of the university responsible for the teaching in one half of a school's curriculum functioned without remuneration.

As a result of the efforts of these men, the graduates of the medical school were universally recognized as among the best qualified and well educated and trained young men in the United States. Obviously, the teaching of the junior and senior students was carried out upon the private patients of the faculty, upon patients on the services of the faculty members on the staff of the Cook County Hospital, and upon an insignificant number of free beds provided by the voluntarily supported, affiliated hospitals.

The attending surgeons at the Cook County Hospital were dependent for their appointments on the intricacies and uncertainties of a civil service examination and, therefore, were quite independent of the department of surgery of the medical school. At any time the complexion of the surgical attending staff at the County could be changed by new political alignments, and the advantages that were then enjoyed could be unceremoniously and precipitately removed. I knew firsthand how the system worked. The appointments were based upon the final civil service grade which depended upon military service, years in practice, contributions to the literature, and the written examination. The County did not have an attending neurological surgeon, and I was the only one in Chicago. I figured that I would have had to get a grade of well over 100 upon the examination to have made a place, but nevertheless I had received a civil service appointment without remuneration. After discovering that every general surgeon on the staff wanted to demonstrate that he could operate upon neurosurgical patients as well as I could and that I had no opportunity to develop a neurosurgical service, I resigned.

I proposed that an adequate number of surgical teaching beds be provided under the immediate control of the medical school; that there be a fund provided for a minimum of twelve fellowships, or senior residents in surgery; that a minimum of fifteen thousand dollars a year be provided for experimental and clinical investigation; that a definite system of education and training of postgraduate students in surgery—that is, a hospital residency program—be instituted; and finally, that financial remuneration on a part-time basis be provided for the members of the faculty of surgery.

This was a revolutionary proposal, and I wonder now why I was not requested to resign from the chair of surgery. But again the proposal was met with polite silence; no argument or discussion, just silence. They regarded the young man's ideas with tolerance; he would learn that the financial support he requested so glibly was not available; besides, why pay for surgical teaching that was present for nothing in such abundance and excellence?

I did not believe, nor do I now, that financial remuneration from a medical school makes a man a better teacher than one who earns his living by his care of patients and teaches without remuneration. However, I do believe that the teachers of clinical medicine should not all be on a voluntary basis. I have observed the schism that existed between the paid teachers in the preclinical subjects and the voluntary teachers of clinical subjects. I have been deeply disturbed more recently by the same kind of division which has developed within the faculty of clinical teachers between those who receive the greater percentage of their income from the medical school and/or a hospital, and those whose income is totally dependent upon the practice of their profession.

In 1938 I lost two of the men who have had the most influence upon my life, my father and Allen Kanavel. My father suddenly developed symptoms of an intestinal obstruction, was operated upon, and found to have extensive metastases. He never complained, and when I took him home on the Burlington's diesel-powered Zephyr, he said that it was the first time he had ever ridden on a purchased ticket. I asked him how he had enjoyed the ride, and he said, "I could have made the same time with steam; his stop here was rough."

Dr. Kanavel was driving his sons, two of the triplets he and Mrs. Kanavel had adopted, with two of their playmates to his favorite fishing stream in California. He attempted to pass a trailer, which swerved in front of him, hiding his view of an oncoming car. He was killed instantly, but the boys escaped unhurt.

Our son, Richard, came to live with Edith, Nancy, and me that summer following the death of his mother. Mainly as a result of the fact that we took him on a trip through the civil war battlefields two successive summers, he wished to go to the summer camp at the Culver Military Academy. He chose to enter the Black Horse troop camp which he attended for three years. As the years have passed, all of us look upon his experience there with the greatest pleasure and with an appreciation of the contribution that the faculty made to his self-confidence, self-discipline, his knowledge of the responsibilities involved in taking care of a horse, and an appreciation of orderliness and routine.

Because Edith had sent him a book entitled *The Gray Knight,* a story of the life of Robert E. Lee, he had become an unreconstructed rebel. He was a great admirer of Jeb Stuart, and for the thesis he had to write his third year to qualify for the gold Tuxis, he described Stuart as the greatest cavalryman who ever lived. Each candidate had to stand an oral examination, while at attention, on the subject of his thesis. Dick was examined by two young officers of the faculty who challenged his position by championing Sheridan. That evening he called us, depressed and discouraged, saying that the two Yankees would certainly not recommend him for the Tuxis. At commencement, the two young officers sought Edith and me out and told us how he had maintained his position that Stuart was the greatest cavalryman in spite of their arguments. Tell him at the proper time, they said, that both of us are Southerners by birth.

I was appointed the editor of *Surgery, Gynecology & Obstetrics,* the second to hold that position, in 1938 shortly after Dr. Kanavel's death. Franklin Martin had died in 1935. His death came from an acute coronary occlusion while he was on vacation at the Arizona Biltmore Hotel in Phoenix. The children, Edith, and I were spending a ten-day vacation there, and Mrs. Martin called me to see him. I telephoned Dr. Kanavel immediately in Pasadena, and he arrived that night. It took Dr. Kanavel's influence and strong persuasive arguments by both of us to get him to agree to the hypodermic injection of morphine that I had recommended. Mrs. Martin received the shares of the publishing company with the provision that upon her death they become the property of the American College of Surgeons. She received twelve thousand dollars a year as president of the company for the remaining ten years of her life; this was the extent of her inheritance.

At their request, I explained the financial affairs of the journal to the board of regents with the help and approval of Dr. Donald Balfour who was a director of the publishing company. Dr. Dallas Phemister, the treasurer of the college elected by the regents, insisted that an auditing firm be employed to study and report upon the affairs of the company. Dr. Phemister, a Chicago surgeon and professor and chairman of the department of surgery at the recently organized University of Chicago Medical School, had been educated and trained by Arthur Dean Bevan. Indoctrinated in a dislike for Martin by Bevan, he was suspicious of the business affairs of the publishing company and was convinced that Martin had grown rich from the publication of the journal. Just why he believed that Martin should not have profited was difficult to understand, but when he learned that only a small amount of money was in reserve to conduct the affairs of the journal, he evidently became more suspicious. The college spent several thousand dollars for the examination of the organization and financial condition of the journal, and the report confirmed completely all that we had told the regents. Dr. Arthur

Allen, chairman of the board of regents, was strongly critical of the expenditure of money "to look a gift horse in the mouth."

Phemister telephoned me a few days after Mrs. Martin's death and in his sly, roundabout way, suggested that Sumner Koch, Michael Mason, and I should discontinue seeing our patients in the offices of *Surgery, Gynecology & Obstetrics.* He seemed pleased when I replied that I had already rented another office and had so informed Koch and Mason and thought they would act in the same manner.

In order to meet the requirements of the internal revenue service, and under the general managership of James Shannon, the Franklin H. Martin Memorial Foundation was created to publish the journal. The earnings are donated to the college for its educational purposes, and since 1945, over $2,500,000 has been contributed to the college. It has been printed by the R. R. Donnelley Company for sixty-six years, and under the general managership of John W. Evers, continues to have the largest paid circulation of any surgical journal.

TEN

THE second of July, 1942, was a hot, humid day, and Edith and I were sitting on a balcony just outside our bedroom overlooking Lake Michigan, hoping for one of the many frequent changes in the weather for which Chicago is noted, when the wind suddenly shifted to come off the lake. The telephone rang, and I heard the high-pitched, nasal, southern twang of Dr. Fred Rankin. He invited me to come to Washington for a conference on July 5.

Rankin, a surgeon from Lexington, Kentucky, had received his education and training in surgery at the Mayo Clinic, particularly from E. Starr Judd, the surgeons' surgeon. He had been appointed by James Magee, surgeon general of the United States Army, as chief of the surgery branch, Professional Services Division, in the rank of colonel.

Rankin brought Dr. B. N. Carter, of Cincinnati, to Washington. Rankin and Carter spoke in general terms of the service and important contribution I could make on the staff of the surgeon of the European theater of operations as the senior consultant in neurological surgery. Rankin said that Elliott Cutler, professor of surgery at Harvard, was going overseas as the consultant in surgery and that James Barrett Brown, the talented plastic surgeon of St. Louis, was already in England.

I remembered Cutler from when I was in Boston. He belonged to an old Boston family, had graduated first in his medical school class at Harvard, was energetic, fast-moving, and fast-talking. He had been appointed as professor of surgery at Western Reserve University in Cleveland and had returned to succeed Cushing. He had served in World War I with the Harvard Base Hospital Unit and had been decorated with the Distinguished Service Medal. I knew Barrett Brown as a casual acquaintance at surgical society meetings and had admired his skill, ability, and imagination in his field of plastic surgery.

I agreed that I was interested in the proposed assignment and took the application blanks that Rankin gave me. Again, all of the changes in my family and professional life kept turning over in my mind, and as my frustration increased, I became more and more anxious to return home from Washington. Finally, I was lucky enough to buy an airline passage, though military personnel priorities were in effect, and was on my way. When we landed in Indianapolis, after a bumpy ride, my seat on to Chicago was pre-empted by a military request, and I was bumped off. I was nauseated by the flight, by the emotional uncertainty of the correct decision, by the fact that I had indicated my willingness to accept the assignment perhaps too quickly, and barely got to the men's room before I vomited. When I recovered, I found a cab driver outside the airport terminal who was willing to take me to Chicago; I was obsessed with the idea of getting home quickly; my disturbing affliction of nostalgia had recurred in a serious attack. I wondered what I would do in England suffering from homesickness. Edith and I discussed the problem from every possible angle; I talked it over with Lewis Pollock, Dean Cutter, and several doctor friends. The consensus was that I should take on the job.

Commissioned in the rank of lieutenant colonel, thanked by Fred Rankin for accepting the assignment, and assured that I would make a great contribution to the war, the impression I got was that there were several general hospitals in the European theater and several would be added rapidly.

Donning a uniform for the first time on August 24, 1942, I became a passenger in a flying boat leaving La Guardia on September 5. The interval in Washington was passed in getting additional immunity injections, having passport pictures taken, being outfitted with a helmet and gas mask but refused the issue of a Colt 45 when the quartermaster sergeant saw my caduceus insignia, reporting briefly each day to the Medical Department Replacement Pool, and attending an unforgettable cocktail party to which I was conducted by Mrs. Henry Field, an old friend from home. It was obvious that Patsy knew that homesickness had already taken its toll, but I didn't know that Edith had telephoned her to look after me.

It was a large room crowded with people, a large mixture of uniforms, many languages being spoken, and a host and hostess known only to Patsy. Utterly unprepared for the surprise, Patsy introduced me to Mrs. Eisenhower and Mrs. Butcher, the general's aide's wife. Mamie Eisenhower quickly realized that the doctor before her was uncomfortable in his strange clothes, ill at ease in the crowd, and awed by the wife of the general whom he was sure he would see at mess daily, and with whom, undoubtedly, he would have the opportunity of talking at table, even though he might well sit at the foot. She graciously steered the conversation so that a rather detailed recital of my life came pouring out. I was convinced that soon I would be living and working close to the commanding general of the European theater of operations when in excusing myself at Patsy's insistence, Mrs. Eisenhower instructed me to tell Ike she sent her love. I next saw her and the general at their home in France in 1951 when he was the commanding general of the North Atlantic Treaty Organization. Edith and I are proud to have had Mamie Eisenhower as our friend since that time.

Patsy took me to a sofa at one end of the room where it was relatively quiet, and on which a tall man, wearing a black glove on one hand, sat. The introduction was mumbled. Patsy left quickly, and the stranger invited me to sit down. The voice was low, the speech typically British, the forehead was high, and unbelieving I heard, "The name's Halifax, Doctor. I take it you have been assigned overseas. We need your hospitals and doctors. Tell me about yourself. If people see us talking, they'll hesitate about coming over and I can rest, listen, and not be required to speak in platitudes. I can be your patient, and you can give me psychotherapy. Agreed?" With only an occasional question as to what my duties would be, to which I admitted ignorance, the time went quickly, and simultaneously we made the move to leave. With a smiling and grateful "Thank you, perhaps we shall meet again," the realization suddenly came that a great opportunity to learn exactly what was going on in the prosecution of the war had been lost. I was naïve enough to think that he would have answered my questions, if he knew. Now, I don't think he knew any more than I did.

After a short refueling stop at Botswood, Newfoundland, the flying boat made an uneventful trip and landed at Foynes, Ireland. I learned about the privileges of rank from a lieutenant colonel on board, who was active in the Reserve Officers' organization, carried a swagger stick, and spoke in a command voice. Each of us had a berth, which he arranged; we were given a breakfast of bacon and eggs at the inn in Foynes; received priority in seating on the plane that took us to Bristol. After a train ride to London, he took me to the Dorchester Hotel and magically got a spacious room for each of us. He realized the utter ignorance that I exhibited about military procedures and manners and decided to manage the medico. Perhaps it was the medical corps insignia that caused him to look after a grateful follower.

Later, I went down to the desk and handed in a cablegram addressed to Edith, announcing my safe arrival. Miraculously, it was accepted and delivered; why I will never know, because certainly it violated security. The brashness of ignorance overcame the strict rules of secrecy and security.

I learned more about my new position from another acquaintance next to whom I sat at luncheon in the officers' mess. He said I would have to learn to sit and do nothing; to realize that I would not be a doctor in the sense that I had practiced surgery; that the best thing I could do would be to find a project in which I could pour my time and interest. For example, a study of the science of ballistics and how fragmenting shells might penetrate helmets; what kind of wounds of entrance and exit machine gun bullets made.

In Cheltenham I was billeted in a private home on an estate that had been turned over to the Americans. I was warned the first night because I had not closed the black-out curtains in my room tightly. The next morning Elliott Cutler took me to meet Paul R. Hawley, chief surgeon of the theater. Hawley had been a member of the London committee that had been made up of representatives of various British supply ministries and representatives of the United States Army who had functioned in mufti in London during the entire year preceding the attack on Pearl Harbor. John C. H. Lee, who had been sent to England as the commanding general of the Services of Supply, had arrived there with another medical officer designated as his chief surgeon, and it was only a fortuitous circumstance that made him appoint Colonel Hawley on the spot after talking with him during a chance luncheon engagement. The original appointee was sent to Ireland as a regional medical chief officer, an example of how the Army functions, but in this instance the result was excellent.

It became evident immediately that for some unknown reason, the speed of action, which had been implied, slowed considerably. There was one United States Army General Hospital in southern England at Oxford, the 2nd General Hospital, staffed by medical officers from Columbia University College of Physicians and Surgeons and Presbyterian Hospital in New York. There was one in the Midlands at Mansfield, the 30th General Hospital, comprised of doctors from the University of California School of Medicine in San Francisco. Another, the 5th General Hospital, had been for some time in Northern Ireland and shortly moved to Salisbury; the staff of this hospital was composed of members of the Harvard Medical School faculty. There was one neurological surgeon in the theater on the staff of the 2nd General Hospital, Dr. John E. Scarff, who needed no help from the Consultant in Neurological Surgery.

Over morning coffee and afternoon tea, we speculated about the slowdown. Perhaps the disastrous experience at Dieppe when an all-Canadian force had attempted to land and was repulsed with serious losses had caused the planners to realize the enormity of the details that had to be met for the build-up operation for invasion across the Channel. Later, it became obvious that the invasion of North Africa had gained precedence over a second front on the Continent. Certainly, I was far away from the mess table with General Eisenhower that I had conjured up in my mind.

It had become the custom for each consultant to make a tour and get acquainted with the United States hospital units as well as the British and Canadian groups. Hugh Cairns, Nuffield Professor of Surgery at Oxford and an old friend who had studied at the Peter Bent Brigham Hospital in Boston, had become a brigadier and consultant for neurological surgery to the Royal Army Medical Corps. There was one important difference in the respective posts of the British and United States consultants. Cairns was responsible for advice in neurological surgery wherever the British Army was fighting, and his mobility and responsibility created a unity that produced results in treatment and policies far surpassing anything that the United States Army attained.

A military hospital for head injuries was located in the buildings of St. Hugh's College for Women in Oxford. This British hospital received only patients who had received craniocerebral injuries of all degrees of severity, and as a result of the careful and scientifically professional service that was given there, they demonstrated conclusively that a high percentage of men so injured could be returned to their military units for duty.

Within the environs of Oxford was the Wingfield Morris Orthopedic Emergency Hospital under the direction of Herbert Seddon, an orthopedic surgeon, who had received a considerable amount of his surgical education and training at the University of Michigan Medical School. The Royal Army Medical Corps found it possible to make use of Seddon without insisting that he be in uniform. To this hospital were sent all of the peripheral nerve injuries from the British military forces and the civilian population. It was immediately obvious that one of the most important contributions to peripheral nerve surgery would one day come from this well-planned and well-organized hospital for study and treatment.

Through his friendship with Lord Nuffield, Cairns had initiated a project at the Morris Garage in Oxford for the construction of mobile surgical units for the Royal Canadian Army Medical Corps. These were three-ton motor vehicles with four-wheel drives and contained an electric generator so that the unit could pull up beside a church or schoolhouse and go to work to help a forward hospital. Each unit carried two folding instrument and operating tables, headrests, sterile drums of supplies, sterile basins, and a water tank. They were not as elaborately equipped as were those originally designed by Cairns, one of which was lost at Dunkirk.

Other projects were under way at Oxford. Zuckerman was working on the effects of blast as observed during the Battle of Britain. In his opinion, blast did not produce cerebral damage but for the most part affected the lungs. He was given the opportunity by Cairns of doing actual field work. He accurately plotted the scene of a bombing, the number and position of the individuals affected, the exact character of the agent, and whether the injured person was stationary or moving, in an effort to determine eventually what prophylactic measures might be instituted. By photographing and measuring the body in all conceivable positions assumed during combat, Zuckerman determined that the head and neck offered a target equal to about 12 per cent of the entire body. Interestingly, a checkup on the actual location and nature of injuries that he had investigated showed a remarkable percentage of correlation with his calculations on the projection of various body areas as targets. While he worked under the auspices of the British Medical Research Council, co-operation with the military was maintained through Cairns.

In contrast, military and civilian projects by the United States were completely independent, and communication was nil. Communication even within the military forces was difficult because of jealousies, as I was to discover.

The Canadian First General, a neurological hospital, was situated at Basingstoke and was built around Hackwood House in 1940. From the beginning it was designed and equipped as a neurosurgical installation. It was superbly organized and administered. In addition to giving excellent care to the wounded, it served as a training place for young general surgeons who could be taught the fundamentals of the immediate care of neurosurgical injuries in forward hospitals. The staff had called attention to the fact that small, apparently trivial, scalp wounds often hid serious underlying comminuted fractures of the skull with destruction of brain tissue; they had treated injuries of the head as long as thirty-six hours after wounding in the Dieppe raid and after careful immediate treatment aided by the use of sulfanilamide. No infections had been observed when the craniocerebral injury had been cleansed carefully, the head shaved, sulfanilamide placed in the wound, a sterile dressing applied, and the wounded man sent back immediately for definitive treatment.

In a memorandum written following this tour, I emphasized that the United States Army records of examination, diagnosis, and treatment of peripheral nerve injuries in World War I were totally inadequate, were incomplete, and were rarely available for study or for use. I pointed out that this should not continue during World

War II and that the records at the Wingfield Morris Hospital could be used as models. This required unified direction from the surgeon general's office in Washington.

Just where the memorandum was sidetracked I never learned, but I suspected Hawley's executive officer because Hawley never saw the memorandum.

This get-acquainted tour emphasized the complete lack of instruments and equipment on hand for neurological surgery in United States General Hospital #2 at Oxford. In an unproductive day visiting two surgical instrument houses in London to determine whether there were any instruments upon their shelves that could be supplied to our hospitals, it was discovered that those instruments available were completely outmoded. The field of neurological surgery and its appliances and instruments had been developed in the United States.

It became apparent that the Army could put supplies into a depot but could not get them out. The Army believed that because an officer was a doctor, it followed that he was capable of getting the correct medical supplies where they belonged. A good stock manager from a mail-order house would have served far better. The principle of ordering a stipulated supply of a particular item for a given number of men every ninety days had resulted in enough thermometers to road-block an invading force and enough hypertonic glucose solution to float the British Navy.

A detailed memorandum of the principles learned by the British in the care of neurosurgical injuries was written and a request made that it be forwarded to the office of the surgeon general for dissemination among military and civilian neurological surgeons in the United States. I hoped that a method of communication might be started that would insure a unified method of care and handling injured soldiers. The memorandum was never recognized. The European theater remained a distinct, isolated entity instead of having a close liaison with the office of the surgeon general.

It became more and more evident that a consultant in neurological surgery should have been responsible, through the chief consultant in surgery to the surgeon general, for the proper organization of the care of neurosurgical injuries in whatever theater of war they occurred. Such a consultant could have been mobile enough to have spent the time necessary in each theater to have organized methods and means of obtaining results that could later have been the basis for valuable contributions to this field of surgery. In the Mediterranean theater there was no senior consultant in neurological surgery because of the wishes of the consultant in surgery; in the European theater there were never more than two qualified neurological surgeons with whom one could consult.

In the middle of September 1942 the 1st Infantry Division, which later was to distinguish itself as it had during World War I, was encamped near Swindon and was preparing to leave for combat in Africa. It became obvious that the cross-Channel invasion had been postponed indefinitely. Each of the consultants gave a talk to the medical officers of the division. The officers' morale was low; they lacked morphine syrettes, blood pressure apparatus, anesthetic agents, and sulfonamides, to name but a few glaring shortages. They were being used as transportation officers and in other capacities; the division surgeon did not attend any of the meetings.

I recommended that a census of the number of neurosurgical injuries in each of the United States hospitals in the theater be kept current, because there was no way of knowing where such patients were or how they were being treated. Many American soldiers, injured severely in jeep accidents in the black-out, were scattered through British Emergency Medical Service hospitals and were receiving treatment for their craniocerebral injuries that was below American standards. An example of an American soldier taken to a British hospital instead of to United States General Hospital #2 at Oxford was cited as a reason for seeking a method to transport such injured soldiers to a United States Army hospital.

On October 13, 1942, the first of seven memorandums to govern the general principles of the treatment of craniocerebral, spinal cord, and peripheral nerve injuries was written and sent to Colonel Ormel Stanley, General Hawley's executive officer. Six of these memorandums were criticized and returned on the grounds of poor English; the seventh was accepted and disposed of effectively by filing.

Stanley had openly and publicly expressed his dislike for the "come lately" consultants who were given ranks that he had gained only after spending years in the regular army medical corps. He exhibited his dislike by issuing a roster of officers for all-night duty to answer the telephone to receive reports of deaths of soldiers in the theater. The roster began with the lieutenant colonel consultants to the chief surgeon, and I served the duty on the first night of the order. General Hawley canceled the duty and the roster when it was called to his attention.

A visit to the 30th General Hospital revealed that no suction apparatus was available to the surgeons and that operations upon one patient with a rupture of the spleen and upon another with rupture of a kidney had nearly resulted in fatalities, although the surgeons had improvised with two bicycle pumps and the strength of an orderly. The first of a series of requests for such a suction apparatus was written immediately and was followed by several others containing minute descriptions of a suction pump available from a supply company in Reading, England, for fifty dollars. The size of the valves, the over-all size and weight, and other specifications were given; in fact, a pump for each of the general hospitals in the theater was available and could have been delivered by hand, if necessary. The only response was the return of the last requisition with a penciled notation from the Supply Division: "I don't know what the colonel is talking about unless it is an all-day sucker."

Many memorandums later, it was evident that the chief surgeon had never seen any of the many recommendations made for the care of neurosurgical patients. They were passed back and forth, or conveniently filed by a hostile medical officer of the Regular Army.

On November 3, 1942, Barrett Brown and I gave the first of a series of lectures at the Eighth Air Force Provisional Medical Field Service School to young air force medical officers. We did not know that a schism existed between the Air Force and the Army, based upon the Air Force's attempts to establish a medical service separate and distinct from that of the Army. On the same trip we visited the East Grinstead Royal Victoria Royal Air Force Plastic Center. We wrote memorandums, upon our return, which recommended the placement of well-staffed, completely equipped, smaller types of hospitals, strategically located within rapid evacuation distance by ambulance from bomber and fighter airdromes, and the assignment of a liaison medical officer from the Air Force, stationed in the United

Kingdom, to the office of the chief surgeon to advise in the eventual disposition of injured air force personnel. At the time the memorandums were written, the struggle for independence in medical organization was taking place, and they could not have been more timely, though they were completely ineffective.

It was more and more apparent that the Medical Department was completely subservient to the Service of Supplies Command and that the chief surgeon had access to the commanding general of the European theater only through the commanding general of the Services of Supply. This fact, learned by diligent study of the volumes depicting the history of World War I, during which the same struggle for direct responsibility of the Medical Department to the commanding general occurred, made it obvious that the Air Force eventually would have its separate medical service. If they did not succeed immediately in such a division, at least it appeared they would conduct their affairs in such a manner.

The first week in November, the 298th General Hospital, the University of Michigan Medical School Unit, the 26th and 29th general hospitals, the units affiliated with the Washington University School of Medicine, St. Louis, and the University of Minnesota Medical School, Minneapolis, arrived in England. The former was kept in England and became housed at Frenchay Park near Bristol; the latter two were sent on to North Africa where the campaign had begun. The Michigan unit's hospital was sadly lacking in equipment and supplies, and much time elapsed before the hospital became effective. I expressed the opinion that the professional staff was working hard, and because of their own efforts they would rectify many of the difficulties that existed, but they needed prompt and sympathetic understanding, and implementation of their needs, none of which were extravagant.

About this time, Major General James C. Magee, the surgeon general of the United States Army, visited the European theater, and the consultants were asked by Colonel Kimbrough to prepare a list of questions that might be asked him. The naïve assumption was expressed that they would be presented at the time of the general's visit and would be answered. Neither part of the assumption proved to be correct.

The questions prepared and submitted emphasized the difficulties that existed in connection with the attempt to establish a medical organization in the European theater patterned on the office of the surgeon general but without any relation to it whatever. It was a disappointment not to have the questions answered, but their formulation did take up some of the time of the consultants.

It was obvious that the consultants were being thwarted at every turn by some of the chief surgeon's staff and without his knowledge. He had instituted dinner meetings with medical officers from other countries, principally from the Royal Army Medical Corps, and the group of consultants acted at his invitation as his aides to entertain his guests. This was only one of the many incidents that led some of the Regular Army medical officers to resent the consultant group. For a time, Colonel Kimbrough, under whom the consultants served, appeared suspicious of their motives until he was emphatically assured that no one of them sought his post and that each consultant desired only to get the job done and to bring to him whatever credit was due.

Ignoring the fact that the Army did not proceed logically, that a memorandum had to be "bucked" by approving signatures step by step, several suggestions were made. The first on the list apparently struck a sensitive, disapproving individual; it was to implement the recommendations of the surgical consultants designed to raise the standards of professional care in United States general hospitals located in the United Kingdom.

Whether or not my memorandum was passed on to General Hawley I never knew, but he instituted regular meetings with the consultant group. At the first meeting he proposed a problem for the consultants to solve and requested that their answers be sent to him. The problem he posed was, How many medical department men would be required to support an invasion to be carried out by a million men, requiring transportation across a body of water twenty-two miles wide? When Brown and I returned to our room, we decided that the general had come to the conclusion that it was necessary to keep the consultants' minds occupied. Perhaps memorandums had reached his desk, and he had decided to give us something to do.

The more seriously Cutler, Diveley, and Middleton took the assignment, the more Brown and I became convinced that we would have as much amusement out of the solution as we could. When Cutler inquired how we were coming with our answer, indicating that he had already turned his in to the general, Brown innocently replied that we were giving our E-32 project a great deal of thought. Cutler's curiosity was immediately piqued, and excitedly he asked what E-32 was. Brown replied vaguely that it was a secret assignment which the general had given us. Cutler was obviously disturbed by the implication that we had been given a separate and distinct, secret problem.

Now we had to set to work in earnest. We decided that we would suggest organization of hospitals that was exactly opposite to that in existence; we would advise several, small, mobile hospitals instead of a large evacuation hospital; we would create a pool of regular army medical officers, who had been trained to wait, and assign reserve medical officers to administer the G divisions and command hospitals. The more we discussed the problem, the more ideas we developed that could be considered bizarre in comparison with the existing organization.

Finally, after weeks during which Brown and I added as much as possible to the mystery of E-32 among our colleagues, the day came when General Hawley said that he had received all the reports except ours. Looking him straight in the eye, I replied that we were still working hard on the E-32 project that he had given us and that it would be ready at the next meeting. He never hesitated in his reply that he could understand the necessity for a few more days. E-32 got its designation from the fact that we lived at the Ellenborough Hotel and our room number was 32. When we finally totaled up the number of personnel, much to our surprise, we were close to the correct answer, and we hoped that our eleven-page typewritten document had given the general a few moments of pleasure in wishing perhaps that he could do some of the unorthodox things we had suggested.

After a thorough study of the neurosurgical aspects of injuries to tank crews, a memorandum was forwarded recommending changes in the helmet worn for head protection, certain aspects of armored tank construction to minimize the occurrence of spinal and other injuries, the evacuation hatch, first-aid equipment, armored ambulances for tank battalions, and the contents of the field chest for use by the medical officer of an armored tank battalion. Within four days a reply came from the chief surgeon, stating that the report had been forwarded to the chief ordnance officer and expressing his interest in the comments and recommendations made concerning the use of an armored half-track personnel carrier as an ambulance, since he had first proposed such an adaptation.

Had this encouraging correspondence occurred earlier, it might have prevented the frustration that prompted sending copies of the memorandums written for three months, arranged in chronological order and with the addressee's name removed, as separate letters to Rankin, Dean Irving S. Cutter of my medical school, and Dr. Howard C. Naffziger, chairman of the department of surgery at the University of California Medical School, a neurological surgeon and a long-time friend. An unwise attempt to bring to the attention of men who, it was believed, might accomplish small changes that would make an organization more effective was stopped abruptly when censors opened the three envelopes and brought the charge of going outside channels of military communication and violating rules that gave the right to a lieutenant colonel to censor his own mail.

The information that court-martial charges had been filed was telephoned to me by Rex Diveley, the consultant for orthopedic surgery, on the day before Christmas, 1942, when I was visiting the 2nd Evacuation Hospital, which had reached its destination in Huntingdon just twelve hours earlier. It was in the temporary, cold office of William MacFee, the hospital's chief of surgery, who had served with distinction in World War I and had been decorated with the Distinguished Service Medal. Bill could not help overhearing Diveley's excited, shouting voice, full of warning and urging me to return immediately. Rex had quickly gained the reputation of knowing everything that was going on at headquarters, and all of us were a bit jealous of his sources of information.

The finish of the conversation left me in confusion, frightened and decidedly insecure. Bill MacFee immediately recognized my discomfiture and said that he knew about the difficulties that existed in the consultant organization and said, "Go on back, ask for an appointment with General Hawley, and simply ask to know what the charges are. Then tell him how you will defend against them. Nothing more."

The timing of events is almost always more significant than the event itself. Later, it was learned that, in anticipation of the result of pressing the court-martial charges, my successor had already been selected in the United States and informed of his mission. However, General Hawley was still to be reckoned with, and our interview was calm, frank, and direct.

Admitting that the method of procedure was improper, I pointed out that the motivating reasons could be found clearly explained in the memorandums. Fundamentally, they concerned the care of the injured. When asked about serving in North Africa, I replied brashly that the records of the men he had transferred to North Africa were not of the highest and that I had no desire to serve elsewhere; in fact, I would resist serving elsewhere. All the difficulties could be solved by a more direct access to him on matters that concerned the treatment of injured men. Finally, to my great relief, General Hawley assured me that there would be no court martial of one of his men, and he was sure organizational changes could be made that would accomplish results more smoothly. This put at rest the worries over arrest, court martial, having buttons cut off my uniform, and disgrace, which had caused two sleepless nights. It also formed the basis for the beginning of a close friendship and association which continued through Hawley's postwar administration as chief medical director of the Veterans Administration, Blue Cross and Blue Shield, and the directorship of the American College of Surgeons.

Early in 1943, my interest was directed to the protection of the heads of airmen. The regular issue steel helmet worn by the United States soldier admittedly furnished excellent protection against craniocerebral injuries and, sometimes more important to the soldier, had many other utilitarian advantages. However, it was not designed for the use of the crews of aircraft or tanks and could not be used to advantage by them, mainly because of its size, shape, and weight. Nevertheless, the desire of a particular copilot for protection to his head from bursting 20 mm. Oerlikon shells led him to remove the liner of his helmet and pull on the outer steel shell over his regulation leather flying helmet. The effectiveness of this protection was emphasized when his pilot, wearing only his leather helmet, was struck in the head by the fragments of an Oerlikon shell that burst between them. The pilot immediately lost consciousness, developed a left hemiplegia and a complete loss in the left half of his field of vision. Although the copilot's helmet was punctured in several places by the high-velocity fragments, it afforded complete protection from even a scalp laceration.

It was obvious that members of an air crew needed a protective helmet that had to meet certain specifications. First, it had to be close-fitting and comfortable so that it would simulate as closely as possible an ordinary leather flying helmet and be considered a personal possession that might gather "good luck" like a favorite, battered felt hat; second, it had to allow free and unrestricted movements of the head in all directions and not interfere in any way with the field of vision; third, it had to be light in weight and afford protection from the heat and cold; and fourth, it had to afford protection, at least equal to that afforded by the regular issue steel helmet, against craniocerebral injuries produced by fragmenting Oerlikon shells, antiaircraft flak, or concussion due to direct, blunt trauma.

I subjected many materials to accurate tests at the ballistics laboratory of Oxford University which was made available by Hugh Cairns. I finally concluded that an acrylic resin, methyl methacrylate, properly manufactured, offered the largest number of advantages for the purpose and most closely met the specifications laid down. This material was obtained, through the friendship of a British civilian, from a plastics firm that had begun to make artificial dentures. There are almost unending variations of the stages that can be reached in the manufacture of the products of an acrylic resin. The properties of the final product may vary within extremely wide limits so that one may think of it as a substitute for glass, a denture, a surgical suture, or a puttylike material. By modifying the amount or character of the plasticizer added, the flexibility, resiliency, hardness, water and weather resistance, flammability, and ballistic protective properties of the material can be varied at will.

The material tested was 4 mm. in thickness and had a velocity resistance, in relation to its weight per unit area, of 440 meters per second when tested with a 52 mg. steel ball fired and photographed electrically. The velocity resistance per unit weight area of the same material of 8 mm. thickness, similarly tested, was 700 meters per second. Velocity resistance per unit weight area of 1 mm. thickness manganese steel, tested under identical circumstances, varied from 500 to 600 meters per second.

The acrylic resin studied had a tensile strength of from 9,000 to 12,000 pounds per square inch; a flexural strength of from 12,000 to 13,000 pounds per square inch; an impact resistance of 0.1 to 0.3 foot pounds, and a Brinell hardness greater than gold. It had a specific gravity of 1.10 so that it almost floated on water, and it absorbed less than 0.5 per cent of water by weight upon immersion for seven days. It was resistant to the rays of the sun and would not soften until a temperature of 190 and 240 degrees had been reached. It was a good nonconductor of heat and cold. It smoldered if a flame was applied to it, but it would not burn with an explosion; if it flamed, the slightest movement extinguished it. When the material was hit directly, the lines of shatter were at right angles to the force and not directly forward as in steel.

Pieces of the acrylic resin were softened in a pan of hot water heated over the shilling-metered gas burner in my room and shaped over a wooden hat mold so that they would conform to the frontal, temporal, occipital, and vertex portions of the skull. These segments were hinged together snugly so that protection would not be lost and yet so that a certain pliability would be gained and a sense of a solid, bucketlike structure would be avoided. The helmet was then covered with the commonly used regulation leather flying helmet and lined with chamois skin. Portions of the protective material were brought down over the ears, and openings were left into which the earphones could be fitted. This afforded further protection and added the distinct advantage of the property of the resin to exclude ambient noises.

The model helmet allowed for complete movement of the head in all directions, provided complete protection of the skull, and in no way interfered with the field of vision. As one molds a derby hat that may impinge slightly upon the parietal eminences and be un-

271

comfortable, so the individual flyer could mold his helmet by applying heat to the protective liner so that it became an integral and comfortable part of him. The pieces of molded plastic could be fitted into pockets of the leather helmet and be removed when it was not being worn in combat. The completed helmet, made of 4 mm. methyl methacrylate, weighed eighteen ounces, and, if material 8 mm. thick was used, affording more protection per unit weight area, the total weight was twenty-seven ounces. I also suggested that similar plastic panels could be inserted into the regular issue flying suit for protection against chest, abdominal, and extremity injuries. I made several flights in a B-17 bomber on practice missions with Captain David Wheeler and his crew, during which the model protective helmet was adjusted and revised until it suited the entire crew.

At this time, General Malcolm Grow, surgeon to the Eighth Air Force, had engaged the services of an armorer in England to devise a metal protective suit of armor for airmen. Ignoring the ballistics tests we had made, he rejected the use of plastic material on the ground that he had shattered a piece of the plastic material with his own .45 caliber pistol. The obvious answer was, of course, that if one got close enough to a heavily armored battleship with a large enough shell, the battleship could be destroyed. Under actual flying combat conditions, it was evident that the acrylic resin would afford real protection. The difficulty with the metal armor was its weight and awkwardness, against which all of the bomber crews reacted unanimously. It was their consensus that General Grow should put it on himself, fly with them, and be asked to bail out over the North Sea, an action that they were allowed ten seconds to perform successfully. Moreover, the pilot, the last to leave the plane, was required to leave through a small window at his side through which he had to propel himself from a sitting position.

No further progress could be made in spite of the support and enthusiasm of the chief surgeon. It was not until late in 1943 that the quartermaster general's office in Washington accepted all of the work performed and the suggestions made. Colonel George F. Doriot and his colleagues were working on a material similar in many respects to the material tested. Through the maze of military red tape, the present air force helmet eventually evolved.

ELEVEN

ONE day in the latter part of April 1943, while walking back from lunch at the headquarters mess, General Hawley stopped me and asked if I would be interested in a trip to the Soviet Union. He added nothing after I returned an unhesitating "yes" and we parted.

On June 28, 1943, the seven members of the mission, the first of its kind ever to go to the Soviet Union, were loaded into a bus at the Swindon railroad station and driven about the countryside until it became dark. We were given dinner at Marlborough and then taken to the airfield that we recognized as the one at Lyneham. The four-engine British aircraft carried the members of the mission and two Soviet nationals, who remained grim and uncommunicative throughout the entire trip. We learned later that they were diplomatic pouch couriers, but also members of the NKVD, the Soviet secret police.

The take-off was at midnight, and flying well out beyond the Bay of Biscay where a plane carrying Leslie Howard, the famous British actor, had been shot down by the Germans two weeks before, the mission landed at Gibraltar the following morning. After breakfast, the British military hospital, a two-hundred-bed unit built in a tunnel that had been drilled out of the rock, was visited; it also served as a bomb shelter if the "Rock" was bombed.

We were off again at noon and flew over the United States 12th General Hospital at Oran, Algeria, and on to Castel Benito, the airport at Tripoli, Libya. The flight followed the route of the advance of the British Eighth Army, and damaged, abandoned material was visible along the road. Jock Munro, who had served as surgeon to the Eighth Army, pointed out some of the interesting sites of advance and retreat of both armies as they fought the desert battle.

We visited the British 48th General Hospital in Tripoli, which they had taken over from the Italians. After tea in a setting of desert sand, flies, bougainvillaeas, and heat at a Royal Air Force staging area, the flight was continued at midnight to arrive at Cairo on the morning of the thirtieth.

In Cairo we visited two British hospitals; the one in a newly constructed modern building that the Egyptians had to close because they could not make it support itself and the other in the building of a former beautiful hotel. The United States 38th General Hospital, staffed principally by the faculty of Jefferson Medical College of Philadelphia, was located at Heliopolis, but we postponed a visit there until our return trip.

On the morning of July 1, after considerable delay while the plane's fuel and cargo were being redistributed at the insistence of the Royal Air Force pilot, on a desert airfield that became hotter and hotter, the leg of the trip from Cairo to Tehran, Iran, began. Without oxygen and at thirteen thousand feet, one of the mission became cyanotic, another had periods of apnea, and a third developed a scintillating scotoma, could not remember names, and had a homonymous hemianopia. All of these symptoms disappeared, and the mission presented a unified, healthy front upon landing at Tehran late in the afternoon. A representative of the British embassy met the mission.

It was hot and dusty on the airfield, which was surrounded by high mountains with snow on their peaks. There were many American soldiers to be seen, and a station hospital was under construction. Water was running in a small gutter along the side of the street, and people were washing their bodies and clothes in it, watering horses in it, sweeping street cleanings into it, and putting it into pails which they were carrying away. The Palace Hotel provided a room for Cutler and me with two iron beds, a wooden washstand with a flowered china bowl, and one water faucet. We sprinkled insect powder on the mattress and pillow in liberal quantities.

Cutler and I paid a visit to Major General Donald H. Connolly, Commanding General, Persian Gulf Command, an engineer who was accomplishing the project of supplying the Soviet Union through the Persian Gulf and Basra, Iraq. General Connolly inquired about the purpose of the visit to Russia, since he knew nothing about the mission. He expressed his doubts of our learning any more than what the Soviet hosts would specifically designate. This was the first inkling that there were difficulties in being allies with the Russians. The general was very specific in stating that it would have been more advantageous for us to have made the trip alone because of the Russians' distrust of the postwar intentions of the British.

There was another delay on the hot, dusty Tehran airfield while petrol was removed from the tanks so that the *Liberator* would be able to gain altitude quickly enough to clear the mountains surrounding the field. After a bumpy, rough trip, we landed in Moscow late on the afternoon of July 2 at a field about thirty miles from the city. We were met by Vice-Commissar of Public Health Vasillii Vassilievich Pairin, Leonid Aleksandrovich Koreisha, secretary of the Medical Scientific Council, and a woman interpreter. Two United States Air Force officers, whom Elliott Cutler believed would be our aides while we were in Russia, accompanied us to a cottage in a woods adjacent to the airfield where we were served tea, bread and butter, sausages, white caviar, and strawberries. On the trip to the National Hotel, where we were quartered, we were told by the air force officers that they were in Moscow with Captain Eddie Rickenbacker on a mission that he was attempting to carry out for Secretary of War Henry Stimson.

Captain Rickenbacker's mission concerned the complaints that the Soviet Union was making about the Aircobra P-39 planes which the United States was furnishing them on lend-lease agreement. The complaint was that they would not stand up in combat. It developed that the Russians had no concept of ground crews to service the aircraft and keep the intricate mechanisms in good working order. It was their idea to fly them, discard them when they broke down, and ask for new ones. They had also complained that the planes did not stand this type of treatment long enough and they were put to considerable trouble in asking for replacements.

After an assignment of rooms at the National Hotel, we found we had a large common sitting room which had a ceiling-to-floor mirror on one wall. The mirror was decorated with gold-painted birds and angels. One evening, after we had been in Moscow for several days, Professor Serge Yudin, an internationally known Russian surgeon who had visited the United States and England and who was chief surgeon of the Sklifossowsky Institute, a large hospital, surreptitiously called upon us around midnight. As he talked, he kept up a constant tapping of the table with his pencil. When asked why he did this, he explained that it would interfere with a clear pickup of his voice. This was a shocking surprise, and after he had gone, we spent hours trying to find the microphone, which was finally located concealed behind one of the angels on the top of the mirror. We had freely discussed our impressions of all we had encountered during our visit and were not quite sure just how our hosts would evaluate our opinions from their transcript.

After a cold-water bath, and this did not vary at any time during our stay, we had breakfast of tea, cherry jam, cheese, caviar, and bread. Neither did this menu change except as we could vary it with instant coffee and hot water heated over a Sterno can which we had brought along.

The business office of the United States embassy was only a door or two from the National Hotel, and both faced Red Square, across which we could see the Kremlin and the new, gaudy, heavily built, yellow-stone Moskva Hotel. All of us called upon Admiral William H. Standley, the United States ambassador, who was charming and interested in learning each man's name and his particular field of surgery. Cutler and I later called upon Brigadier General Philip R. Faymonville who had been in Russia on four tours of duty, for ten years. Faymonville was the lend-lease administrator and, in a frank talk with us, made his position perfectly clear. He was under direct instructions and orders from President Roosevelt, delivered by Harry Hopkins, to supply everything possible to the Russians without thought of getting something in return. He said that other branches of the United States Government wished to barter with the Soviet Union, using lend-lease material as leverage, on the grounds of protecting the interests of the United States. It was obvious that the military attachés and embassy officials were in direct conflict with Faymonville and believed him personally responsible for a situation that was intolerable to them in dealing with the Russians, without accepting the fact that he was carrying out specific orders from the President, and failing to consider that his own personal views might be entirely different. Faymonville's knowledge of the Russian language, his long residence in Russia, and his familiarity with their music and customs made the Russians friendly to him. This was to be seen at the social gatherings that were given for the mission and at which he was present. However, this made him all the more suspect of favoritism by his colleagues when the war had finished and when the relationship between the United States and its former ally underwent a change.

British Ambassador Clarke-Kerr indicated that the mission had been made possible by his friendship with Dr. Serge Yudin, who had suggested such a visit by United States and British surgeons. This version of the origin of the mission was at variance with Ambassador Winant's—that it had been arranged by him as the result of discussions between members of the National Research Council and the Medical Research Council of Great Britain. The truth probably is that all had a hand in the proposal and that priority of ideas would be difficult to establish. Each of us received one thousand rubles from the British embassy, but we could use the money only for gratuities to the hotel employees, because there were no shops or stores where we could purchase any kind of an article without a ration card.

We visited VOKS, the Soviet society to promote cultural relations with foreign countries. Large posters of Churchill, Stalin, and Roosevelt hung side by side in the large museumlike room of the building to which we were taken by Pairin and Koreisha. Oil paintings of Soviet soldiers in various units, cartoons, and large photographs of Charlie Chaplin and Paul Robeson completed the display. On the return trip to the hotel, a stop was made at a park where there were pictures of the party leaders lining the walk, a Ferris wheel and various airplane rides for the children, an area for dancing to the music coming from the loudspeakers distributed through the park, and a children's library.

We discussed when and how we could get our visit under way and decided to follow Admiral Standley's admonition to be patient. We walked around Red Square, Lenin's tomb, the Kremlin, and the Church of St. Basil, a Byzantine structure, highly colored and resembling a gingerbread cake. This was our first unaccompanied trip of any distance on the streets, and people stopped and looked at our clothes and uniforms; sometimes they would approach shyly and feel the material. The guards, walking along the top of the walls of the Kremlin, were either curious about us or were very alert to their duties. There were no taxicabs, and only the Intourist organization could supply transportation.

We had several discussions about drawing up our own agenda for procedure and talks with the people's commissar for public health. We wished to see the surgical treatment of the war-wounded in the forward areas and at the bases and to see and discuss Soviet research projects and ways of exchanging information. There were pleasant periods of conversation with each other, but it was like shadowboxing in a gymnasium. Finally, we did write a memorandum that would explain the desires of the members of the mission and left it with the people's commissar for public health.

On July 4 we spent the morning viewing a large collection of captured German war material—guns, planes, trucks, and medical supplies—gathered together on the bank of the Moscow River and looking much like a world's fair. Groups of soldiers and civilians were taken through on tours and given lectures on the material displayed and the superiority of Russian equipment.

We spent the afternoon of the fourth at Spasso House, the official home of Ambassador Standley, which had been occupied also by his predecessors, Bullitt, Davies, and Steinhardt. Captain Eddie Rickenbacker was present and brought up the question of the damage airmen were receiving from high-altitude frostbite, interesting the ambassador in the discussion. We looked at two Mickey Mouse movies, drank Coca-Cola, and ate hot dogs. The ambassador took me on a conducted tour of his house, showed me his bedroom, and pointed out the windows in the house adjacent where a constant watch, even on his personal ablutions, was kept by members of the Russian secret police.

That evening we attended the ballet *Swan Lake,* with Dudinskya, the première danseuse. The audience consisted of workers from factories who had purchased tickets from allotments given to their factory. When we went into the lobby between acts and returned, we had difficulty in regaining our seats from individuals who had moved into them from less desirable ones. The ballet was beautifully performed, but the odor of a mixture of perfume, powder, perspiration, and mustiness that came into the theater when the curtain was up was almost overpowering.

Eventually, on the fifth of July, the mission was received in the office of the people's commissar for public health, Georgii Andreevich Meterev. There were seven mission members and seven Russians; there were three of the mission in uniform and four of them in uniform. We found that this desire to have a balance or a superiority in numbers was almost an obsession. The Soviet military included Lieutenant General Efim Ivanovich Smirnov, of the Soviet Army Medical Service, who was thirty-eight years of age and corresponded to our surgeon general, and Nicolai Nilovich Burdenko, the chief surgical consultant to the Soviet Army, not a regular medical officer, and with the added great distinction of being a member of the Academy of Sciences. The meeting began with a formal speech by the commissar, who described the existing organization for the treatment of battle casualties and provided a typewritten program of activities for the coming week.

General Smirnov's medical organization was responsible for the care of soldiers in combat units, in army hospitals, and through all evacuation steps to the base area. The care of the wounded in the base area, as well as the care of all civilians, was the responsibility of the Commissariat for Public Health. The methods of treatment were identical in both organizations in order to insure continuity in the patient's care when he was transferred from the combat zone to the rear. The line of demarcation between these two areas was never unchangeably fixed. When a patient received a certificate of fitness from the civilian doctors, he was transferred back to the military authorities for reassignment. Patients requiring long convalescent care remained under the jurisdiction of the civilian authorities in hospitals that were required to devote their chief attention to the treatment of the war-wounded. The commissar for public health said that 70 per cent of all wounded were returned to the combat zone for duty, a figure designed to impress us with the toughness of the Russian soldier, and if true, it was impressive.

The next day we began our tour of the facilities that our Russian hosts wished us to see, and nothing beyond that was possible. The Botkin Hospital, the Sklifossowsky Institute headed by Serge Yudin,

279

the Central Institute for Traumatology and Orthopedy, the Institute of Neurological Surgery, a clearing hospital of the Commissariat for Public Health, two front-line hospitals near Vyazma, a hospital for the lightly wounded, the Central Institute for Blood Transfusion, the Central Institute for Medical Research, and a final meeting with the commissar filled our time. At no time was any member of the surgical mission asked to relate experiences of the British or United States in treating the wounded.

Elliott Cutler had insisted upon taking a million units of penicillin as an introductory gift, like taking wampum to the Indians. The drug had just been released for use and was scarce. It was received coldly with the statement that it was nothing new to them and was available for the care of their wounded. This was the first bald demonstration of their facility for lying to support their claims to priority and superiority.

The best impressions of the Soviet methods of treatment were obtained in their care of fractures. They had a line of continuity in the treatment between surgeons at the front and in base hospitals that represented the same institution and methods. Yudin at the Sklifossowsky Institute had cared for over two thousand compound fractures of the femur during the war with Finland. They preferred to splint the limb in the field with wooden, wire, or Thomas splints at the place of the first definitive treatment. The wound was widely excised and sulfanilamide was placed in it. Often the wound was sutured open by uniting the skin edges to the deep fascia, and skin-tight plaster was then applied directly to the wound and skin; the cast was not split, and inspection windows were never used. Watson-Jones and Yudin began an interesting discussion in a give-and-take friendly exchange of opinions until Watson-Jones indicated that it was difficult to believe the successes claimed. Whereupon, Yudin pleasantly inquired if Watson-Jones had ever treated two thousand compound fractures of the femur, and when the reply was in the negative, Yudin stated again that he and his associates had and these were the best methods and results.

The Soviet Army Medical Service used large amounts of citrated whole blood and little or no plasma. An excellent technique was employed to collect the blood in the larger cities, but chiefly in Moscow, where two thousand pints a day were obtained. Donors were given a special food ration and a small amount of money, but it was solemnly claimed that 85 per cent of the money was returned voluntarily through gifts to the government for airplanes and other military purposes. The name of each donor was placed on each container, and the name of the recipient was given to each donor, thus insuring a personal relationship and a feeling of participation in the war effort by the donors.

General Burdenko was the head of the Institute for Neurological Surgery and claimed that sixteen neurological surgeons were at the front in charge of 3,200 beds and that there were 3,700 beds for neurological surgery patients in the rear. He had a right hemiplegia and from the interpreter's expression evidently had difficulty at times in expressing himself.

An incident occurred during our visit to the institute that revealed more of the Soviet mind than was being disclosed surgically. Burdenko demonstrated a microscopic slide that purported to show the excellent regeneration which had occurred as the result of the experimental use of a Formalin-fixed nerve graft in the repair of a peripheral nerve injury. The specimen was poorly stained and showed nothing conclusive; I turned away without comment. Through the interpreter Burdenko insisted upon a comment about the demonstration stating that he had a copy of Pollock's and my book on peripheral nerve injuries. He indicated that an opinion would be highly appreciated. The answer was, of course, that it had been proved during World War I, and subsequently many times, that such Formalin-fixed grafts were completely useless. I asked Burdenko how many patients had been operated upon and to demonstrate one who showed a return of sensation or motion in any area in which overlap from adjacent uninjured nerves did not occur. He replied with a smile that twenty-five patients had been so operated upon, that all had recovered, and that they were unavailable for demonstration because they were at the front in combat.

The other members of the mission, and in particular, Cutler, were not hesitant later in indicating that my doubting attitude might well impair the entire success of the mission and, if carried into other fields, might even destroy the alliance between the Western nations and the Soviet Union and allow Germany to win the war. I said that if the Russians stopped fighting, they would do so using our equipment. The sequel to the incident occurred later at the dinner we gave to our hosts in the National Hotel. During the cocktail hour I saw Burdenko rearranging the place cards at the table; we had spent a great deal of time placing our guests according to protocol and rank. Our guest list had been altered arbitrarily by the Russians to whom it had to be submitted; several of the doctors with whom we had been impressed were taken off the list and replaced by total strangers. As I sought my place at the foot of the table, I was unsuccessful until I reached the seat on the left of Burdenko near the head of the table. Cutler made frantic signals indicating that I was in the wrong place and only subsided when I picked up the place card and showed him my name on it. He was immediately suspicious that I had made the switch, and the other members of the mission were fearful that I was persisting in an attempt to offend our Soviet hosts. Ambassador Standley, who sat opposite, viewed the incident with amusement and finally told Cutler to "ease off and sit down; you just think this is your party."

During the dinner Burdenko summoned our interpreter and asked again my opinion of the Formalin-fixed grafts, and again I said that they had been proved unsuccessful beyond any doubt. Whereupon Burdenko said he agreed completely but then inquired why the other members of the mission, particularly the British, had been so complimentary in their praise of the demonstration. He said that this was an example of how difficult it was to trust and negotiate with people who did not always bluntly state their views and position. Ending with a firm, pumping handclasp, he stated that henceforth there would be no difficulty in understanding my opinions, raised his glass of vodka, and we drank a toast.

During our tour we were shown and told about several clinical methods that were emphasized as completely new and original ideas, including the treatment of shock by the suboccipital cistern injection of potassium phosphate solution to stimulate the vasomotor centers in the medulla.

We visited Dr. Lena Stern's laboratory to observe an experimental animal treated for shock by this method of cisternal injection. Allowing for all of the difficulties that are inherent in the demonstration of any experiment to a group, the basic technical methods employed were so crude and inaccurate as to throw complete doubt upon any conclusion that had been expressed. Dr. Stern was one of the few women Academicians, and her apartment, automobile, food, and gasoline rations could not be compared with those of the average citizen. It was plain that Academicians had been placed in a separate, high category in the existing class struggle.

It was apparent that women held equality with men in the Soviet Union as members of the street repairing gangs and of other construction groups on the country roads, and as soldiers and officers in the Army. Several women junior officers were seen with artillery and infantry insignia, but we were told that there was no woman with a higher rank than colonel in the line services, although in the medical service the inspector general was a woman.

On the eleventh of July we began a trip to the front-line hospitals near Vyazma. Preparations were in progress for opening an extensive and decisive campaign along the Orel-Kursk-Byelgorod line that extended directly south of Moscow. Vyazma was about 125 miles southwest of Moscow and represented a point to which the Soviet Army had driven back the Germans from their advance on Moscow.

Our entourage consisted of several automobiles containing the members of the mission and their hosts. But there were two additional cars which served as transports when the cars in which we were riding broke down, and this occurred four times going and coming. Extra cans of gasoline were carried in the seats with us, and the rugged, jolting ride was only a part of the rigors that it is said every doctor-soldier should be trained to expect. At each crossroad we were stopped and waved on after identification by women soldiers armed with rifles, whose demeanor and expression left no doubt as to their ability and willingness to use them.

At about five o'clock in the afternoon we arrived at a casualty clearing station, well camouflaged in a thick forest. We were shown through the wards and then were served vodka, strawberries, caviar, and smoked fish in a Mongolian tent. Faymonville had briefed me on the drinking of toasts in vodka in the Russian fashion. It consisted of making up one's own mind about how many vodka toasts could be tolerated and then going through the motions, substituting wine or water if possible, or otherwise simply raising the glass. It became obvious at this first stop that if the Soviet rules were accepted, not a member of the mission could be victorious in a drinking contest.

At ten o'clock that night we arrived at a large evacuation hospital in a pouring rain and pitch-darkness; this hospital, too, had been placed in a thick forest and seemed to be constructed of logs. A sumptuous dinner had been prepared, with an exact protocol of seating arrangement along one side of an enormous table which occupied a large dining hall. Jock Munro, the senior-ranking military member of our group, sat in the center of the table, and on his left was a young, blond, Amazon-like, beautiful Russian woman with the rank of major of infantry. Lower ranks and civilian representatives graduated downward to the ends of the table. Vodka, wine, champagne, and enormous quantities of all types of food were served while representatives of various republics of the Soviet Union, dressed in their native costumes, entertained us with folk music and dances.

The toasts came thick and fast, and, as was customary, by the time it came down to me, there was little left to toast. The ruling heads of government, the Red Army, and the women of the Soviet Union had been honored so that a few well-delivered mumbled words with the correct emphasis and gestures sufficed. It was evident that the young woman major had considerable capacity for vodka and a technique of eating large pieces of bread between toasts. It was also apparent that Munro was slowly but surely becoming unable to accept her challenge. Impulsively, and with the thought that I might be of some temporary assistance to Munro, using pantomime gestures, I invited her to dance to the Ukrainian music in the hope that the exercise might slow down her vodka-consuming abilities. As a matter of fact, her vigorous dancing burned up the alcohol more rapidly and only exhausted me. She was physically superior to any one of us and apparently was devoting herself single-mindedly to carrying out an order, because when I escorted her to her seat, she bowed stiffly, turned to Munro, and raised her glass in an invitation to drink with her.

Suddenly, the dinner terminated when Munro abruptly rose from the table and uncertainly started to leave. I quickly sensed what was wrong and took his arm; the other had been grasped quickly by his dinner partner, and together we got outside. She assumed charge, and supporting him between us, we began a precarious journey in the rain along a narrow boardwalk. Suddenly, Munro lurched toward me, and losing our balance, we fell into a shallow drainage ditch. Quickly and surely, the lady major pulled him to his feet, supported him, and gave me a helping hand. We continued on our uncertain way to the ward in the hospital where it appeared we had been assigned beds for the night. In spite of my protests by sign language that we could now manage to get our clothes off, our energetic friend insisted upon helping me get Munro's clothes off and putting him to bed.

During the night I awakened with a severe, persistent, abdominal pain which seemed to be in my side, but which I could not localize. I awoke vomiting and in a cold perspiration. Soon, I had six attending physicians, each of whom had a different diagnosis of my illness, varying from an acute intestinal obstruction due to a malignancy to overeating strawberries. A Russian nurse came to the bedside, and I made motions that I hoped would indicate that I wanted a hot-water bottle; quickly, she nodded her head and returned with it, placed it, covered me up, shooed my colleagues back to their beds, and turned out the lights. I was vaguely aware of her gentle, capable hands with their coarse, rough skin, rearranging a newly warmed bag at intervals. When I was awakened by her in the morning, she insisted upon shaving me and serving me with a cup of tea before she allowed me to get out of bed, and then helped dress me.

The log-and-plank hospital was a remarkable structure. It had been erected by officers, nurses, and enlisted personnel, and I saw the nurse who had taken such good care of me using a hand ax, as she, with others, worked on a window frame in a recently added portion of the hospital.

At breakfast of tea, smoked meats, bread, and the customary strawberries and caviar, the Russian medical officer of the same rank, who sat on my left at the dinner, sat down and inquired how I felt. We were both embarrassed by an incident that had happened early in the course of the dinner the night before. I had reached my limit of drinking toasts in vodka and had substituted water in my glass. In a lull, he had risen, and although I could not understand him, it was obvious by his gestures that he was severely criticizing me for not drinking each toast in vodka. In answer, I called over our interpreter and asked her to repeat in Russian what I was going to say. I rose, bowed to him, and reminded him and our other hosts that if he was our guest in the United States, he would be permitted to drink as often and as he pleased, and I intended to do the same. She looked at me in amazement, and perhaps thinking of the stockings and soap she knew I had planned to give her when we departed, she translated my remarks accurately enough to have their effect. The lieutenant colonel promptly rose to his feet, bowed to me, kissed me on both cheeks, then shook hands with me, and we had a pleasant exchange of smiles, hand signals, and nods the rest of the dinner. Now he said that he wished again to apologize, and his halting English was understandable, whereas the night before he did not speak or understand English. He said that there was no real necessity for accepting the Russian rules about drinking toasts, but if they were accepted, then the Soviet people went all out to drink their guests under the table. It was again plain that they felt the necessity for asserting their superiority in every line of endeavor; this explained their claiming priority for medical and scientific advances, their insistence that they had manufactured penicillin, their trial balloons to see just what reactions they would obtain with their preposterous clinical claims.

Several days after our return from the Vyazma front, we received word that finally arrangements had been made for us to confer honorary fellowships in the Royal College of Surgeons of England and the American College of Surgeons upon Burdenko and Yudin. Gordon Gordon-Taylor had been persuasive in obtaining permission from the council of the Royal College to confer the honorary fellowship for the first time outside the confines of their college, and the regents of the American College had agreed to a similar exception in a token contribution to improve the co-operation between the surgical professions of the Western countries and the Soviet Union. We had failed repeatedly to get the Russians to agree to a time and place for what we wished to be a dignified and auspicious occasion. We had discussed the possibility of an audience of doctors before whom the presentations could be made. We realized that Serge Yudin was not a member of the Communist party, and we assumed that his stature and reputation as a surgeon was sufficiently recognized internationally that he was being tolerated. We learned that all of the properties of his family had been confiscated; he had the rank only of a colonel when he alternately served at the front, and yet it was hard to realize that the Russians would obstruct our paying a generous tribute. Suddenly, a time and place had been set; we gathered in the office of the People's Commissariat for Public Health; there were exactly the same number of Soviet officials as there were members of the mission and no other guests. The British and United States ambassadors had not been invited, and both Soviet recipients prominently displayed their stars of the Order of Stalin on their coat lapels. It was a ceremony completely unworthy, in its setting, of the fellowships from the distinguished Colleges of Surgeons of England and America, both of which had broken a precedent in conferring their honorary fellowships in a foreign country.

We made a return visit to Yudin's Sklifossowsky Institute; visits were made to the Pirogoff Clinic and to the Balneological Institute, where it was claimed that a pine oil water and Odessa mud were miraculous curing agents; a visit to the Central Institute for Blood Transfusion where, accidentally, we learned that our constant Soviet companion, physiologist Pairin, the vice-commissar for public health, understood English perfectly, though he had never uttered one word of English while in our presence, and communication with him had been difficult. We wondered in retrospect just what he was reporting about our frank conversations with each other while in his presence. We arranged through the embassies to attend the ballet from Otto Nicolai's opera *The Merry Wives of Windsor* and Tchaikovsky's opera *The Queen of Spades* and again were impressed by the high quality of the performances.

At a meeting at the Central Institute for Medical Research, Rock Carling, Wilder Penfield, and I spoke about the free exchange of research information between the British, Canadian, and United States research councils, but there was not the slightest sign of encouragement that the Soviet Union would join in.

The last week of our stay was a difficult one for our hosts as well as for us. They had completed their agenda, and we were at loose ends; the time allotted to us had been overstayed. It was impossible to walk about alone, because the ever-present NKVD representatives were always nearby; there were no shops in which to purchase mementos of the trip, and the members of the mission had become slightly weary of one another's frailties. We had been sent back to the hotel by our host at dinner, the ranking British military attaché, so that his car could return to his compound, and we would be safe in our hotel before ten o'clock because, as he said, it would keep him from having to get us out of jail for being out beyond the curfew hour; the NKVD showed no respect whatever for the signs of his military rank that his car carried.

The real obstacle to our leaving was the fact that no airplane was available to take us back to our starting place. The British and Soviet authorities had been negotiating an agreement whereby, in the summer months, one route would be flown by way of the Mediterranean, Cairo, and Tehran, as we had come, and another directly across Europe from London to Moscow. One aircraft by each route each week was the schedule. In the winter months two planes would fly the southern route. The British believed the agreement to be firm, but flew two planes in one week in July via the southern route, instead of one directly across Europe, because of operational difficulties, which would quickly straighten out. The Soviets considered this a violation of the agreement and refused to allow any plane to enter Soviet territory by any route.

A week passed with British Ambassador Clarke-Kerr frankly admitting that he could get nowhere with the Russian Foreign Office. United States Ambassador Standley finally demanded passage out of Russia for the two United States citizens, and on July 23 all of us were taken from the National Hotel to the airport at five o'clock in the morning. We could see the two-motored American-built plane sitting on the field. A large red star decorated its side. After waiting two hours for Walter Citrine, a British trades union leader, and his companions who had also been in Moscow studying Soviet labor relations, we boarded the plane, whose motors were still idle. Without preliminary revving of the engines, the plane taxied to the end of the field and took off. The flight was never above one thousand feet, because an order had been issued to the antiaircraft crews to shoot any plane above that height, without attempting to identify it. Stalingrad was circled at five hundred feet, and all that could be seen standing was one stone chimney. That evening about 5:30, our Soviet pilot dove the field at Tehran, and with the smell of scorched rubber tires in the air, we were unceremoniously deposited on the air strip. We had been removed from the Soviet Union.

TWELVE

FOR some time prior to the mission to Russia, I had been studying the effects of high-altitude frostbite. An airman had been examined at the 2nd General Hospital with tremendous blisters upon the backs of his hands. At first the opinion had been expressed that these were burns, because his aircraft had crashed on landing and burned. Careful questioning elicited the fact that he had been at a waist gun position, which at that time was an open window. He had worn his electrically heated flying suit at the time but had taken off his gloves to urinate. The parts of the suits, it was found, were wired in series, and thus the entire suit was turned off completely if one portion was disconnected. The aircraft had been at an altitude of considerably over thirty thousand feet, and the outside temperature was minus thirty degrees.

Instances of cold injuries to the hands, occasionally to the feet, in isolated instances to the buttocks, and only once to the cheeks and ears, multiplied rapidly through April, May, and early June of 1943. Exposure to low temperatures and air blasts at high altitudes with failure of oxygen supply and, most important of all, failure of, or lack of, electrically heated clothing were the important etiological factors.

I made color photographs of the striking lesions, which were resulting in the complete disability of the airmen, and studies were begun to devise the proper treatment and to prevent the injuries. General Hawley requested that the data upon twenty-five patients be presented to General Grow, and made the appointment for me. Ushered into Grow's office, I stood unrecognized for fifteen minutes while he carried on a discussion with Herbert Wright, a urologist from Ohio, who was on his staff, about his own experiences with frostbite when he was in Russia following World War I. Grow emphasized that it was not a serious problem and was the result of the carelessness of the airmen.

Becoming irritated by the total lack of courtesy and obvious antagonism that Grow exhibited, I interrupted to place on his desk copies of the patients' stories and color photographs of their lesions, which included complete casts of the skin of the fingers which had been shed, dry gangrene amputation stumps, and bullae of all degrees of severity. I said that I had been ordered by General Hawley to deliver the material and turned to leave. When I reached the door, I was called back, asked to take off my overcoat and sit down. A lengthy discussion followed with a persistently antagonistic attitude prevailing on Grow's part. He doubted that the electrically heated clothing was wired in series, and called Colonel Harry G. Armstrong, director of the Eighth Air Force Central Medical Establishment, into the discussion. Colonel Armstrong said frankly that he had no idea how they were wired.

Following this experience, permission was granted by General Hawley to designate the 2nd General Hospital as the center to receive patients with cold injuries and to establish a laboratory and special wards for their study. Early in May 1943, capillary microscopic studies were under way, and mildly injured patients who had recovered without loss of digits were being studied at fixed low temperatures to see if they could be returned to flying duty with safety. Permission was requested to go to operational Eighth Air Force fields to make capillary microscopic studies upon airmen immediately upon landing. Many methods were investigated in an effort to prevent the injuries, and it was recommended that the clothing be wired differently and that the open waist gun positions be protected. All requests to visit airfields were denied by the Eighth Air Force. Finally, these patients became so numerous as bombing activities increased during May and June that the chief surgeon discussed the situation directly with Lieutenant General Frank M. Andrews, commanding general of the theater. Unfortunately, General Andrews was killed in an airplane accident soon after, and again it was necessary for General Hawley to brief his successor, Lieutenant General Jacob L. Devers. Eventually, permission was obtained, and observations were made over a two-week period, aided by John E. Scarff, the neurological surgeon to the 2nd General Hospital. Patients continued to suffer the effects of cold injury, and during the two-week period at the bomber station where observations were made, thirty patients had cold injuries requiring hospitalization for varying periods of time. One medical officer at a bomber station denied that any of his personnel had received such injuries until their names, ranks, and serial numbers were supplied to him during the discussion. It was obvious that Grow had indoctrinated his medical officers and inoculated them with his antagonistic, closed-mind attitude.

On a Sunday morning in August, the week after my return from the surgical mission to Russia, General Hawley asked me to meet him at the 2nd General Hospital in Oxford. He said that he was bringing General Henry Arnold, commanding general of the Air Force, and Major General David N. W. Grant, the air surgeon, to visit the wards where the airmen with high-altitude frostbite were being studied and treated. General Grow was in the party and for the first time was seeing the ward and the patients. As Arnold went from bed to bed, Grow told him of how "they" had discovered the condition, how "they" had set up the ward and laboratories; he was taking credit for all that had happened; he was deliberately lying. My face evidently showed my astonishment, anger, and determination to set the record straight because Hawley pulled me aside and said that I should not remonstrate, just to be quiet, that he had known Hap Arnold for many years, had served with him, had taken care of his children, and that Arnold was in possession of the facts.

The following week I received orders to go to Washington and present the entire story, including the color photographs of the high-altitude frostbite injuries, the clinical histories of the patients, and all other data to Surgeon General Kirk. Hawley also instructed me to present the data on the protective helmet. After a delay of forty-eight hours at Prestwick, I flew back in a bucket seat transport plane that carried pilots who had ferried combat planes from the United States to the Eighth Air Force.

General Kirk and his staff were interested in the material that had been collected and immediately arranged a meeting with the air surgeon's executive officer, Colonel Walter Jensen, who Kirk said was the smartest medical officer assigned to the Air Force.

General Kirk came out of his office and said that he would drive me to the Pentagon, since he was going there to pay his respects to Secretary of War Stimson on his birthday. As we were leaving the building, we were stopped by General Grow. Kirk looked from one of us to the other. Evidently, he did not know Grow, and so I introduced them. Grow stammered that he was just coming up to see him. Kirk said, "Did you expect to see me without an appointment?" Grow answered that he had just arrived in Washington and it was important that he see him. Kirk looked at him quizzically and with a grin said, "Davis has already shown me the high-altitude frostbite material, and I'm sending him down to see Walt Jensen. Why don't you come down with us? Come on, get in the car." Kirk directed me to sit in the back seat with him and asked me about Hawley and the hospitals in the theater as well as about our trip to Russia. As we entered the Pentagon, Grow abruptly left us, and Kirk directed me to the air surgeon's office and then went on his way.

Jensen and his staff were evidently expecting me because they were assembled in his office. He was cordial, pleasant, and expressed their interest in the material that I had brought. During the presentation, Grow entered and listened. When I had finished and before Jensen and his staff could ask questions, Grow objected strenuously to any implications, he said, that he and his staff had missed the injuries in the first place, had continued to disregard them, and had failed at any time to study them. Jensen heard him through and replied that the facts, not the implications, needed no defense. I angrily said that he had placed every kind of an obstruction in the way and just why I didn't know, because I wasn't bucking for his job, nor any other job in the Army. I pointed out that had he co-operated when Hawley had sent me down to present the material to him in the first place, he and his staff could have received all of the credit, if he thought any was due. Jensen interrupted my tirade to ask if he understood correctly that General Hawley had sent me down with the material to show it to General Grow and inform him about the patients. Before I could answer, Grow said that "they" knew all about the situation when I appeared. Jensen said that was strange because the air surgeon's office had never been informed about the patients and continued saying that he thought Grow owed me an apology. Grow mumbled that there were no hard feelings on his part, but I said that there were hard feelings on my part and they concerned the dishonest statements that had been made and were continuing to be made. I gathered up my material and started to leave but was stopped by Jensen who kindly said that he and his staff wanted to know more and would I answer some questions over a cup of coffee. Grow left, and the rest of the afternoon was spent pleasantly discussing the condition, how it had been studied, what the methods of treatment had been, and what could be done to prevent it.

The Air Force eventually requested copies of my color photographs of the injuries produced by high-altitude frostbite and made educational posters designed to instruct airmen on proper protective measures. Properly wired clothing was issued, and the side-gun apertures on aircraft were closed in. The plastic material for protective armor was field-tested by the Marine Corps and the Navy, and finally, on September 15, 1951, the Army Medical Corps announced that a plastic-protected vest would stop a .45 caliber bullet fired from a distance of three feet. This armored protective clothing was eventually used in the field during the Korean War with great success.

I was completely ignorant about the unusual character of the orders I had received to proceed by air from England to the United States. Paul Hawley wrote them personally, I learned later, and the freedom of movement that they provided caused eyebrows to be raised in the surgeon general's office. I had lost thirty pounds in weight and still suffered from the symptoms of amebic dysentery and a kidney stone that first occurred in Russia. After presenting the material on the helmet and the high-altitude frostbite in Washington, I returned home and was admitted to the army general hospital located in the old Chicago Beach Hotel. From there, I was sent to the Percy Jones Army General Hospital at Battle Creek, Michigan, and ended in the Walter Reed Hospital in Washington, from where I was discharged from the Army.

I regretted being unable to return to the European theater of operations and take part in the Normandy landing, but I was glad to be back at my hospital and medical school resuming my practice, administering the department of surgery, and teaching. Deservedly or not, I had been promoted to a colonelcy and received the Legion of Merit. Edith had worked in radio during my absence to help support herself and keep our children in school. Her experience in the theater made her a valuable asset to the producers of "Betty and Bob" and several other radio programs. I had missed Nancy's commencement exercises at Smith College but had arrived back to visit Dick in his first term at Princeton.

As a result of Dick's earlier attendance at the Chicago Latin School for Boys with the children of Mayor Edward J. Kelly, Edith and I had become their friends. The Democratic mayor often said that he knew I always voted the Republican ticket but that my vote was canceled by that of my Virginia-born Democrat wife. I learned many things about the workings of city, county, and state governments from Ed Kelly. A tall, redheaded Irishman with a quick wit, uneducated beyond grade school, he attracted people mainly, I think, because they identified with him in his mispronunciations of words and his laboring-class background. They boasted of how he said "vitamums" and introduced Admiral Halsey as Alderman Halsey.

The office of mayor of Chicago is politically more powerful than that of the governor of Illinois. I was nonplussed one evening when the Kellys had been invited to our home for dinner and I answered the doorbell to find Dwight Green, then the Republican governor, and his wife. I was sure Edith had erroneously invited them for the same night. There was no hesitation as they greeted each other warmly, and my embarrassment quickly disappeared. After dinner, they were in earnest conversation and the governor asked to use our telephone. When he returned, he said quietly to the mayor, "I've taken care of it." Until then, I thought that political rivals must be dyed-in-the-wool enemies but soon learned that this is more apparent in campaigns than it is in the day-to-day administration of government.

Dick once accompanied us when he was in his teens to Eagle River, where the Kellys had a summer home. On a rainy Sunday afternoon the mayor, Dick, and I took a walk in the woods. Suddenly, and much to my confusion, Dick asked him how he got into politics. He said that when he was a boy back of the yards, there was no YMCA, and so he and his friends rented a vacant store for five dollars a month, got some chairs, dumbbells, exercising pulleys, and tables. This was their club. He said, modestly I thought, that for some reason he was elected president and organized their baseball team. The veteran Irish alderman of the ward asked Kelly and his friends to ring doorbells throughout the ward and urge his election. The mayor said, "We put him over in a hard campaign." By the next aldermanic election Kelly had passed his twenty-first birthday, and the club decided he should run for office against the alderman.

"Dick," said the mayor, "that was the first time I was short-penciled."

"What do you mean, Uncle Ed?"

We sat down on a log, he took a piece of paper from his pocket, made out a specimen ballot, printed in names of candidates and the voting squares. Then he cut his pencil down to a short stub which he held concealed between his fingers and explained how the ballot could be invalidated by extending the lines of the X outside the square. It was a graphic teaching demonstration, easily understood. "The next time I ran it was for mayor of Chicago."

This offered me an opportunity for a question that he might or might not answer. Harry Truman was running for President against Thomas Dewey. The Democrats had nominated Adlai Stevenson, a Princeton University graduate from stylish Lake Forest, for governor, and Paul Douglas, a professor at the University of Chicago who was an alderman in the city council, for United States senator. So I brashly gave my opinion that the Democrats didn't expect to win Illinois against Dewey or they wouldn't have nominated Stevenson and Douglas. They could afford to lose these two offices, since they controlled City Hall and the states attorney's office, the second most powerful office in Cook County. I said I thought they were put up as pigeons to be shot down. After the defeat, the party could take the position that they had nominated two fine, upstanding citizens who were rejected, and at the next election they could go back to the professional politicians in the party. Kelly's answer was that Paul Douglas was a smart man, a professor, with a brilliant mind; Stevenson, a fine citizen, whose family had been politically oriented in Illinois for years. I persisted by asking him to tell me about Douglas who served in the city council. "Well," he said, "one day we were having a meeting of the council finance committee on the budget when a knock came at the door. When Douglas opened the door, some of my Irish aldermen told him to get out, he wasn't a member of the committee. I invited him in to hear what he had to say. His plan to save money for the city was to furnish bridge tenders with jeeps. The tender at the Michigan Avenue bridge could open and close it, jump in his jeep, skip Wabash Avenue, and go to the State Street bridge. This would cut the number of bridge tenders by half. The trouble was that Douglas forgot about the second boat." To a practical realist like Kelly, this was a stupid proposal. After a thoughtful moment of silence, he said, "If Dewey will make a strong, aggressive speech at the stadium next week attacking Truman, we will lose. If he doesn't, we'll take Illinois by about fifteen thousand votes." Dewey didn't make the speech, and Stevenson and Douglas were elected.

Shortly after, Irene Castle McLaughlin stirred up a controversy about the use of dogs by medical schools for teaching and research. She appeared before the council and got the support of the Hearst papers in her antivivisection crusade. An alderman named O'Halloran introduced a bill into the council that would prohibit the use by the medical schools of unlicensed, unclaimed dogs consigned to the city pound. I was asked by Andrew Ivy, professor of physiology at Northwestern, if I could get an appointment with the mayor for representatives of each of the medical schools to present an ordinance in opposition to the O'Halloran bill for his consideration. Kelly readily agreed.

I went with the committee of four, introduced them, and the mayor told A. J. Carlson, the famous physiologist at the University of Chicago, how much he admired his work and his knowledge about "vitamums." There ensued a deadly silence which I broke by urging Ivy to give the mayor our proposed bill. He read it through carefully and said, "This seems to me to be all right. I'll have the corporation counsel look it over and put it in the right language." Carlson's expression of thanks for the committee was interrupted by Italo Volini, then dean of the Catholic medical school, who began a tirade against the Hearst newspapers and their treatment of fine doctors and scientists. He referred to the cardinal, who was in favor of the proper care and use of animals for research. The mayor heard him through patiently and then said, "They wrap today's garbage in yesterday's newspapers, and the cardinal doesn't run the city of Chicago." I quickly ushered the committee out of his office.

One week later, the telephone rang at 9:30 at night, and the mayor asked if he, his corporation counsel, and Alderman O'Halloran could stop at our house for a cup of tea. Could I, he asked, get some of the members of the doctors' committee to meet with them? Luckily, I found Ivy still in his laboratory. Around our dining room table, Kelly handed the proposed ordinance to Ivy, who read it carefully and said that it was excellent and would be quite satisfactory. Kelly turned to O'Halloran and said, "Introduce it at the council meeting tomorrow and it'll be the O'Halloran ordinance, but the next time don't go off base because some society dame flatters you."

The irony of the situation came two weeks after our bill was passed when the physiologists wanted me to ask the mayor to have the bill amended to improve one facet that they had overlooked. I knew the mayor well enough to know that it would have proved to be an unwise and futile request. He would have expressed himself forcibly about endangering what had been accomplished against real opposition.

My research interests became directed toward the problem of the surgical treatment of hypertension and the efforts to control essential hypertension by removing portions of the sympathetic nervous system. This was the type of high blood pressure for which no cause could be demonstrated. Herbert Barker, a young internist colleague, had instituted the treatment of his patients with a drug, thiocyanate, which was quite successful. We found that in those patients who were resistant to the drug, removal of the sympathetic nerves made the drug more effective. We took the problem into the experimental laboratory and produced hypertension in animals by partially occluding the arteries to the kidneys with a metal clamp. We then gave the dogs thiocyanate before and after removal of the sympathetic nerve supply and followed the systolic blood pressure in the animals.

Both Barker and I thought of the possibility of the existence of an occlusion of the renal artery in man as the cause of the hypertension for which no other cause could be found. We knew that women often developed high blood pressure in the menopause, that older patients with arteriosclerosis had hypertension, and that younger individuals often had rises and falls in their blood pressure which fluctuated with their emotional stresses. It was only after the introduction of a method of introducing opaque material into the vessels that supplied the brain and demonstrating them on X-ray films that the same technique was applied to the blood vessels in the abdomen and thorax. By this method, various degrees of occlusion of the arteries that supplied the kidneys were demonstrated. So the category of essential hypertension has disappeared, and the administration of thiocyanates and surgical operations on the sympathetic nervous system ceased.

It is easy to be critical of medical and surgical attacks upon disease processes in the light of the latest contributions to diagnostic procedures and the resultant advanced methods of treatment. It is also easy to be a Monday morning quarterback, or second-guess the strategy of a baseball manager. I am sure that many of the patients Barker and I were treating had occlusions of one or both renal arteries and could now be helped by vascular transplantation operations or by removing the obstructing material from the vessel.

I was elected to the board of regents of the American College of Surgeons in 1950. Paul Hawley was selected by the regents to be the director of the college, its chief administrative officer. Hawley was pleased to have been chosen and to become associated closely with the problems of the practice of surgery. He had served as chief medical officer of the Veterans Administration with General Omar Bradley, as the administrator, and as medical director of Blue Cross and Blue Shield after retiring from the Army Medical Corps.

The regents had elected Arthur W. Allen, of Boston, as their chairman. He initiated the move to replace the committee of three, which attempted to administer the affairs of the college following Martin's death, with a director who would carry out the policies of the regents and who would suggest avenues of activity by which the college could help influence the practice of surgery.

The board of regents always hold one of their meetings just preceding the annual Clinical Congress of the college at which scientific papers are read and exhibits of educational interest for the Fellows are shown. At the meeting in New York City in September 1952, certain members of the group of science writers and reporters who were covering the meeting requested the opportunity to discuss in a frank manner with the regents the perennial problem of fee-splitting between surgeons and physicians who refer them patients. Hawley had rekindled the concern of the regents over this unethical practice with which the college had concerned itself since its founding.

The splitting of the surgeon's fee with a physician who refers a patient to him is an inducement, which in its simplest form I had encountered while in practice in Galesburg, and in its many variations is a violation of a principle of professional ethics. A finder's fee in business and in the legal profession is acceptable, but a kickback is a violation of the trust that the patient's doctor will examine and give him his best judgment, uninfluenced by a desire for financial gain. The regents had steadfastly sought obedience to the ethic which emphasized that doctors attending a patient should submit separate and independent bills.

Fee-splitting, unheard of in many parts of the United States, was deeply rooted and, in fact, was the accepted mode of practice in other sections. In some areas local medical societies were attempting to change the code of ethics to make fee-splitting ethical under spurious situations easily met.

The conference with the science writers was unprecedented. Never before had the responsible officers of the college, or any other national medical organization, had the willingness and courage to submit to a round-table discussion of the unethical problem with press representatives. The questions put by the press representatives were sharp and pointed. They wished to know what was so bad about the practice, what the college was doing about it, and what the patient-public could do.

Finally, one of the science writers said sarcastically that it was futile to talk with the surgeons present because they all were lily-white, lived in ivory towers, and had no personal experience with fee-splitting. There was an embarrassed silence until I spoke. I had been warned not to speak to a fellow surgeon in Galesburg by my senior partner, I said, shortly after beginning practice, because he was offering a fifty-fifty split of the patient's fee while we were offering only a forty-sixty division. I said that I had received no teaching about professional ethics in medical school; I had never heard of the American College of Surgeons, but if they wished to speak only with someone who had personal knowledge of fee-splitting, I was available. My fellow regents were visibly surprised, but after a moment a chuckle that grew into laughter spread around the table.

I said that there was no question in my mind that fee-splitting was being practiced in Chicago and the surrounding areas and in some areas was on the increase. I knew that there was evidence of canceled checks and statements in the director's office that would support my statement. It was also emphasized by the regents that fee-splitting worked to exclude the young, well-educated and well-trained, ethically conscientious surgeon who sought to establish a practice in a community. Having carried out a policy to encourage young physicians to seek education and training to become a surgeon, the regents were deeply concerned. Fee-splitting worked against the immediate best interests of the patient by introducing a financial consideration into the choice of a surgeon, rather than professional competence, and against the general public benefit that came from elevation of the quality and improvement of the results of surgical treatment.

Three hundred thirty-eight newspapers carried stories about the conference, and thirty-six ran editorials. The majority commended the college for bringing the practice into the open, branding it for the fraud it is, and inspiring public respect and confidence in the medical profession. The Chicago newspapers ran editorials praising the position of the college, and one quoted me in a headline over their story. Three months after the meeting in New York, I was awakened by a representative of the City Press Association who informed me that charges had been preferred against me, seeking my dismissal as a member of the Chicago Medical Society. He was astounded that I had received no notification before the president of the society, who had been a student of mine, released the news to the press.

Approximately 150 physicians, all members of the society, most of them general practitioners and a large number from the staffs of two hospitals, signed petitions charging me with making statements for personal publicity advantages, releasing misleading information, and making statements detrimental to the entire medical profession. The charges were published on December 18, 1952; I did not receive official notification of the charges until January 19, 1953. I refused to appear until I had a copy of the petitions and the names of the signers. One name was that of a doctor who had served his internship at the Cook County Hospital with me, and upon whom I had operated and removed a large benign tumor from his brain which allowed him to return to his lucrative practice.

I was not allowed to appear before the society's Committee on Ethical Relations accompanied by an attorney to defend myself. I prepared my own defense and was accompanied by Warren Cole, professor and chairman of the department of surgery at the University of Illinois Medical School, an old and respected friend.

In the meantime the Chicago newspapers commented editorially. Said the Chicago *Sun-Times:*

> Too frequently it has been the policy of individual busi-nessmen and certain business organizations to complain bitterly against criticism rather than do their part toward correcting the conditions criticized. It doesn't take a partic-ularly smart man to recognize that this is the wrong ap-proach.
>
> Chicago doctors currently are supplying another example of this type of attitude. . . . If they had asked the Chicago Medical Society to make an impartial investigation of the matter and then make public its findings, they would have attracted public support. As it is, one gets the impression that they are attempting to cover up, that they would silence all further criticism by those on the inside who know the facts. . . .

The Chicago *Daily News* commented:

> Physicians as a group . . . still have much to learn about the art of public relations. An illustration is the ill-timed and unwise attack on Dr. Loyal Davis. . . . The ouster ef-fort seems to be a sanctimonious attempt to silence a critic without bothering to refute his charges. The energy would

301

be much better spent in combatting the evil of which Dr. Davis complains. It is the Dr. Davises, and not their attackers, who gain public support for the profession in its battles over the drives to socialize medicine. . . .

The Chicago *Tribune* said:

One of the principal aims of the organizers of the American College of Surgeons, many years ago, was to wipe out fee-splitting. . . . The evil has been lessened, but, as the conversations in New York make clear, it has not been eradicated.

Dr. Davis was not sounding off on some curbstone when he said that the practice seems to be increasing in Chicago. He was speaking at a news conference with science writers, organized by 13 officials of the College, who spoke in its name, to organize public opinion against a practice that hurts the public.

The medical gentlemen who want to take reprisals against Dr. Davis are trying to indict the prosecutor. Dr. Davis is not given to rash or ill-considered statements, and if he says that fee-splitting exists in Chicago, his statement will be generally accepted as the truth. The medical society should be taking measures to stamp it out and the more responsible members, it can be predicted, will do so. . . .

In the hearing before the Committee on Ethical Relations of the society, the truth or falsity of my statement was not discussed; nor was there any discussion of fee-splitting in the later meetings of the council of the society which considered the report of the committee. The debate was confined to whether or not I was guilty of unethical conduct as a member of the Chicago Medical Society in making a public statement as a regent of the American College of Surgeons without the permission of the society. The American Medical Association had never been able to accept the fact that the American College of Surgeons was an independent organization; as a matter of fact, this same objection was raised by the Medical Association to the founding of the American Surgical Association.

302

Actually, the resolution then pending before the council of the Chicago Medical Society proposing that the code of ethics be redefined to make fee-splitting ethical supported my statement. This resolution ultimately resulted in reaffirming the American Medical Association's Principles of Medical Ethics, coupled with a request that the house of delegates consider amending the code to define proper conduct, responsibilities, and bill procedures where two or more physicians take care of a patient.

The five members of the Committee on Ethical Relations voted 3 to 2 to find me guilty of unethical conduct; the minority submitted a strongly worded report in protest. At its first meeting the council approved the committee's majority report and then tabled it. At the second meeting the council rescinded approval of the majority report by a vote of 42 to 32. Action was then taken to drop the charges. A nonspecific resolution was passed deploring the use of the public press in fighting unethical practices. The punishment for conviction of unethical conduct is expulsion, suspension, or censure. No one of the penalties was imposed upon me. During the time the council was considering my expulsion, two eminent jurists on vacation in Arizona assured me they would be happy if they could act as my attorney in any suit I wished to bring against the Chicago Medical Society if I were expelled.

The board of regents of the College of Surgeons issued a statement in the *Bulletin* of the college which, among other things, said:

> The American College of Surgeons has always contributed to the education of the profession and the public to the end that the care of the patient may be improved. The Regents of the College believe that the public is interested in the ethical principles which should be applied between the patient and the surgeon with reference to financial arrangements, the indications for surgical treatment and the qualifications and identity of the surgeon.
>
> A small minority of the medical profession chooses to circumvent its moral and ethical responsibilities and strongly resents any action which calls the attention of the public and the profession to its wrongdoing. This group

desires to keep the knowledge of these unethical practices from the public and to silence all doctors of good will who decry conduct which is prejudicial to the best care of the sick. . . .

The Regents of the American College of Surgeons believe it to be their duty to inform the profession and the public concerning these ethical and professional principles by all the methods of communication now available. They will continue to speak as a body, charged with the formation of policy for the American College of Surgeons, to maintain the high standards of surgical practice which the College has fostered. In these efforts, the College invites and hopes for the co-operation of all other medical organizations.

So ended the episode, and happily I was spared the thorny crown of martyrdom, but I earned the dislike of the Chicago Medical Society and the American Medical Association.

Dr. Evarts Graham, of St. Louis, who had performed the first removal of the lung for cancer, began his surgical practice in Mason City, Iowa, but soon returned to Chicago because of the prevalence of fee-splitting. He had been educated by Arthur Dean Bevan and Frank Billings at Rush Medical College, and his father was a doctor. They convinced him that Franklin Martin was a selfish, ambitious, untrustworthy man who promoted the Clinical Congress of Surgeons and the American College of Surgeons for his own purposes. He was highly critical of the college for not raising its requirements for admission and was a prime mover in founding the American Board of Surgery which established standards for surgical residency educational programs and conducted examinations leading to certification by the board that the candidate was a qualified, educated, and trained surgeon.

Graham accepted election by the board of governors as a regent of the college. He accepted his responsibilities as a regent with the same vigor and aggressiveness he had shown in opposition to the college, and was elected by his fellow regents as their chairman. The reputation and influence of the college in initiating and supporting measures to improve the care of surgical patients grew rapidly and progressively under his chairmanship. I felt sure that Franklin Martin was observing and chuckling over the actions of this convert with the greatest pleasure. They were much alike: opinionated, energetic, good friends to those whom they chose discriminately, and unrelenting enemies. Both had the ability to admit an error of action graciously.

I accompanied Dr. Kanavel to my first meeting as a member of the Society of Clinical Surgery in St. Louis, and Evarts Graham was the host. At the dinner I overheard Kanavel and Graham discussing the details of the Theodore Roosevelt shooting episode in Milwaukee. Graham was convinced that Murphy had stolen the patient from Bevan; Kanavel insisted more strongly than was his custom that he didn't know the facts and said that if he wanted to hear them, he should come to our room at the hotel when dinner was finished. I was told about the challenge on our way back to the hotel. Graham came, I told him what I had learned from my research into the occurrence, he listened attentively and asked a few pertinent questions. He finally rose, said he was glad to have the facts straightened out, and admitted his error.

He was more subtle on a later occasion. There was a committee of the regents who recommended surgeons to the board, whom they believed to be worthy of the honorary fellowship of the American College of Surgeons. These were awarded and citations read at the annual meeting when the candidates and the newly elected president were initiated into fellowship and office. The only time this tradition had been broken was on the occasion of the surgical mission to Russia when Elliott Cutler and I obtained the permission of the regents to honor Yudin and Burdenko with honorary fellowships.

Graham was highly enthusiastic about a sectional meeting of the college to be held in the British Isles and without consulting the committee, chose surgeons for honorary fellowship and announced their names to the board of regents at a meeting held in Cleveland. He requested that the regents approve his action. I voted against the proposal and said that he had not consulted the committee, that his action was dictatorial, and that to confer honorary fellowships at meetings other than the convocation and in such numbers might well set a custom that, in my opinion, would lower the honor it carried.

Graham became angry and charged me with being a party to conferring honorary fellowships outside the United States. I replied that it was true but I believed the circumstances to be quite different. We had a shouting match which he ended by adjourning the meeting for luncheon. Many of my fellow regents said they agreed with me completely but were silent when I asked why they had not expressed themselves in the meeting and voted their convictions. It was hinted that I would not serve another term as a regent; Graham would see to that. I replied that we would see what kind of a man he was if he couldn't take opposition and insisted upon being a dictator.

As I went into the room where luncheon was being served, there was a vacant chair next to him, and I sat down beside him. He looked at me and said, "You need a drink." I replied that perhaps he did, too, and we should have one together. He accepted enthusiastically. He left the table before all of us had finished our lunch, urging us to finish and get back to business. When I reached my seat, there was a rolled piece of white paper tied with a red ribbon in front of me. Graham quickly called the regents to order and said that he had conferred an honorary fellowship on me for stating my views and voting my opinions, but, he added with a smile, the action of the board would stand. From that time on, we had the most pleasant relationship, and on many occasions he commissioned me to present in writing to the board, policies that he had discussed with me and that we believed the board should consider.

One of the most dramatic of these resolutions of policy concerned the issuance of certificates of qualification by education and training in surgery by the International College of Surgeons. These were given to men who had failed to become certified by the American Board of Surgery, and there was evidence that they were easily obtained. The International Board of Surgery was functioning without the sanction of the Advisory Board for Medical Specialties under whose auspices all of the recognized qualifying boards were acting. The resolution of the regents called attention to the significant contributions made in the elevation of the quality of care and treatment of surgical patients to the highest level yet obtained by the standards adopted and applied by the existing American boards for certification in general surgery and each of the surgical specialties. The regents could find no logical justification for the establishment of other certifying boards in the same fields. It was the opinion of the regents, clearly expressed in the statement, that the application of standards fixed by the board of the International College of Surgeons was not in accordance with the generally accepted principles of education and training upon which competence in surgery should be evaluated. It was futile to believe that most patients would be able to distinguish between two standards for the certification of surgeons who were qualified to operate. The regents deplored the creation of certifying boards other than those approved by the Advisory Board for Medical Specialties and regarded such action as a menace to the existing standards in the practice of surgery and to their further elevation.

The regents advised the Fellows of the American College of Surgeons not to support in any manner the establishment and perpetuation of any certifying boards other than those approved by the Advisory Board for Medical Specialties and not to support any organization that sponsored such boards.

Later in the month of December 1951, after the resolution was adopted and circulated to the Fellows, Norman Littell, general counsel for the International College of Surgeons, United States Chapter, told the director, Paul Hawley, that the resolution was a direct attack on the International College and would have to be revoked. He claimed that it was a violation of the antitrust laws and that it invited legal proceeding for treble damages. He alleged that several resignations from the International College had resulted.

The International College of Surgeons was the brain child of Dr. Max Thorek, a Chicago surgeon. In 1937 *Time* magazine had commented that Dr. Thorek saw in Mrs. William Randolph Hearst a likely patroness for a new International College of Surgeons which he was to help an old Manhattan friend, Dr. Harold Lyons Hunt, get on its feet in the face of denunciation by the American Medical Association's mouthpiece, Dr. Morris Fishbein. Thorek had received the greatest opposition from Dr. Rudolph Matas, a scholarly, excellent surgeon and teacher, professor of surgery at Tulane University, who was active in the organization of the International Society of Surgery.

Fishbein, who had been retired as editor of the *Journal of the American Medical Association,* wrote an editorial in *Postgraduate*

Medicine, commenting upon the resolution passed by the regents of the American College of Surgeons. He said that the hostilities toward the International College of Surgeons waged by Rudolph Matas and Paul Hawley had been renewed. He attributed the growth in membership of the International College, which he failed to verify, to its director-general, Max Thorek, who spoke many languages, was dynamic, a master showman, and who had gained the respect and cooperation of many surgical leaders in foreign countries.

Thorek had been refused fellowship in the American College of Surgeons on more than one occasion in spite of his bizarre and questionable efforts to obtain the support of members of the local credentials committee. I was a member of this committee early in my professional practice when Edith supplemented my income by her radio appearances. I received a call from a doctor asking me to come to the American Hospital, which Thorek had succeeded in building with the financial help of the stagehands union, to see a young boy who had received a craniocerebral injury. I went, examined the boy, and talked with the parents and their doctor, assuring them that I believed their child would recover completely. I realized that we had been joined by Dr. Thorek. When I had finished and asked the father and mother if there were any questions they wished to ask, Thorek interrupted and said to the father, "You have received advice from the finest neurological surgeon in Chicago, or in the United States. Now pay him his fee." The father handed me a check for five hundred dollars. I tore it in half, gave it back to him, and said that I was in the habit of setting my own fees and that my consultation fee, taking into consideration his circumstances, was twenty-five dollars and I would send a statement for that amount. I learned later that John Wolfer and Philip Kreuscher, two other members of the credentials committee, had similar experiences.

On another occasion Thorek appeared at our office with his photographer assistant and insisted that Franklin Martin allow him to photograph him. Martin could not resist the smoothly stated appeal to his ego and posed. The camera angle, lights, and focus were set by the assistant while Thorek kept up a running command and finally squeezed the bulb. A Fellow of the Royal Society of Photography bitterly resented Thorek's election to fellowship, telling me that all of his photographic results were the product of his assistant. The photographic portrait of Franklin Martin that resulted from that afternoon's performance is the best existing photograph of him.

Dr. George Lull, then secretary and general manager of the American Medical Association, attempted to arrange a meeting between representatives of the two colleges in the hope of preventing legal complications with the attending publicity which might be damaging to the medical profession. Graham refused to meet with representatives of the International College when the organization was threatening the regents individually and the American College with a legal suit. Anyone who knew Graham well would understand that as chairman of the committee that organized the American Board of Surgery, he would take the establishment of the International Board of Surgery as a personal affront. He was somewhat offended, I thought, that the attack had not been made against him alone instead of the board of regents.

Finally, the board of trustees recommended to the house of delegates of the Medical Association that it reiterate its previously established position that the American Medical Association recognizes and approves only one certifying board in each of the specialties of medicine, namely, those boards established by the Advisory Board of Medical Specialties and the Council on Medical Education and Hospitals. The statement of policy that "it is not in the interest of medicine or of the public for other medical organizations to establish certifying agencies" was finally adopted by the house of delegates during its meeting in December 1952, a year after the board of regents had passed its resolution. Soon after, the International Board of Surgery was abolished, and the threatened legal action was dropped.

Six years later, the regents became aware of letters that were circulating to doctors soliciting their participation in the founding group for the "American Board of Abdominal Surgery." These came from Dr. Blaise Alfano, the organizing spirit of the American Society of Abdominal Surgery. Many requests for information about the proposed new board came to the offices of the American College of Surgeons. In the official *Bulletin* of the college, the regents issued a statement in October 1958 that said there were nineteen existing American specialty boards that had gained official status through sponsorship by recognized national societies of the particular specialty, and by the corresponding scientific section of the American Medical Association. Subsequently, each proposed board had been elected to membership in the Advisory Board for Medical Specialists and had received approval from the Council on Medical Education and Hospitals. The regents pointed out that sponsorship had not been achieved by the American Board of Abdominal Surgery and even though it was obtained, it did not assure approval by the Advisory Board for Medical Specialties. The statement was republished in June 1959.

Shortly thereafter, Alfano began his attempts to obtain sponsorship of the scientific section in general surgery of the American Medical Association for his board. The officers of that section asked him to outline the origin of the board, furnish the names of the surgeons responsible for its inception, names of the officers, the numbers of diplomas issued, the criteria for approval used by the regional credentials committees for certification. None of this information was furnished.

Alfano and his colleagues then took more direct and aggressive action. They attended the business session of the section in general surgery at the New York meeting of the Medical Association in 1961, and by sheer numbers of those present, the group elected their candidates as chairman, vice-chairman, and secretary of the section, in opposition to the slate recommended by the executive council of the section. This was the first time a political note had been introduced into a scientific section of the association. The meeting had been deliberately and efficiently packed by Alfano's adherents. After the election, a resolution was passed that gave approval of the section to the American Board of Abdominal Surgery.

These high-handed methods incensed the majority of the surgical profession, and an organized drive was begun to insure attendance at the next meeting of the section on general surgery to be held in Chicago in June 1962. The response from both groups was so great that the administrative staff of the American Medical Association had to provide a meeting hall that would hold more than a thousand for the business session. Such goon tactics were a surprise to the then chairman of the board of trustees of the American Medical Association, Dr. Hugh Hussey, he told me. As the result of a well-organized campaign, with a meeting chaired by a partisan, with speeches that were politically effective but extravagantly garnished by untruths, the "good guys" were again defeated by the "bad guys." Again belatedly, the Committee on Medical Education and Hospitals of the house of delegates dashed the hopes of Alfano and his colleagues for recognition of his self-constituted board, and at the next meeting of the section on general surgery, the slate of officers supported by Alfano was defeated.

The urge for status symbols leads in many directions among all professions and human relations. The ease with which men with particular gifts and talents can attract followers has been exemplified through the ages. Doctors, in particular, are "joiners," motivated in various ways. Some join because the new organization gives them an opportunity to talk and they like to talk; others, because meetings held in foreign countries make it possible to travel with proper support of an income tax deduction. Still others, who are unable to meet the qualifications in education and training established to elevate the care of patients, find that without the early sacrifices that are necessary, they can hang a certificate upon the wall of their office which can be displayed to an unsuspecting and undiscerning public.

Doctors should always be proud of belonging to a profession that stands alone in the enforcement of adherence of its members to a high code of ethical conduct which guides the relationship between its members and their patients and which dates back to the Hippocratic oath. The Principles of Medical Ethics of the American Medical Association contains the code of ethics to which all medical organizations subscribe. However, neither the principles nor their interpretation by the judicial council of the Medical Association have always been clear and precise; violations by the more enterprising members of the profession have been frequent. Therefore, the board of regents of the American College of Surgeons, in no way a subsidiary organization of the Medical Association, has made its own interpretation and requires its Fellows to observe a more stringent course of ethical conduct than that specified in the principles. The regents have held that the college has the right to do this in the interest of the welfare and best professional care of the surgical patient and disciplines its Fellows for infractions.

Evarts Graham had become so concerned with the affairs of the American College of Surgeons that he showed evidence that he believed he, alone, was capable of administration. He had served four terms of three years as a regent, and his chairmanship became more dictatorial, a beneficent dictatorship to be sure, but occasionally touched with humor which he did not recognize. On one occasion near the end of a morning meeting, Dan Elkin and Alfred Blalock attempted to slip out before adjournment to meet their wives for luncheon. As they quietly and surreptitiously attempted to leave, Graham fixed them with a glare and in a loud voice said, "Where are you going, the meeting isn't over. Sit down!" They did so promptly, but Dan said in a voice loud enough to provoke laughter, "I only wanted to go to the men's room."

The nominating committee of the board of governors rebelled when a member of the advisory committee of the regents, and a sitting regent, used all of the pressure he could bring to bear upon them to renominate Graham as a regent. This they refused to do, and Graham became bitter. As a result, the regents proposed that in the future, except in unusual circumstances, a regent could serve a total of three terms of three years each. Also, they established the rule that the advisory committee to the nominating committees of the governors and Fellows should consist of the last three past presidents of the college, who presumably had no further ambitions for office.

I. S. Ravdin was chosen as chairman of the board of regents succeeding Evarts Graham. Of Hebrew parents, a native of Evansville, Indiana, Rav, as he was universally addressed by his friends, was the son of an ophthalmologist. He often told of how, as a boy, he saw Allen Kanavel come courting Miss Olive Rosencranz, who lived across the street from his home. Rav had successfully conquered the animosity and jealousy that accompanied his success in his residency, direction of the experimental laboratory, and attending staff position at the hospital of the University of Pennsylvania. His ability as a surgeon was never questioned, nor were his talents as a teacher and administrator. He had risen to the John Rhea Barton professorship of surgery and chairman of the department against the odds imposed by his ancestry but helped tremendously by the charming intelligence of his wife, a fellow medical school graduate and classmate. He developed a wide spectrum of close friends and acquaintances among the business and industrial community of Philadelphia which he employed to great advantage for the benefit of the university and its hospital. He had served with distinction during World War II in the Burma-India theater of operations and repeatedly boasted of his experiences with Lord Louis Montbatten and General Joseph Stilwell.

I had the pleasure of serving as vice-chairman of the board of regents with Rav, and as a result, our friendship, which had begun as members of the Halsted Society, became closer. I understood the necessity for him to exaggerate the importance of his own role when he recounted his experiences, and often I pointed this out to his critics. But I also knew that in a discussion of principles he expressed himself logically, could accept an opposite opinion with flexibility, and was faithful and loyal to the final expression of policy by the regents. I also knew that often his forceful and rapid expression of a question for discussion carried his own opinion and that, as a result, many of his fellow regents did not express their own views. Often, I whispered to him to call upon certain of the regents to express themselves before a vote was taken.

During his chairmanship the International Federation of Surgical Colleges was organized to foster a free exchange of views in surgical education and patient care among nations. Each college was taxed for support as a body according to the size of its membership and had a representative on the council. It was hoped that somewhat as a surgical United Nations it could function for the relief of surgical and medical catastrophic events throughout the world. Its progress has been slow, hesitant, and thus far unproductive.

During a regents' meeting Rav was called by Leonard Heaton, surgeon general of the Army, and asked to consult about the abdominal symptoms of President Eisenhower. He took part in the subsequent surgical operation that restored the President to health.

Rav finished his contributions to the American College of Surgeons as its president and then had a distinguished career as vice-president in charge of medical affairs at the University of Pennsylvania, where

313

a hospital building dedicated to his name stands as a tribute to his excellence.

I succeeded Ravdin as chairman of the board of regents and was thrust immediately into a controversy between the college and the American Medical Association regarding the methods of implementing the ethics of professional practices. In 1955 I had received an honorary fellowship in the Royal College of Surgeons of England, a great honor which had come unexpectedly. Edith and I enjoyed the hospitality and warm friendship of Sir James and Lady Paterson Ross when we went to London to have it conferred. In 1957 another great honor had come to me in my election as president of the American Surgical Association, the premier surgical organization in the United States, in which membership was highly coveted. This was followed in 1958 by the honorary fellowship of the Royal College of Surgeons of Edinburgh, the oldest surgical college, chartered by James IV in 1505.

THIRTEEN

SPECIALIZATION does not preclude the art of the practice of medicine or treating the patient "as a whole." Over the years there are some patients whose symptoms prove to be more interesting than others; there are others whose personality captures interest; there are still others who can never be forgotten because of the humorous or tragic circumstances that accompanied their treatment.

The combination of the short, heavy, bull-necked, red-faced, rough-handed mechanic and the dark-haired, frail, younger wife with an aesthetic face was enough to stimulate interest in their problem. She did all the talking, and soon the reason was obvious. Her husband, she said, suffered with severe pain on the right side of his face which came on suddenly, lasted a few seconds, reached a climax, and then, as suddenly, disappeared. Eating, talking, shaving, the slightest touch of his face beside his nose, would start the pain. She had insisted that he come for an examination. The story and the trigger zone from which his pain could be started were typical of tic douloureux, or trigeminal neuralgia. I explained in detail, drew a diagram of the nerve, told them the cause was unknown, that I might have my first attack while talking to them. She nodded her head and said that his first pain came while they were in a movie theater, and it caused him to cry out. I said that the only relief was to cut that portion of the nerve inside the skull that would never regenerate; his face on that side would be numb for the rest of his life. Then, we did not have experience with a combination of drugs that often control the pain. When I explained the operation in detail, he got up abruptly, grabbed her hand, shook his head, and said, "Let's go." She was embarrassed, pleaded with him to stay, have the operation, reminded him of the severity of his pain, cried, apologized for taking up my time, and started to leave. I stopped them and said that when his pain persisted in its severity, without relief, he would make up his own mind; to call me and we would operate upon him. It was his pain, no one else's. The pain alone would not kill him; it was up to him to decide how long he could tolerate it.

The call pleading with me to admit him into the hospital came the next night. He was a co-operative patient, did well during the operation, and was so relieved of his pain that he ate his dinner that evening. He was warned to stay quietly in bed until we allowed him to sit up, dangle his legs, and finally we would allow him out of bed. I had opened his skull, released cerebrospinal fluid. It was necessary to allow the intracranial mechanics to readjust. The next day he cajoled a voluntary nursing aide to bring him a chocolate ice cream soda from the hospital gift shop, and when we made rounds, he was standing by his bed, smacking his lips over it. The possibilities of what might happen to him, so soon after his operation, frightened all of us, and we quickly put him back in bed. I scolded him harshly and at length. He looked at me sullenly but never challenged my orders to stay in bed until we told him he could be out.

A few days later, the resident and interns began to laugh as we came into the ward where Steve was. They told me what had happened while they were cutting his sutures and dressing his wound. He told them that he had a garage and was an expert automobile mechanic; that he would repair and tune up each of their cars free of charge any time they wished. Then he offered them a bonus if they would get me to bring my car to him so he could put sugar in the transmission. He was serious, not mad, they said; this was evidently the only way he could work out to get even for the scolding I had given him before all of the other ward patients for something he was convinced had not harmed him and which he had a right to do. Later, his wife heard the story and told him he should be ashamed for disobeying my orders and for being so childish as to want to get even. When he left the hospital, he grinned, thanked me for our care, said that he didn't know how he had stood the pain as long as he had, and returned regularly and faithfully for his postoperative checkup examinations. He took great pride in discovering other patients with trigeminal neuralgia and referring them for operation.

The telephone rang at midnight and awakened me from a sound sleep. The woman's voice said, "I have a brain tumor, and I want

316

you to operate on me." It took me several seconds to become alert enough to ask the proper questions which might explain this unusual call from a total stranger at such an hour. Her name, she said, was Alice Hatch; she had suddenly begun to have convulsive seizures; she had been diagnosed as having a brain tumor in New Haven, where her only son was at Yale University. Why hadn't she stayed there and received treatment? She was a widow, lived in Chicago, barely earned a living doing interior decorating, and most important of all, her friend, the sister of a former mayor of Chicago, would be glad to pay her hospital bill. I examined her the next morning, she was admitted to a private room, and all of our diagnostic tests indicated that she had a benign brain tumor sitting on the surface of the right side of her brain. She had put off consulting a doctor about her convulsive seizures until she had become hemiparetic on the left side, dragged her leg when she walked, and had practically lost the use of her arm. She was interested, she said, in living, not whether or not she would regain the full use of her arm and leg.

As I visited her the afternoon before the operation, I found her sitting up in bed, dressed in a stunning white negligee, with a silver tea service, which she had borrowed from the office of the women's board, on the bedside table. She was pouring tea for three lady visitors. Upon invitation, I, too, had a cup of tea, was introduced to her friends, and was embarrassed by the fulsome praise with which she told them about my abilities as a surgeon. Finally, she commanded them to leave with an imperious gesture and ordered me to remain. She wasted no time but immediately and directly came to the matter that obviously concerned her.

"Doctor, I have no money to pay my hospital bill or your fee. My dear friend, the former mayor's sister, will pay all of my hospital expenses."

I interrupted and said that I had often operated upon patients who could not pay a professional fee.

"Doctor, you interrupted me. I was about to say that the story of my life will be the payment of my fee to you. I know you are interested in people, aside from their illness; I have read your biography of Doctor Murphy. My life has been just as interesting. You see, I am the unrecognized daughter of a beautiful young French countess and the son of the Turkish ambassador to France. I'll give

317

you all the facts and materials before I leave the hospital. Now you go home, have a good night's rest, and don't worry about me; together we'll make the operation a success."

I left her room with admiration for her assurance, self-confidence; with wonder about the truth of her story; and with suspicion that she evidenced some of the symptoms of a frontal lobe euphoria.

The operation was successful; she quickly recovered and was gaining improvement in the movements of her left extremities with rehabilitation and physical therapy exercises when she left the hospital. "I will bring all of the documents when I come to see you next Friday on my regular physical therapy day. When you have read them, I am sure you will feel fully repaid."

The story that developed from the letters, photographs, and newspaper clippings I was given, punctuated by comments from Alice Hatch, was this:

In the summer of 1882, a childless widow, Mrs. Bonfield, answered an advertisement published in the *New York Herald* seeking a home for a female child. After a series of interviews, she received a little girl, between two and three years of age, from Dr. J. Marion Sims, a distinguished gynecologist of New York and founder of the Women's Hospital. The child was brought from France in November, 1882, by a nurse with whom he had placed the child. Dr. Sims told Mrs. Bonfield that the child had been born in Paris of aristocratic parentage, and that for a time it was necessary to keep the child's existence, and its parentage, a secret.

Dr. Sims, a South Carolinian by birth, graduated from the Medical College at Charleston, South Carolina, in 1834 when he was 21 years of age. He began practice in Lancaster, South Carolina, and married the daughter of a doctor with whom he entered practice. He and his family became infected with malaria and with the help of friends moved to Montgomery, Alabama, where he built a one-story, eight-bed hospital and entered practice. He developed the operation for vesico-vaginal fistula which was common among female slaves due to a disproportion of the size of the head of the fetus and pelvis in protracted labor. His patients were miserable, uncomfortable, constantly wet with irritating and malodorous urinary excretions, and were regarded as incurable. As the results of his technique, using a vaginal speculum and silver wire sutures, became known, his reputation increased. He moved to New York in 1853, with the hope of escaping the recurrent attacks of malaria which caused him to become intolerant, impatient, fretful, easily angered, jealous of his rights and alert to the slightest encroachment upon his discovery of a successful operative technique.

Sick, emaciated, fragile and worried, he entered practice in New York and, with the help of Henry Luther Stuart, founded the Women's Hospital located at 83 Madison Avenue. Dexterous, bold, self-reliant, ingenious with a restless and active mind, Sims made many professional enemies. When the Civil War broke out, his strong southern sympathies led him to make reckless remarks. His popularity and practice, which came from patients below the Mason-Dixon line, dwindled. He left for Europe, travelled and visited clinics in Scotland, Ireland and London, where he demonstrated his operation. He went to France where he received an enthusiastic reception and began a practice, which he continued from 1862 to 1868. He became the physician to the Duchess of Hamilton; lived in a chateau at Baden-Baden; was presented to Empress Eugenie, became her physician at St. Cloud and was made a Knight of the Legion of Honor of France.

He returned to New York in 1868 and was appointed senior consulting surgeon at the Women's Hospital and a member of the Board of Governors. He returned to France in 1870 and served as Surgeon-in-Chief and was in command of the Anglo-American Ambulance Corps which consisted of eight American and eight British surgeons. He returned to New York and the Women's Hospital where he had violent arguments with the Board of Governors, who had adopted a resolution refusing admission of cancer patients and limiting observers at operations. He offered his resignation in 1875 which was accepted and his application for reinstatement later was refused. He continued to practice in New York but at intervals spent months in Paris and Rome operating upon patients.

It was, therefore, possible that J. Marion Sims had firsthand knowledge of the birth of the child in 1879 or 1880. My skepticism partially disappeared when I read the handwritten letter addressed to Mrs. Bonfield and signed, J. Marion Sims. I compared the signature with that of Sims on other letters in the medical school library. It was authentic.

> 12 Place Vendôme
> Paris
> Dec. 12, 1882

My dear Mrs. Bonfield:

My daughter Mrs. Carr forwarded to me your letter of the 30th Nov. and we are all glad to hear such a good report of yourself and the precious little Alice.

As I have so long had the responsibility of her management in my hands I feel as much interested in her, and her welfare as if she were my own flesh and blood.

I hope and pray that she may be only comfort and happiness to you as long as you live.

We go to Rome in a week. But will be at home again next summer. I wonder if we shall have the pleasure of seeing you and your dear baby in New York then, or shall we some day see you here?

My wife joins me in kindest regards and best wishes for you both.

Believe me, dear Mrs. Bonfield, yours most sincerely,

> J. Marion Sims

The story went on:

Mrs. Bonfield married a close friend of her late husband, Jesse B. Barton, an attorney in Chicago, who legally adopted the child and named her Alice Barton.

320

Mr. Barton read an item in the *Chicago Tribune* of October 17, 1900, which concerned the death of Prince Felix Hohenloe, a cousin of Queen Victoria. The gossip column, however, was concerned with the marriage of his son, Prince Kraft Hohenloe, to the niece of General the Marquis de Gallifet. The story said that the young lady had been the heroine of a sensational elopement shortly after debut in society when she married Paul Musurus Bey, Secretary of the Turkish Embassy in London, son of the Ambassador to England, and a brother of Princess de Vrancovan. The young couple fled to London where they were married and lived. The young bride's guardian, the General, and her mother persuaded them to return to France when she informed them she was pregnant. She was assured that all would be forgiven. Upon landing in France, they were seized by the police, she was delivered to her relatives and Musurus was expelled from France, with a warning that he escaped criminal proceedings for abduction solely because of his diplomatic position in England. The marriage was annulled on the grounds that it was contracted without the consent of the guardian and the mother of the girl, Marguerite Maria Madeline D'Imecourt. Later, the story said, Mlle. D'Imecourt married Prince Kraft Hohenloe but the marriage was not a happy one. The Prince lived at Neustadt near Vienna, where he was stationed as a Captain of Austrian cavalry and his wife was confined in one of her own chateaux, not far from Nancy, where she was maintained under restraint. The columnist wrote: "There are no children born to this marriage, though there was a girl by the former union of the Princess with Paul Musurus Bey. Only the D'Imecourt family know what has become of this child."

Mrs. Barton remembered that Dr. Sims had told her that the young mother was given chloroform for the delivery and when she awakened was told that her child was born dead.

Jesse Barton now became dedicated to a search to establish the identity of his adopted daughter, who was a young lady, denying at all times any desire to establish her as a legal heiress to Princess Hohenloe's fortune. He wrote William A. Prickitt, the United States Consul in Rheims, asking if he could determine the date of the marriage of Paul Musurus Bey and Mlle. D'Imecourt; asking for photographs of Princess Hohenloe before her marriage and at present, and what the reasons were, if any, for the seclusion of the Princess. Mr. Prickitt wrote to the editor of *The Figaro,* asking for enlightenment about the two marriages. He received a short, curt, impolite reply which revealed nothing. He explained this to Mr. Barton by saying that the Princess Hohenloe was a niece of General de Gallifet, late Minister of War, and that he and the editor were intimate friends.

Eventually, Prickitt sent photographs of Marguerite Maria Madeline D'Imecourt taken at the ages of ten, sixteen, and as Princess Hohenloe in 1889.

"Don't you see the likeness to my photograph as a little girl, Doctor?" I had to admit that the resemblance was striking, particularly the large, prominent eyes.

"My father continued to write letters, following every lead he got." The bundle in my hands was convincing evidence of Mr. Barton's persistence.

He had verified the date of the marriage between Paul Musurus Bey and Marguerite D'Imecourt in London as October 13, 1879. He learned that Paul Musurus had remarried and was living in Paris at 35, avenue de la Grande Armie. His letter to him was never answered.

Alice's father pressed Prickitt to make an attempt to get Princess Hohenloe to become interested in the question of whether or not a daughter born to her was living. If he could get her to admit that she was attended by Dr. Sims, if she would compare her photograph with that of Alice, with the assurance that there was no attempt to seek financial gain, the question could be settled for once and all.

Mr. Barton wrote Harriet Hubbard Ayer, editor of the home page of the New York *Herald,* who answered his question about the Marquise de Fontenoy, who had written the article that appeared in the Chicago *Tribune.* She replied that the marquise was a clever writer who wrote strictly for money and she might not be the most reliable source of information. This was an unusual comment; a bit like the pot calling the kettle black.

Prickitt continued to send back information driblet by driblet. Princess Hohenloe had been divorced from Kraft Hohenloe, after agreeing to pay him a large sum of money. She had subsequently married a German, Baron de Wangenheim. She resided at 30 Kasernen Strasse, Brunswick, Germany. The Baron was intendant of the Ducal Theater in Brunswick and held a high and important position at the Ducal Court.

On June 24, 1903, Barton wrote directly to the baroness giving her all of the facts in chronological order, stating that he believed her to be the mother of his adopted daughter, Alice. He enclosed photographs of Alice taken at various ages and said that if she had been attended by Dr. Sims, and had been led to believe that her child was born dead, he believed that a scrupulous examination of the photographs would convince her that her child was alive. If, he said, on the other hand she had knowledge of the existence of her own infant, or that she had seen her child who had later died, then the photographs would be false evidence. In any case, he insisted she would respect his feelings in the matter if she would agree to receive his representative who would present his credentials, the letter, and the photographs.

On February 29, 1904, the United States consul in Brunswick, Talbot J. Albert, wrote Barton that an entertainment that was to have been given to the attachés of the Ducal Theater on the evening of February 27 had to be postponed on account of the baroness's illness from a heart attack. Barton never received a reply from the baroness but continued his search for proof. On November 15, 1904, he wrote John K. Goudy, consul general in Paris, asking him to verify the possible date of Alice's birth as March 28, 1880, by consulting the Registry of Births. In addition to giving the name of Dr. J. Marion Sims as the attending obstetrician at the birth, he supplied the name of Constance Boucherre, the nurse to whom Sims gave the child immediately upon delivery. If the date of the marriage in London of Marguerite D'Imecourt and Paul Musurus Bey was correct, and if the birth date was correct, there would be added reason for the young couple to have eloped to legitimatize the birth.

Barton was not discouraged or deterred in his project to establish his adopted daughter's parentage. He wrote Dr. John A. Wyeth, of New York, Sims's medical executor and son-in-law, on April 22, 1907. Barton said that Dr. Sims had told his wife the date of the child's birth; that the mother of the child was very young; that the child, at the time of the adoption, resembled its mother strongly; that great secrecy was maintained to conceal the fact that a child was born; that the child's mother, her mother, and an aunt occupied an apartment in Paris, without servants, and that he was called to attend the young woman; that when the child was born after chloroform anesthesia, he gave the child to Madame Boucherre; that he returned to the mother and when she had regained consciousness, told her that the child was born dead; that if the child's identity became known, it would create serious family trouble; that Madame Boucherre and her husband had taken the infant and cared for it in their home in Sens sur Yonne. Barton related all of the steps he had taken to establish Alice's parentage and asked Wyeth if he would search through Dr. Sims's papers and books of account to find the name D'Imecourt or Gallifet, possibly some memorandums or copies of letters between Dr. Sims and some member of the young mother's family. He received no answer from Dr. Wyeth.

Barton took his wife and Alice to Kissingen where the consul in Brunswick had informed him the baron and baroness had moved. Their search in Kissingen was fruitless. In reply to Barton's letter of complaint, Consul Albert said that indeed the Von Wagenheims had moved to Kissingen from Brunswick and had leased a villa. He chided Barton for not having inquired at police headquarters or the post office, where they might have been registered.

"I remember how frustrated my father was because he couldn't find my real mother. I don't know just why he gave up when he was so close to them in Kissingen or just what he planned to do if he located them. My foster mother was interested and tolerant of his efforts but was satisfied to let the matter drop. I was sure that

I was the child born to Marguerite D'Imecourt and Paul Musurus Bey. I understood why my real mother thought of me and my foster father as impostors; she believed what she had been told by Dr. Sims and her family. I suppose she was convinced that we were trying to establish proof so that I could inherit some of her fortune."

"You would have liked that, wouldn't you?" I asked.

Mrs. Hatch was frank. "Yes, I would. I have always had the feeling that I was born to enjoy luxury. I hope the story has repaid you for your surgical skill and care." I assured her that it had; in fact, it has continued to repay me because I, too, would like to have the unmistakable proof of her parentage.

I think it is unfair to judge Dr. J. Marion Sims in the light of present-day professional ideals and standards. Certainly, today obstetricians do not reveal the parents of infants born to unwed mothers for whom they arrange adoption. But the adopted parents do not make the persistent efforts that Barton made to determine the parentage. I doubt if Barton would have done so had it not been for his chance reading of the gossip column in the newspaper.

Evidently, Sims was a man of strong opinions, ambitious, perhaps flattered by patients of social and court standing, using the reputation he had achieved abroad to strengthen his influence among his professional colleagues in New York. He was brought into the situation after the marriage had been annulled; there was reasonableness in the request to prevent further harm to the young woman's future. However, if all the facts were true, it remains that the young mother was not told the truth about her child, a responsibility that was shared by her family. It could be assumed that the young woman was never happy in her subsequent marriages, certainly not that to Kraft Hohenloe. Perhaps she lost her true love, and one wonders if she was torn between her intuition that her child was living and the apparently unassailable statements that her child was born dead.

This tale of romance and intrigue was balanced by experiences that dealt with pragmatic, realistic people. I was asked by Dr. Karl Meyer to come to the West Side Hospital to care for a patient with a gunshot wound of the head. Dr. Meyer, a fine surgeon and long-time medical warden of the Cook County Hospital, whom I had known from the time I was an intern, was a member of my surgical faculty at Northwestern. He told me to go right ahead and take care of the patient and advised me to bring any special instruments I thought would be necessary. Edith and Jeannette Jones, my surgical nurse, went with me. I took Edith to a waiting room where she could be comfortable and read her book; Jeannette went to the operating room to get the instruments sterilized, and I examined the patient. He had a craniocerebral wound in the right frontal area, and brain tissue was visible among the clotted blood and matted hair. I told his red-haired, attractive wife that he should be operated upon; that he was not unconscious; and that I believed he had an excellent chance for recovery. She listened attentively, asked no questions, and directed me to go ahead.

I carefuly debrided the wound, after shaving the head meticulously, removing loose brain tissue and irrigating the wound carefully. The X-ray films had shown that the missile had not been retained; it evidently had entered and exited in an unusually favorable tract. Loose bone fragments were removed, and I had no difficulty in obtaining a tight closure of the scalp. The patient responded well after he recovered from the anesthesia and showed no evidence of a motor defect.

I went to see his wife to tell her what we had found and how her husband had responded. Again, she listened carefully, thanked me for my care, and said: "Doctor, my husband's name is not Barker under which he was admitted to the hospital. He's Frank Parker, and he's been mixed up with booze running by airplanes from Canada. He's a licensed pilot. I'm Nellie Parker. We grew up together in a small coal mining town in Pennsylvania. Frank drove into the parking lot behind our apartment building this evening, and as he got out of the car he was shot in the head. I heard two shots; one missed. Frank didn't have a chance to protect himself. Now, I want to pay your fee; I've heard how you take care of your patients and continue to see them after they've recovered. I want you to do that for Frank. How much is it?"

Her directness and frankness confused me. In fact, I was somewhat embarrassed to have been taken into her confidence so quickly. Before I could answer, she said to her sister, "Get a thousand-dollar bill out of the upper drawer." She gave it to me, saying, "I hope this is satisfactory." It was the largest fee I had ever received for an operation.

Nellie brought Frank for postoperative examinations regularly. He was striking in appearance: tall, blond, had a rugged face with an attractive smile, and he was extroverted. On one visit he earnestly tried to get me interested in buying shares in a gold mine in Colorado. His sales talk was eloquent, low-pitched, and convincing. Nellie knew her husband well. She opened the door to the examining room, grabbed him by the arm, and said, "The doctor has finished with you this time. Come on, you should be ashamed of yourself, trying to sell the doctor that phony gold mine stock."

I didn't see Frank Parker for several months but read in the newspaper that he had been convicted for participation in a mail fraud and was sentenced to the federal prison in Atlanta. Some time later, Nellie called for an appointment and told me that Frank was in bad company in the Atlanta prison. She would like to have him transferred to Leavenworth. She asked if I would give her a letter recommending the transfer because of Frank's convulsive seizures. She said he would get better medical care, she had been told, in Leavenworth. Nellie was not completely satisfied when I wrote a letter that simply stated what I had found and done at operation and what I had observed in my repeated postoperative examinations. I tried to find out what happened to Frank and Nellie after he had been paroled from Leavenworth. Finally, a Christmas card came from that small coal mining town in Pennsylvania. Frank's seizures were controlled with sodium dilantin; they had a small general store, and Nellie had found the happiness she looked forward to when they were first married. Maybe the frontal lobe destruction that the gunshot wound had produced had affected a lobotomy and Frank's personality had been changed.

The next name on my office appointment list one afternoon was Mr. Williams. When I asked him to come in, a big man well over six feet tall rose from his chair, and with him came a round-faced, plump boy whom I judged to be about twelve to fourteen years of age. Mr. Williams told me that two years previously his son had a brain abscess, the result of a middle ear infection, which had been treated at a hospital in New York City. They did not now live in New York City, and he wanted my opinion as to whether or not the high altitude in Colorado would be detrimental to the boy if he were to spend the summer on a ranch. I got the history of the middle ear infection and as much as they could tell me about the surgical treatment of the brain abscess and then asked the boy to come into the examining room, take off his clothes, and get up on the examining table. I left the door open into the consulting room, and Mr. Williams stood there as I began to examine the boy. I found nothing abnormal, but as I asked him to hold his arms outstretched before him to test his motor power and co-ordination, I noticed a large, heavy, gold ring on the middle finger of his left hand. I examined it with interest. It appeared to be ebony; at least the background was black. In the center was a face that I recognized as that of Al Capone. Mr. Williams interrupted the silence. "My name is not Williams; it's Diamond. This is Sonny Capone, Al's boy. We didn't know whether or not you'd see us. His father and mother are concerned about the high altitude on Louis Alterie's ranch." I knew Alterie to be one of Capone's men who was a braggadocio. I also knew that Lieutenant Mickey Naughton had slapped his face, arrested him, and marched him from Madison Street down State Street to the lockup at Eleventh Street. Alterie lost face with the boys after that episode.

I could find no physical or neurological signs of a brain deficit; the boy had no convulsive seizures. I told them I saw no reason why he shouldn't spend the summer in Colorado. The boy's face lighted up and he was obviously happy. "Mr. Williams" thanked me and brought a large roll of bills from his pocket. "How much do we owe you, Doctor?" I said it was a pleasure to see the boy so well after a brain abscess operation. This was before the advent of the antibiotics, and we had to depend upon the abscess becoming walled off within a capsule so it could be drained successfully. This didn't happen too often. I said there would be no fee. Diamond smiled broadly, put the money back in his pocket, and said, "I understand, Doctor. Al will appreciate your opinion." Al Capone was then in Atlanta prison. I didn't know whether I was consulted because of having operated upon Frank Parker, or who had referred them to me. I

328

quickly decided, rightly or wrongly, that acceptance of an examination fee would establish a patient-doctor relationship that I didn't want to promote.

Molly Netcher was the widow of the owner of the Boston store and was in her seventies. As a young Irish girl, she had gone to work for Netcher as a cashier, later married him, had two sons, Irving and Townsend, and after her husband's death ran the store efficiently. Irving and Townsend became playboys and never entered the family business. Their mother remarried a man more intellectual than her first husband and encouraged and supported his stamp collecting hobby.

Lewis Pollock was called one evening by her family doctor because she had fallen in the bathroom, struck her head, and had become unconscious. It did not take Pollock long to decide that she had either a middle meningeal artery hemorrhage or an acute subdural hematoma. He sent her to Passavant Memorial Hospital, called me, and by eleven o'clock that evening we had her in the operating room, had turned an osteoplastic flap and evacuated a large extradural middle meningeal artery hemorrhage. I secured the bleeding vessel, and as I was replacing the bone flap and closing the scalp incision, she began to regain consciousness, and I had to reinforce the local anesthetic that I had used.

The morning after the operation, I went to her room, introduced myself and my house staff. She was sitting up in bed and had a breakfast tray before her. She had a rugged face with a growth of hair on both cheeks. She was a large woman and acknowledged my introductions with a nod and a shrewd look at each of us, as she continued to eat. I told her special nurse that I did not want her elevated so high in bed and she was not to be out of bed until I gave the order. This was met with silence, but she did smile slightly when I said that inasmuch as she had a hearty breakfast, there would be no restrictions upon her diet.

Pollock had detected a slight weakness of the left arm, left leg, and left side of the face when he had examined her. These signs had all disappeared. She did not ask what we had found nor what we had done; she certainly was aware of her head dressing.

329

The following day I received a call from her son Townsend who said he had flown in from California; that he wanted to see his mother right away. I told him there would be no objection from me, and I informed her nurses that he should be allowed to see his mother. The next day when I made rounds her nurse said that he had come to the door, she had answered his knock, and her patient had asked who it was. When she told her it was her son, she refused to see him. Later that morning Townsend came to the hospital, and I took him to see his mother's room. She nodded to him and didn't reply when he said he was glad she was doing so well. Finally, he became embarrassed by her silence, as I did, and left.

Mrs. Netcher left the hospital after ten days with her scalp wound healed and a wrap-around scarf to cover her head and her short-cropped hair. I asked her to come back in two weeks so I could check her condition postoperatively. She wanted to know why she had to do that; I explained in detail, but when I finished I was not sure that she would come. However, she did come and was in excellent condition.

I told her I wanted to discuss my fee with her; that her family doctor would send her a bill as would Dr. Pollock, both of whom had saved her life by their prompt recognition of her condition. I said that I would take these facts into consideration in setting her fee and would she discuss the matter with me? In her deep, coarse voice, which I had not heard at any length before, she said that I should send her my statement; that she would decide whether or not it was excessive. After a pause, she added that she had won a legal suit brought against her by a gynecologist because she refused to pay him. She thought he charged her too much for an operation. "He settled for a smaller fee," she said with a broad grin.

"Mrs. Netcher, if you think the fee I charge you is too high, in view of the fact that you sold the Boston store for fifteen million dollars and I helped save your life, I refuse to haggle with you. I shall be glad to contribute my services and skills to you for nothing, and you can brag about that to your friends."

She got up abruptly, her anger was obvious, but she stood silently for a moment looking at me. "I believe you would," she said. "My secretary will be here tomorrow; discuss your fee with him, and whatever you decide will be satisfactory." She patted me on the shoulder as she left the room. I never saw Molly Netcher again, and her secretary said he had never known her to be so agreeable about a doctor's bill before.

Through the years of my surgical practice, I was stimulated and encouraged by my relationship to my patients. I was taught to think of my opinions and decisions about my patients as I would if they were my own mother, father, wife, sister, brother, or myself. What would I want for them? Allen Kanavel also taught me to call myself to my own attention, because those things within me were the most important factors that would govern the realistic actions that I had to perform daily.

I believe that every patient and his relatives must understand clearly what his doctor believes his condition to be and what action he believes should be taken. Often, pain and mental suffering are in large part due to the apprehension of not knowing just what the doctor is thinking. Often, it is necessary to be repetitious, oversimplified, and patient, but the successful treatment of disease is based upon confidence and respect between doctor and patient.

FOURTEEN

THERE comes a time when a surgeon should take stock of himself and decide that it is time for him to stop operating. This is made easier when one holds an academic position and the age limit for retirement from the active teaching faculty has been set by the university. It is also less difficult for the surgeon who has developed other interests during his years of practice and teaching.

I was taught that surgery is the application of the knowledge of the basic biological and physical sciences to the care of the patient. It is not an exact science in the narrow sense. It is also an art. The surgeon must translate his knowledge and apply his skills by a series of mental, moral, and physical acts into their highest potential for the care of the individual patient under certain limited circumstances and at a specific time. Age inexorably slows some or all of these actions. I decided early that I did not wish a committee of my peers in the hospital to tell me that I shouldn't operate. I would make that decision for myself and did.

There were several factors that made the decrease of my surgical practice and teaching responsibilities pleasant. I had established a professional partnership with two of my former residents, and as my practice diminished I decreased my one-third of the partnership income. This arrangement allows me to examine patients, refer them to Dan Ruge and Nick Wetzel for operation, be present in the operating room, follow the patients in the hospital, consult with them about their patients and the problems arising from hospital and medical school relationships. I need have no fear that fatigue will impair my surgical technical skills or judgment during a long neurosurgical operation. I can be judicial in offering advice in the administrative problems that I recognize as being cyclic but that they believe are completely new.

My work as editor of a surgical journal has kept me in touch with the advances in surgery and with the young surgeons throughout the world upon whose contributions this progress is based. That position led, I am sure, to the offer from the W. B. Saunders Company, the foremost medical book publishers, to edit the *Christopher Textbook of Surgery* through four editions, the last of which appeared in 1968, five years after I had retired as chairman of the department of surgery at Northwestern University Medical School and chief of surgery at Passavant Memorial Hospital. I continue to be taught and to learn from the manuscripts submitted to the journal and which I read and decide upon weekly.

In 1963 I had been professor of surgery and administered the department for thirty-one years. I had been responsible for the teaching of surgery to thirty-one classes of undergraduate medical students and to fifty graduate students, or residents, in surgery and neurological surgery. I subscribed completely to the belief that surgical teaching entails detailed supervision at the bedside and in the operating room until the students' ability is unquestioned; that his responsibilities should be graded dependent upon his ability and dedication, including the opportunity to make independent decisions and judgments. I believe that one of the greatest dignities of being a surgeon is the opportunity to pass on to the next generation the teaching, training, encouragement, and personal aid that I received from my seniors and that I cannot hope to repay in any other manner. The young men I have helped to become better surgeons than I have shown and continue to evidence their appreciation. This has been a most pleasant experience.

By chance, at this same time, I was elected president of the American College of Surgeons and so continued my interest, as the nineteenth regent, in that organization. The presidency is less exacting and exhausting than the chairmanship of the board of regents. One of the prerequisites of the office is a beautiful, gold-ornamented red and blue presidential gown which appeals to the male ego of every holder whether or not he frankly admits it. Besides, there is an annual luncheon for the ex-presidents who are members of the advisory council to the board of regents at which our opinions are sought. This gives us an opportunity to express our viewpoints freely without having to weigh the results if they were acted upon.

I finished a three-year term as the first president of the James IV Association of Surgeons from the United States in 1972. This is an organization with only one purpose: to provide financial support for young surgeons, not residents, to travel from foreign countries to the United States and vice versa and exchange views with their contemporaries about surgical practices and teaching. The membership is limited to one hundred active members throughout the world, and there is an annual meeting where necessary business matters are settled but which is characterized by friendship and good fellowship. No scientific papers are presented. One of the qualifications for membership is that the candidate be a surgeon who expresses his opinions without regard for his self-advancement. We are proud that we have provided support for more than thirty young surgical travelers and have the help of interested laymen.

Another factor that contributes to a pleasant experience in a less active professional surgical life is an interest in sports. Denied successful participation in high school and college by my physical abilities and youth, I have gradually become a sports buff. I tried to take part in football, baseball, and basketball through our son, Dick, when he was in prep school. I attended many of his teams' practices; I collected money from the parents of the Chicago Latin School to buy sweaters for the football team; Edith and I gathered students from the Girl's Latin School and drove them to the games to provide a cheering section. Fortunately, I didn't cause him to give up athletics in disgust at my enthusiasm. I continue to attend football games, watch sports on television, and try to improve my golf game by taking lessons, practicing, and buying new putters, wooden and iron clubs.

Often, "the old man" is said as an excuse for his foibles, as a term of affection, or to denote respect. Sometimes it is used, particularly by the young, in derision.

Just because I've reached a chronological number of years larger than the insurance actuarial figures, I doubt that I have automatically become an old man. Certainly, I envy the rubber muscles of youth, because mine have lost some of their elasticity. I have to warm up my joints by hitting a bucket of golf balls before I go to the first tee.

I suppose my grandchildren would have justification for saying, "He's getting old," if I unqualifiedly criticized the clothes they wear, their hair styles and their speech, and did not recall and confess that I had my hair cut in a pompadour style and that I once wore peg-top trousers which had cuffs three inches wide. It was the style, too, to wear high, starched collars which left room only for a small knot of a narrow red tie. I tried hard to look like the man in the Arrow collar ad. I have to think hard to remember what "Twenty-three, skiddoo, kiddo," "Up in Mabel's room," and "Tell it to Sweeney" meant, or how they were used. It isn't difficult to equate "That's slick" with "It's groovy." I'm sure my father didn't approve of either my clothes or my speech, but, wise man that he was, he regarded them with tolerance and silence, realizing that the fad and fashions could disappear and a new cycle would begin just as it had in his youth.

There were acts of meanness, violence, arrogance, ignorance, and destruction my father's generation would not tolerate. I believe my children and grandchildren have no right to ask me to tolerate their excessive displays of disapproval of accepted and well-established norms of social and professional behavior. Tipping over privies was an act of destruction that my parents believed exceeded the spirit of Halloween; delivering oneself of an opinion instead of asking a question that would stimulate a discussion was an act of ignorance and arrogance; to avoid communication with one's parents deliberately was dishonest; to lie was the cardinal sin. I believe these principles still apply.

I must confess I become impatient with youngsters who confidently know wherein my and their parents' generations failed and exactly what's wrong with the world though they conveniently avoid saying how they would correct the failures. They seek and accept security from parents and grandparents to provide transportation, tuition, clothing, and reverse-charge telephone calls, but they are against the social and economic realities that provide the money for these mundane benefits.

I suppose it can be said I'm old because mini-skirts reveal bowed legs, knock-knees, bulging calves, and legs like pipestems in a coffeepot instead of stimulating my imagination as to what lies beyond, or that stringy, long, unkempt female hair suggests that the umbilicus may be full of debris. And that the long hair, scraggly beards, dirty shirts, sandals, and ragged blue jeans of male medical students seem to me to be symbols, as were the frock coats, heavy watch chain draped across the vest, detachable cuffs, and neatly trimmed, clean Vandyke beards of their great-grandfathers in medicine, of their ignorance of the art and science of medicine behind which they hide.

My hair does stand on end when I overhear an intern newly graduated from medical school arrogantly tell an excellent internist with a large practice, who was discussing the treatment of a patient with the young man, that in the neophyte's opinion, based on his experience, the internist was treating the patient incorrectly. But I become more upset when that dedicated, thoughtful clinician accepts the undisciplined, insolent statement without a proper reply. I gag at the indecisive, appeasing, pusillanimous actions of administrators of universities, colleges, medical schools, and hospitals. Perhaps it takes age to know that their actions will lead to the defeat and destruction of those ideals of freedom and dissent that they mouth so loudly.

I should like to believe that I have discarded the casual disbeliefs of youth; that I now evaluate my personal and professional experiences at a slower, calmer, and more judicious rate; that my opinions are now based on a nonemotional, nonpersonal, logical consideration of all of the possible solutions to a problem; that I can reflect upon actions and thoughts taken in my youth, not with regret, but with an appreciation of how they could have been better.

I should like to believe that I have contributed to the happiness, future, success, and well-being of my family, professional colleagues, students, and patients. If these are the thoughts of an old man, I accept the accusation. But if at some time in the future my relatives, my contemporaries, and my young friends in surgery speak with each other about my failings, my virtues, and my accomplishments, I shall have made it.